D0340896

Feb 17

THE PROMETHEUS BOMB

THE PROMETHEUS BOMB

The Manhattan Project and Government in the Dark

NEIL J. SULLIVAN

Potomac Books

AN IMPRINT OF THE UNIVERSITY OF NEBRASKA PRESS

All rights reserved. Potomac Books is an imprint of
the University of Nebraska Press.
Manufactured in the United States of America.

Library of Congress Cataloging-in-Publication Data
Names: Sullivan, Neil J., 1948– author.
Title: The Prometheus bomb: the Manhattan
Project and government in the dark / Neil J. Sullivan.
Description: Lincoln: Potomac Books, An imprint
of the University of Nebraska Press, 2016.
Includes bibliographical references and index.
Identifiers: LCCN 2016020649
ISBN 9781612348155 (cloth: alkaline paper)
ISBN 9781612348902 (epub)
ISBN 9781612348919 (mobi)
ISBN 9781612348926 (pdf)
Subjects: LCSH: Manhattan Project (U.S.)—History.
| Atomic bomb—United States—History. | Atomic
bomb—Government policy—United States—History.
| United States—Military policy. | Science and state—
United States. | BISAC: HISTORY / Military / World
War II. | HISTORY / United States / 20th Century.
Classification: LCC QC773.3.U5 S86 2016
DDC 355.8/25119097309044—dc23
LC record available at https://lccn.loc.gov/2016020649

Set in Minion Pro by John Klopping.

For Joyce, Kate, Tim and Olivia, and Mo

[CONTENTS]

[ILLUSTRATIONS]

[ACKNOWLEDGMENTS]

Understanding government power has been a lifetime interest. How do communities organize themselves so that they can solve problems and promote common interests? How do we balance the interests of the community and the individual? What processes do we use to make decisions so that we can act efficiently while also giving proper consideration to people who may not have the wherewithal to participate in civic life? I am grateful to all the people who have helped me appreciate the complexity of those questions, beginning with my parents, who kept the spirit of Franklin Roosevelt alive in our home.

At Baruch College–City University of New York, Diane Gibson, Rita Ormsby, Steve Savas, and Jerry Mitchell are friends and colleagues who set the standard for teaching, scholarship, and service. Thousands of students over thirty-eight years have inspired my curiosity and reflection about public affairs. Students and faculty are served by a staff that is a privilege to know.

Jane Dystel and Miriam Goderich are my friends and agents who took an inchoate sentiment and helped me turn it into an idea. Their contribution to seeing the essential political issues in the curious world of the atom was especially welcome.

Other companions have been enormously helpful through their thoughts about government, science, writing, and other subjects germane to this book. Jean Huff is a fellow writer and attorney who has been encouraging through her own example. Kenny Greehan serves the City of Yonkers with distinction and has had intriguing observations about the wonderful city where my family and I live. Joe Cianciulli is our chairman of the Yonkers Zoning Board of Appeals, a post from which he has paid particular attention to the interests of the people who so often are ignored in their struggles.

After ten years on the zoning board, my education continues on the Westchester County Planning Board, and I am grateful to my colleagues there. Pete Bradley is a friend and neighbor who has helped me keep focused while navigating the book.

James Jond is my friend and teacher who is not responsible for my failure to master his lessons on the golf swing. Deborah Roche has given me some clarity about why I struggle with James's wisdom, and, whatever happens with par, her friendship is a great gift.

Peter Woll, my Brandeis mentor, remains my dear friend whose counsel has been invaluable. Walter Modrys, sj, has read the early chapters and has provided particularly insightful comments. Peter Michaels has let me interrupt numerous rounds of golf, to answer questions about science that many people learned by the fourth grade. Dave Lockhart has been very gracious in discussing the book, another friendship with grand lunches in Hyde Park. Vic Quiroz has helped me keep the book in perspective with other priorities so that it becomes another form of teaching and service. Dan O'Connor, MD, distinguished himself in both elements of C. P. Snow's *Two Cultures*, and he's missed by all who loved and admired him.

Kristen Rowley at the University of Nebraska Press was an early champion of the book. Tom Swanson and Emily Wendell are the editors who have guided the manuscript through the publication process. Jeremy Hall has provided the haircut the manuscript needed, through superb copyediting.

The Prometheus Bomb is a book about World War II, and that conflict is as close as some of the people dearest to me. Dan Fenn left Harvard for the Army Air Corps in 1943 to serve in the European theater. He returned to Cambridge, was appointed to the White House staff by President John F. Kennedy, became the founding director of the Kennedy Presidential Library, and continues teaching at Harvard and elsewhere, still the youngest person in whatever room he's in.

Tim Ireland served our country through the "long, twilight struggle" of the Cold War and the current challenges. He and his sister Kathleen have been treasured friends since our college days. Their father, Dr. Robert Ireland, served in the Pacific during World War II as a surgeon before returning home to marry the wonderful Joan and to extend kindness to those who knew him.

Colin Cooke was a friend, writer, and neighbor who sang as the sole chorister at the coronation of King George VI, served as an engine machanic in the RAF during the war, and whose first born, another Colin, can boast of being the founder of our neighborhood's Sunday Cigar Seminar.

Al Nocella is the son of Staff Sergeant Nocella, another Al, who was drafted in 1940 with the expectation that he would be serving until 1942. Pearl Harbor extended his service for the duration, and he was sent to Europe in March of 1945. He returned to America after the war, married the marvelous Eleanor, and raised three splendid children.

Ron Yoshida has been a friend since our days at Loyola High School in Los Angeles, where we took classes from Mr. Bill Lenihan that put the questions about government, history, and writing in a permanent place in our lives. Ron serves the country by helping people in the Middle East work on education reform. His parents, Robert and Yoshiye Yoshida, both born in the United States, were sent to internment camps during World War II because of the country where their forebears were born, a distinctly un-American act. They returned from the camps to raise a wonderful family and contribute to their friends and neighbors.

Emile Vaessen, born and raised in Belgium during the war, is the son of Leonie, who smuggled small arms for the Resistance and raised her six children while the Gestapo occupied their home. Emile's cousin, Ivan Hotchamp, died a hero's death, executed during the war for his Resistance efforts. Emile himself was saved by U.S. Army doctors after a gasoline explosion. He has been a devoted husband, father, and grandfather and has built a successful business of his own—that success is especially reflected in the regard and affection that his friends have for him.

Closer to home, Joyce is the daughter of Thomas H. Murray, who went to the Pacific at the age of seventeen. He returned; married the delightful Carolyn; raised six children, including the extraordinary Joyce; and brought particular joy to family, friends, and neighbors through his participation in community theater and a town garden.

I have been blessed beyond measure by sharing life with Joyce. Kate and Tim showed up and visited for about twenty years, staying connected now with the adventures of their marvelous and admirable lives. Kate has taken the family back to the West Coast, where she is forging a career in animation. Tim is also west of the Hudson, in New Jersey. He gave our family a Brazilian branch through his marriage to Olivia, our third child, who is developing an online presence in the art of cooking while Tim pursues Information Technology. Through much of the time researching and writing the book, our beloved cat Mo was a center of attention as he battled the illness that took him from us. He taught the great lesson that what matters most in life is doing the next act of kindness. I dedicate this book to my wonderful family.

THE PROMETHEUS BOMB

Introduction

$E=mc^2$ in the hands of Adolph Hitler. In the summer of 1939, that nightmare was on the minds of two Martians as they drove through the North Fork of Long Island hoping to get the signature of the one man who might forestall catastrophe.

Leo Szilard and Edward Teller were fellow Hungarians, fellow physicists, and fellow Jews who fled Germany after they received PhDs and before the Nazi vise tightened. Both delighted in the tale that so many geniuses hailed from their native Budapest because they were descendants of visitors from the neighboring Red Planet passing among us as Magyars.[1]

As they raced along Route 25, Szilard and Teller knew that German scientists were among the pioneers of quantum physics, that ample quantities of fissile uranium had come under the control of the Reich, and that the combination of knowledge and material could produce a bomb that would lead to swastikas flying over the capitals of Europe.

Making a right turn onto Skunk Lane in Cutchogue, Szilard and Teller were a couple of miles from the summer residence of Albert Einstein. The drive was a return trip for Szilard, who had visited Einstein a few weeks before with Eugene Wigner, another Hungarian physicist. Szilard's familiarity with the area meant that he and Teller would find the house on Old Grove Road without getting lost on Nassau Point, the custom for first-time visitors looking for the great man.

The purpose of the trip was to try to wrap up a letter that Szilard needed to send to somebody in authority to sound the alarm about a Nazi bomb. He realized that, if he contacted a public official directly, the reaction he could expect would be, "Who the hell is Leo Szilard?"

Not only was Einstein the most famous scientist in the world, but he also knew everybody. And somewhere in his collection of admirers was the person to whom the letter should be sent.

The queen of Belgium was a possibility. Her country had colonized the Congo, where vast supplies of the crucial element uranium-235 were held, a relatively easy target for Nazi extraction. Einstein had met her, but he thought a minister in the Belgian government was a more sensible choice. Learning of that idea, Wigner countered that, with Europe on the brink of war, immigrants contacting a foreign official without going through the State Department could be hard to explain to a congressional committee.

Showing that genius has its limits, Einstein and company prepared to ask Charles Lindbergh to carry the message to Franklin Roosevelt. They soon realized that the Lone Eagle was busy crafting a national address that trumpeted the wisdom of isolationism and, unable to repress his antisemitism, hinted at the patriotic duty of the barons who controlled American media to refrain from luring the nation into war.

Alexander Sachs turned out to be their man. He knew FDR personally, having written speeches on economics for him in the 1932 campaign. Sachs determined that the letter was too important for him to limit himself to being its postman. He told Einstein and Szilard that he not only would deliver the letter himself but would explain its contents to the president, lest its message die a common bureaucratic death.

Weeks passed with no word from Sachs. What could possibly be holding up a matter of such urgency? Sachs was looking for the right moment when the president would have the time and focus to absorb the ominous news. The opportunity came finally in the middle of October. After hearing Sachs, FDR commanded, "This requires action," setting in motion what would become the Manhattan Project.

None too soon. Six weeks before, the German army had rolled into Poland, turning a question of theoretical physics into a race for the decisive weapon of the war.

The Prometheus Bomb reveals a vacuum of leadership in the research and development of nuclear weapons during World War II. Who assessed the costs and risks of building the atomic bomb? Who chose the most effective strategy for building the weapon? Who decided how to pay for it? Personnel issues? Location? Security? Who balanced all those considerations against competing claims elsewhere in the war effort? The answer is many people, thus no individual. Franklin Roosevelt made the ultimate decisions in the Manhattan Project, but his inability to comprehend the science at the heart of the effort meant that his determinations consisted of best guesses and trust in subordinates rather than informed judgment.

The Manhattan Project was the first case of a new type of challenge for the American republic. Our government must now fashion public policy for issues where a small group of brilliant scientists affect the entire population with discoveries and inventions that could secure or threaten our existence and our future. Bioengineering can target the human brain, alter livestock beyond nature's constraints, and create artificial life. Economic development and convenience in one part of the planet may trigger environmental disasters elsewhere. Combinations of robotics and artificial intelligence (AI) may force us to consider the meaning of *human*. In these and related questions, who should make the critical decisions, and by what process? The question is especially urgent with the nation's survival at stake.

In the American community, public policy had been the realm of politicians and bureaucrats. Those officials supervised even great engineering projects. Without grasping all the details, they understood rail transportation within cities and across the nation. A ditch through Central America? Sure. Flying machines? You bet. The Manhattan Project introduced new actors in policy making because Franklin Roosevelt had no capacity to supervise Nobel Prize winners while they penetrated the essence of matter and energy. The president did have capable subordinates like Vannevar Bush, Leslie Groves, and Henry Stimson. Their backgrounds in engineering, warfare, and diplomacy prepared them to manage the alpha males in science, industry, academics, and the military who tackled perhaps the greatest engineering challenge in history. But not one of those aides alone had sufficient knowledge or authority to oversee every aspect of the Manhattan Project.

The collaboration of experts from different fields repeatedly faced complications from contending personalities and professional cultures. It fell to American government to control the turmoil of those rivalries, to keep the talent and resources focused on a weapon that might be necessary to America's survival, and to do so without abandoning the values for which the nation fought.

In this case, "American government" means Franklin Roosevelt. We will see him set a tone for the people in his administration that facilitated a bristling exchange of ideas followed by confidence, win or lose, in the decision reached. Army brats worked with scions of the Eastern Establishment. Some Nobel physicists worked relentlessly on an atomic bomb that they later argued should not be used. Some military officers counseled against dropping the bomb on Japan and were countered by career politicians using a different calculus. Nobody won every bureaucratic battle, but strong egos had the humility to accept the decisions that they had opposed. Politics, even in the most urgent circumstances, was an art practiced energetically and gracefully, a reflection of FDR.

The story of the Manhattan Project is a story of war, so it is a tragedy. Heroes abound, and they can be celebrated without becoming depressed about our own times. The 1940s also included nature's usual share of deplorables and knuckleheads, so we can look back for inspiration and encouragement rather than despair that we fall short of our own heritage.

We find much to consider in that retrospective: Leslie Groves, the army engineer, returning from his initial meeting with Vannevar Bush, the MIT engineer, bewildered by Bush's own befuddlement. For his part, Bush was on the phone stopping just short of trying to get Groves fired. We find Henry Stimson, the patrician secretary of war, bristling when Dwight Eisenhower explained why we shouldn't drop atomic bombs on Japan, a position with which Stimson agreed. We read that Stimson and Groves contended for weeks over targets in Japan and then that Groves expressed gratitude to the secretary for arguments that reduced casualties. We puzzle that all but a handful of members of Congress were kept in ignorance about the Manhattan Project while Soviet spies strolled about Los Alamos. Not puzzling at all, we see Congress furiously reengage at the end of the war to battle the executive for control of policy and programs. We discover the public implications of the great friendship between Franklin Roosevelt and Winston Churchill, especially poignant for being forged in war. We read as the story shifts from FDR pressing through rapidly declining health to secure the postwar world to Harry Truman picking up the mantle, carrying through to the war's conclusion, fighting a revived Congress, and laying the foundations for the Cold War.

If we struggle to assume honor, wisdom, and courage in America's public officials, we might at least assume sincerity. The questions remain: How did a president and a few members of Congress manage scientists whose work was incomprehensible? Could a public, whose taxes sustained that scientific work and whose lives were jeopardized in some of the experiments, know about the endeavor when secrecy was paramount? If they did know, how could they understand the issues before them? In short, how can we trust or control experts when we have no idea what they're talking about?

We live with the legacy of the Manhattan Project beyond even the thousands of nuclear warheads that are stockpiled about the planet or the efforts of turbulent regimes and terrorist groups to obtain those weapons. Building the bomb also established patterns of authority, models of organization, and a culture of secrecy that were harbingers for a type of public choice that has been with us since a shattered Japan surrendered on the deck of the USS *Missouri*.

Until the Manhattan Project, public works in America confined their potential catastrophes to folks in the neighborhood. If the dam burst, the train derailed, the schoolhouse caught fire, or the bridge collapsed, the immediate pain was local. If you didn't live below the lake or next to the tracks, if your kids weren't in that school, or your car on that bridge, your reaction would be relief and compassion: "Glad it wasn't us" and "Oh, those poor people." The Manhattan Project changed that calculus by introducing a new kind of disaster, one that removed the physical limits of tragedy.

Releasing the energy within the nuclei of atoms meant that the initial explosions and the subsequent radiation could conceivably reach every corner of the globe. Natural barriers such as oceans, mountains, and deserts once protected some people from the conflicts of others. Neutrality or a treaty with a powerful noncombatant state might keep a nation safe. But given enough countries at war and enough nuclear weapons at their disposal, nature would provide very few places to hide, and a treaty would likely be incinerated in the first exchange.

In the nuclear age, billions of people have been affected by the decisions of a very small band of officials. Just as significant, if the public did have access to the key issues, the opportunity would have been pointless. In a nuclear war, retail clerks, ballerinas, and Wall Street traders would not understand the weapon that killed them, but they would be every bit as dead as the geniuses who conceived the bomb. So, are we condemned to government in the dark where the most ominous decisions in science, ones of life and death significance for all of us, remain in the hands of a gifted few?

Two thousand years ago, Juvenal asked a question that James Madison would have appreciated: *Quis custodiat ipsos custodes?* Who guards the guardians? In our system of government, the answer is, "We do." But how do we do so when the guardians' work involves concepts and vocabulary that the rest of us are unable to understand?

Ask a financial adviser where to put your money. Talk to a guidance counselor about the middle school years. Call the Building Department about adding a deck to your house. Listen to a mechanic tell you whether your car is worth that repair. Entirely common experiences, but never mundane. Routine though these interactions are, we generally need experts to help us navigate them.

If we're baffled by municipal bonds, the adolescent brain, rear yard setbacks, or power trains, more complexity is coming in the years ahead. Who will decide if we should be the objects of surveillance by satellites of the National Security Agency or by drones of the local police? Craig Venter's labs have fashioned synthetic bacteria. How far into the animal kingdom can that technology penetrate? Robotics, artificial intelligence, and genetic engineering will force us to wonder about the meaning of *human* with more urgency than we do when considering hominid fossils from the Rift Valley.

As C. P. Snow famously put the matter, "It is dangerous to have two cultures which can't or don't communicate. In a time when science is determining much of our destiny, that is, whether we live or die, it is dangerous in the most practical terms. Scientists can give bad advice and decision-makers can't know whether it is good or bad."[2] He concluded that we were following the news from science, "as though listening to a foreign language in which one only knows a few words."[3] The danger to which Snow referred began with atomic fission.

The Manhattan Project was the first of a new type of public choice: life and death on a national scale. The effort began out of a fear that Germany would be the first combatant to develop an atomic bomb. Even after we saw that we would not be the target of an atomic attack, we pressed ahead as the bomb consumed resources, pushed aside other priorities, engendered secrecy, and likely ensured that we would never again disband our military after hostilities ceased.

Building the new type of bomb was an intriguing story with great significance for the outcome of World War II and for the future of life-altering science in our nation. The history of the Manhattan Project can be especially instructive as we again strike a balance in our government between authority and restraint in the face of scientific challenges the framers of the Constitution could not have imagined.

[ONE]

A Squash Court in Chicago

On a November day in 1942, two guys had a conversation about blowing up Chicago. Enrico Fermi and Arthur Holly Compton were Nobel Prize–winning physicists and key figures in the Manhattan Project. Their plan to conduct the first controlled nuclear chain reaction in a facility outside the nation's second largest city had been frustrated by a labor dispute, so they were looking for an alternative site.

Fermi proposed that they run the experiment at the University of Chicago, where he and Compton were employed. Well aware that 3.4 million of their neighbors lived relatively near the test, their discussion first needed to rule out a couple of potential disasters.

One was a reactor explosion equivalent to the fate that awaited Hiroshima. Fermi and Compton allowed that "some new, unforeseen phenomenon" might intrude, "some unknown process" that would accelerate the reaction beyond their control, but Compton double-checked Fermi's math.[1] They concluded that they would be able to slow the reaction to a safe level if an X factor appeared. They were willing to take even "superfluous" precautions to guard against such a catastrophe.[2]

The second possible disaster was a massive leak of radiation without an explosion, the kind of event that occurred at Chernobyl in 1986. Compton described that scenario as "intolerable," and added he that "the outcome of the experiment might thus greatly affect the city."[3] Indeed. More numbers crunched, and the two were confident that Chicago would not be in danger.

For those familiar with such positions, the tension rises when we learn that Compton was also an academic administrator. It crossed his mind while talking with Fermi that perhaps he should notify the university's president Robert Hutchins that the two Nobels had decided to proceed with the most famous scientific experiment ever attempted in a squash court.

Compton recognized that "according to every rule of organizational protocol, I should have taken the matter to my superior. But this would have been unfair."[4] Why? "Based on considerations of the University's welfare the only answer [Hutchins] could have given would have been—no. And this answer would have been wrong. So I assumed the responsibility myself."[5]

Robert Hutchins, unqualified in Compton's eyes, had begun his undergraduate studies at Oberlin at the age of sixteen. He left two years later to join the ambulance corps on the western front in the Great War. He returned and finished his bachelor's degree at Yale in 1921, received his law degree from the university in 1925, and was appointed dean of the Yale Law School two years later. In 1929, at the age of thirty, he was named the president of the University of Chicago, where he promoted the study of the Great Books, overhauled undergraduate education, eliminated a very successful football program for being inconsistent with the university's purpose, and cultivated a popular following unusual for a college president.

When a decision was needed on proceeding with an experiment to release unimaginable energy from the fundamental elements of matter on the campus of the University of Chicago, Arthur Holly Compton decided to keep Robert Hutchins in the dark. Beyond the risk to Chicago, some physicists wondered if a chain reaction of atom splitting might continue past the campus, the city limits, the nation's borders, around the world, into space, and then to every corner of the universe. An interesting question, but as Compton himself claimed, "President Hutchins was in no position to make an independent judgment of the hazards involved."[6]

Hutchins wasn't worth a conversation? He didn't know other physicists and mathematicians who could have advised him after checking the numbers yet again and again? He couldn't have learned enough about the risks to make a reasonable and thoughtful judgment? If in doubt, he couldn't have contacted another president, Franklin Roosevelt, to plead that this one was above his weight class?

In Compton's account, written in 1956, he alone decided that Fermi should proceed with the chain reaction. His recollection implies that Robert Hutchins could be informed after the fact, but Compton's recollection was flawed. Under Hutchins's leadership, the university had become a research lab for the army, and Hutchins knew full well that the object of that research was to be an atomic bomb.[7]

Hutchins had asked the university administrators and trustees to support his decision to cooperate with a government program that would be identified as the Metallurgical Project. He provided them with no specifics, not even mentioning the word *uranium*. He added that the venture would be extremely expensive, uncertain in outcome, but potentially decisive in winning the war.

A trustee asked if the project might be physically dangerous to the university or the city, and Hutchins replied that he would have to find out. He reported a few weeks later that "he had been told that such danger appeared to be unlikely but could not be excluded."[8]

Hutchins asked that his decision be endorsed on grounds of trust. Trust in him personally, just as he trusted the judgments of the public officials and scientists who had come to him with the urgency of the task and little in the way of details about the research. The man who championed the Great Books determined that the fight against totalitarianism required subordinating the traditional values of the liberal arts. In short, Robert Hutchins knew much more about the Manhattan Project than Compton was perhaps aware.

Even if Hutchins had not willingly turned the University of Chicago into a war plant, he could not have been ignorant of Fermi's work. The apparatus in which atomic nuclei would be split could not have been smuggled into the squash court in a gym bag. The device, known as Chicago Pile No. 1 (CP-1), had to be constructed over several weeks, and it was enormous.[9] Four hundred tons of graphite, six tons of uranium metal, and fifty tons of uranium oxide were arranged in a complex lattice structure under Fermi's supervision. Layer upon layer was brought to the underground site and put into its proper place. Dozens of people were involved in the construction and the subsequent operation.

Hutchins certainly would have been aware of such a significant development on his own campus and could have brought the effort to a halt if he had not been satisfied about the safety and importance of the venture. Compton may have thought he bypassed Hutchins, but he did so only because Hutchins let him. Nonetheless, we have to wonder why Hutchins permitted such a radical experiment to proceed without apparent personal intervention.

A few weeks after the chat with Fermi, Compton briefed other members of the Manhattan Project at a meeting in Washington DC. The S-1 Section of the Office of Scientific Research and Development (OSRD), an agency whose roots trace to the beginning of World War II, was comprised of key officials in the latest administrative scheme for determining the feasibility of an atomic bomb.[10]

The accounts of the meeting at which Compton discussed the planned chain reaction in the squash court reveal that administrative forces reflected passionate collisions among the personalities who were trying to figure out the potential of atomic energy as a factor in the global conflict on which the future of civilization depended.

James Conant, the president of Harvard, was a liaison from the White House to the S-1 Committee. He reported directly to Vannevar Bush, who was FDR's chief administrator for the Manhattan Project; Compton claimed that, upon hearing about the upcoming experiment in the squash court, "Conant's face went white."[11] In his own memoirs, Conant included the quote, adding that Compton wrote "with understandable poetic license."[12] On the essential point of whether to block the experiment, Conant concluded, "I think we all felt that the construction of the pile was so far advanced that it was too late to call a halt."[13]

Gen. Leslie Groves, the principal contractor for the project, was at the same meeting; when he heard that Compton had given a green light to the chain reaction within the city limits of Chicago, he rushed to check if the original site in the Argonne Forest outside the city might yet be available. Compton noticed that "it was evident that Groves did not like what we were doing in the least."[14]

After the war, Groves wrote that due to the risk of the chain reaction, "I had serious misgivings about the wisdom of Compton's suggestion."[15] He allowed that "there was no reason to wait, except for our uncertainty about whether the planned experiment might not prove hazardous to the surrounding community. If the pile should explode, no one knew just how far the danger would extend."[16] He let Compton know of these concerns "but . . . did not interfere with his plans."[17]

Groves took heart that preliminary work was providing some empirical evidence that Fermi's project would be safe and effective. The university was already being used for limited purposes related to the chain reaction even when the Argonne Forest outside Chicago was expected to be the site of the full test. Groves wrote, "It did not seem possible, with the control system to be used, there could be an accident."[18] Fair enough, but Compton himself had acknowledged that it was impossible to rule out every risk since the experiment was unique in the history of physics for releasing forces never before tapped.

With so much at stake, Groves elaborated without clarifying, "At this time, the exact status of responsibility for the operations of the Chicago laboratory was still a bit hazy to some, but not to Bush, Compton and me. Compton was in direct charge. The over-all responsibility was now mine."[19] *Direct charge* and *over-all responsibility* can be expressed on an organization chart, invoked in a memoir, but remain murky in practice.

An elaborate structure of bureaucratic authority combined with brilliant scientific and mathematical calculations ruled out all kinds of hazards in the Manhattan Project, but they could be helpless against the human factor. When thinking about the chain reaction in the squash court, the worst fears of Compton, Hutchins, Conant, and Groves were understandably focused on their incomplete comprehension of the atomic nucleus. But to see the real danger to Chicago from Fermi's experiment in December of 1942, we need to jump to August of 1945 and the end of World War II. After the bombings of Hiroshima and Nagasaki, in the high desert of New Mexico, we learn that the threat to Chicago lay not in abstruse physics but in the mundane. If a catastrophe had emanated from the squash court, it would not have been because Fermi's math was off but because of a most common experience painfully familiar to anyone: human beings don't always follow the rules, and sometimes we drop things.

Harry Daghlian Jr. was a twenty-four-year-old graduate student in physics at Purdue University who moved to Los Alamos for the

Manhattan Project and to further his studies toward his PhD. His responsibilities included a task known as "tickling the dragon's tail," in which materials that could trigger a nuclear chain reaction were brought into close proximity to determine the amount and arrangement of the materials that would generate such a reaction.

At this point in 1945, atomic bombs had been built and used, but the Manhattan Project was still crude in the sense that its scientists didn't know, with the precision that scientists want to know everything, the exact process of atomic fission. In other words, the purpose of the project had been accomplished without a complete knowledge of the process. How did things vary depending on whether the fuel was U-235 or plutonium? How did the reaction change when different materials were used to generate fission? How did these other materials have to be employed to trigger the reaction?

Harry Daghlian's job was to help answer those questions.[20] On August 21, 1945, two weeks after atomic bombs were dropped on Hiroshima and Nagasaki and a week after Emperor Hirohito's surrender speech, Daghlian was working with a sphere of plutonium to measure the critical mass when bricks of tungsten carbide (WC) were placed in various configurations about the orb.

When the elements of atomic fission are separate from one another, they are said to be *subcritical*. When brought together so that the reaction is stable (i.e., the neutrons released equal the neutrons lost to energy or absorption by adjacent material), the reaction is *critical*. When the neutrons released exceed those lost (i.e., when the chain reaction accelerates to split ever-more atoms in the fuel), the reaction is *supercritical*.

On the morning of the twenty-first, Daghlian built one partial cube with WC bricks to enclose the sphere, and he noted the exact distance and configuration between the bricks and the plutonium sphere when it reached a critical point. In the afternoon, he returned, built another partial cube in a different design, and again found a critical reaction.

After dinner, he attended a lecture and apparently got an idea about a way to assemble a complete cube to contain the sphere. If he had followed official procedures, he would have gone home, gotten a good night's sleep, and returned in the morning to test the new notion with colleagues present. As it was, he went back to the lab after hours and alone. Robert Hemmerly, an army private, was present, serving as a guard to prevent theft and to keep an eye on things. His duties did not extend to enforcing the protocol for scientists doing research.

Daghlian and Hemmerly exchanged pleasantries, and Daghlian retrieved the plutonium from a vault. Probably twelve hours after his workday had begun, he started placing the wc bricks about the sphere. A monitor emitted clicks that increased in frequency as the materials approached a critical point.

In the space of about a half hour, he fashioned four layers of bricks and proceeded with greater care as he built the fifth layer. Just before 10:00 p.m., he held a brick in his left hand and moved it over the center of the cube. The monitor issued a flurry of clicks that indicated a supercritical reaction was imminent, meaning that a dangerous release of radiation was possible.

Startled, tired, frightened, perhaps remembering that he wasn't supposed to be the lone scientist in the lab at that time, Daghlian tried to jerk the brick to a safe distance from the sphere. Instead, he dropped it.

The brick fell onto the sphere, the worst possible outcome. Daghlian reached with his right hand to grab the brick. The room filled with a flash of blue light, and Daghlian felt a tingling in his right hand. He then dismantled more of the structure to return it to a safe level, and he informed Private Hemmerly that they both had been exposed to radiation.

Another graduate student had just arrived at the lab, and she drove Daghlian to the hospital, where signs of acute radiation poisoning appeared almost immediately. His right hand began to swell, and debilitating nausea set in. After two days, his condition seemed to improve, but new symptoms soon showed.

His right hand was severely burned and blistered. The damage to his hand anticipated similar effects to his arms, neck, face, and internal organs. Blisters had to be sliced open, drained, and have the dead skin scraped away. Despite general anesthesia, Daghlian suffered the torments of the damned.

Ten days after the accident, nausea and abdominal pain returned but then abated. He was given intravenous fluids that seemed to cause a dangerous drop in blood pressure and a spike in his heart rate to 250 beats per minute. Treatments for one condition aggravated others, and his doctors were limited to easing some of the symptoms with no hope for a recovery.

Harry Daghlian died on September 15, 1945. "By the end, his appearance had changed dramatically because of a significant weight loss that had started on day 6 and had increasingly worsened. In addition, all of the epidermis of the abdomen and lower chest had been lost, as well as the hair from his upper chest, beard and temples."[21]

Thousands of people in Hiroshima and Nagasaki were suffering the same fate at the same time, and thousands of people in Chicago had been in the same peril on December 2, 1942, not because of some strange, unknown aspect of physics but because somebody might have dropped something in the squash court.

On May 21, 1946, nine months after the WC brick slipped from Harry Daghlian's hand, Louis Slotin, a friend and supervisor of Daghlian's, was working with that same lethal plutonium sphere.[22] In an experiment different from the one the previous August, the device was in two parts, and Slotin's task was to keep the two hemispheres separate while he brought them close enough to achieve a critical state.

A year before, Slotin had assembled the core for the test bomb at Trinity. His skill and ease in working with the deadly material led his colleagues to refer to him as the Chief Armorer of the United States. He had a reputation for being somewhat reckless even though Fermi himself warned him that he would be dead within a year if he persisted in the criticality experiments. Any overconfidence should have vanished during the days he spent at Daghlian's bedside, seeing the horror related to the awful word *necrosis*. As it was, Slotin was planning to leave Los Alamos and return to the East. On May 21 he was training his replacement with six other scientists present.

Slotin explained to them that, if the two sections touched, the disaster of the previous August would repeat. To prevent that calamity, wooden blocks were supposed to be placed between the two hemispheres. The blocks would be removed and replaced with ones ever thinner until criticality was imminent.

Having performed the exercise more than twenty-five times, Slotin returned to his reckless impulse. Rather than go through the cumbersome business of swapping out wooden blocks, the instrument that Slotin used to maintain the separation was a screwdriver. By adjusting the angle of the tool, he could raise or lower the top hemisphere at will, directing it in a kind of deadly dance, the music supplied by the changing tempo of the clicks from the radiation detector.

Again, the human factor. Slotin raised the handle of the screwdriver, driving the upper hemisphere higher and farther from a fatal encounter with the bottom part. He then raised it higher still but past a point of stability. Somewhere beyond 45 degrees, forces on the screwdriver shot its tip off the lower hemisphere. The top of the sphere crashed onto the bottom; when the two halves touched, the device became supercritical. The awful flash of blue light filled the room, and all eight men realized they had been exposed to dangerous levels of radiation.

They drove themselves to the hospital, where a medical team, notified of the radiation release, awaited their arrival. Those who were farther from the sphere received significantly less radiation than those who were closer, but Louis Slotin was aware that he had received a fatal dose. Nine days after the accident, he died.

The safety of Chicago was a paramount consideration of the top officials in the Manhattan Project. They checked one another's math; conducted preliminary experiments to confirm their calculations; and planned to take, as Compton put it, "superfluous" care with the chain reaction. At no time did they take into account the factor universal and eternal: people take shortcuts, and people drop things.[23]

On the morning of the chain reaction, Enrico Fermi left his apartment on the coldest December 2 in Chicago's history. Over forty of his colleagues from the Metallurgical Laboratory headed to the university. They ranged from Nobel laureates to a "suicide squad" of graduate students who were charged with throwing suppressants on any fire that developed.

Fellow Chicagoans were going to work and school, bracing against the subzero temperature. Wartime gas rationing put an uncommonly large number of them on buses and the L. Some of them, having suffered through mediocre baseball seasons for the Cubs and White Sox, would have discussed the Bears of the National Football League with any travelling companions. Led by quarterback Sid Luckman, the team was undefeated with one game left in the regular season. December 2 fell on a Wednesday, so conversations would have finished analyzing a shellacking of the Cleveland Rams 47–0 the previous Sunday and then turned to the prospects against the rival Chicago Cardinals the following Sunday.

If sports didn't divert the pain and anxiety of war, such thoughts might have weighed on millions who were going about routine matters in terrible circumstances. Loved ones were fighting at Guadalcanal while plans for the holidays proceeded. The anniversary of Pearl Harbor approached, and families would have drawn hope from the news that German forces had been surrounded at Stalingrad and repelled in North Africa.

The war was close in an emotional sense and in the inconvenience of rationing, but its reality may have seemed far away on Pacific islands and an African desert. Little did the plumbers, bankers, teachers, and bus drivers know that a short distance from where they labored, the nature of war was about to be transformed.

Ten years after the chain reaction, Enrico Fermi himself wrote one of the more useful accounts of that morning's experiment.[24] His reflection was published in the *Chicago Sun-Times*, so it was intended for a general audience. Fermi neglected to write about the critical place that he had in the Manhattan Project, and perhaps he didn't reflect on the significance of his role in its relationship to the issue of controlling experts in a democracy.

As we have seen, administrative officials had concerns about the chain reaction in Chicago, but they deferred to someone who understood the science far better than they. They deferred to Enrico Fermi, who won that confidence despite being in the United States for only four years and despite being a native of a country with which America was at war.

Fermi earned that trust despite a very strange story even for the very strange field of nuclear physics. He had come to the United States after receiving the Nobel Prize in December of 1938. Fermi's wife Laura was a Jew and subject to antisemitic laws recently passed in Italy. The family took the occasion of the award in Oslo to escape to America.

Fermi was receiving the Nobel for something he hadn't actually done, while his major accomplishment passed unnoticed. The award specified that he had created *transuranic* elements, new elements heavier than uranium, at that time the heaviest element in the periodic table. In fact, he had not found those elements, but in 1934 he had accomplished atomic fission using neutrons rather than protons as the instruments for splitting the uranium nucleus. Other researchers had split nuclei using protons, but those positively charged particles faced resistance from protons in the nucleus, so an excessive amount of energy was required to penetrate the positively charged nucleus, compared to using neutrons, particles without any charge.

In December of 1938, about the time the Fermis were meeting the king of Norway, two German physicists, Otto Hahn and Fritz Strassman, replicated Fermi's experiment. They found that the uranium atom split into two roughly equal parts, and a barium isotope was created. Of greatest significance, the total weight of uranium and barium was now less than that of the original uranium nucleus.

The prewar climate in Europe confounded the emerging scientific discoveries. Otto Hahn, realizing the significance of the findings, sent the results to a colleague Lise Meitner. While the Fermis were passing through Norway to escape the totalitarian threat, Meitner, a Jew, was in Sweden, having escaped Germany herself. Working with her nephew Otto Frisch, she reviewed the efforts of Hahn and Strassman and concluded that matter had been transformed into energy. Frisch borrowed a concept from biology and called the process *fission*. Fermi had confirmed physics' most famous equation, $E=mc^2$.

In his *Sun-Times* article, Fermi acknowledged how unconventional was the clandestine collaboration of the work on fission. As the developments in physics coincided with the threat of another war in Europe, Fermi and his colleagues agreed to stop publishing their research.

Fermi explained, "We were afraid these findings might help the Nazis." He well understood the radical change that secrecy introduced: "Our action, of course, represented a break with scientific tradition and was not taken lightly."[25] The decision sacrificed the customary benefits of collaborative research, and it also denied interested parties an opportunity to ask about the safety and benefits of the work.

Events were moving very fast. Meitner and Frisch also found that neutrons were released during fission, and they in turn might split adjacent nuclei. The possibility of a chain reaction of fission was apparent. As the Fermis sailed to America in January of 1939, Meitner and Frisch informed Niels Bohr of the news. Bohr, another Jewish physicist, was preparing to sail to America himself.

On January 26, 1939, a month after Fermi received the Nobel Prize in Oslo, he joined Bohr in Washington DC to present the discoveries to a conference of American physicists. By that time, Fermi had taken a position at Columbia University, where he worked with Leo Szilard, Walter Zinn, and Herbert Anderson to convert theories of fission into machinery that would produce an actual chain reaction.

After working in New York for several years, Fermi moved his operation to Chicago to join the Metallurgical Institute at the university, another component of President Hutchins's war factory. He arrived in the summer of 1942, with America only months into World War II and Fermi only months away from attempting the first experiment of a nuclear chain reaction.

In his subsequent *Sun-Times* article, Fermi described Chicago Pile No. 1 and the process of atomic fission, comparing it to a rubbish fire lit by spontaneous combustion. Concerning a critical point, he wrote, "The atomic pile is controlled and prevented from burning itself to complete destruction by cadmium rods which absorb neutrons and stop the bombardment process. The same effect might be achieved by running a pipe of cold water through a rubbish heap; by keeping the temperature low the pipe would prevent the spontaneous burning."[26]

Readers of Fermi's newspaper article learned they had been safe on that cold December day because the chain reaction "was designed to proceed at a slow rate" in contrast to an atomic bomb designed "to proceed at as fast a rate as was possible."[27] In other words, the atomic pile was a nuclear reactor capable of producing energy, rather than a bomb capable of destroying a city. Such at least was the hope, but perhaps any relief for the reader might have been tempered by the conclusion: "Otherwise, the basic process is similar to that of the atomic bomb."[28] Fermi also left out some pertinent points.

For one, the pile was constructed without blueprints.[29] No comprehensive engineering design was followed. Rather, physicists would tell craftsmen what they wanted, and laborers would build the ensuing structure. Fermi's Columbia University colleague Walter Zinn was in charge of the construction. As Richard Rhodes characterized the labor force, "For crew Zinn had half a dozen young physicists, a thoroughly able carpenter and some thirty high school dropouts earning pocket money until their draft notices came through. They were Back of the Yards boys from the tough neighborhood beyond the Chicago stockyards and Zinn improved the fluency of his swearing keeping them in line."[30]

These young men built the pile layer by layer through grueling manual labor. As Rhodes described it, "Graphite dust blackened walls, floors, hallways, lab coats, faces, hands. A black haze dispersed light in the floodlit air. White teeth shone. Every surface was slippery, hands and feet routine casualties of dropped blocks."[31] Some of the graphite blocks contained the uranium fuel; others did not. The content depended, as so many things did, on the calculations of Enrico Fermi.

In the morning of December 2, Fermi took his place on a balcony where fans had once watched doubles matches of squash. From that vantage, he monitored the experiment and issued directions on its course. The mechanism that engaged the uranium pile was the removal of the cadmium control rods. Preliminary work indicated that the pace at which the control rods were removed from the pile would control the rate of the chain reaction.

George Weil was the young physicist in charge of withdrawing the last control rod from the pile. He was to do so by following instructions from Fermi, who calculated the exact length of removal in relation to the increased activity within the nucleus of the fissile material. By confirming that the level of the reaction matched his prediction at each point that the cadmium rod was pulled, Fermi could be confident that he controlled the experiment as long as Weil did as he was told. Here, again, the possibility of the human factor.

On the face of it, pulling a rod out of its housing shouldn't be an especially challenging task. "Another six inches, George." And Weil would draw out the rod to coincide with a point on some kind of adjacent ruler that indicated six inches. Nothing to it, except . . .

Weil was thirty-four years old that day in the squash court, and other men that age are employed in professions where, despite extreme tension, their hand-eye coordination, ability to concentrate, and control of their nerves are beyond the imaginations of the rest of us.

Yet from time to time, those young men drop passes that quarterbacks put right in their hands. They walk the opposing pitcher, with the bases loaded. They let lazy fly balls bounce off their mitts. They put up air balls from the free throw line. They send a wrist shot into the stands when the goalie is completely out of position. They rifle a winning volley into the net. They miss putts the length of a small dog.

Sometimes the errors are mental. They make the catch but jog off the field with two outs while the tying run scores from third. They miss the hit-and-run sign and watch their teammate get thrown out at second by ten feet. They ground a pass to stop the clock . . . on fourth down. They call time out when they have none left. They sign an incorrect scorecard. And in the cruel calculus of sports, sometimes the blunders become as immortal as the heroics.

Elite athletes make notorious mistakes for two reasons: fear and carelessness. The pressure of the moment can sharpen the senses to perform brilliantly, but if that pressure passes a level of confidence, it can trigger ineptitude and the calls to sports radio to inform, "My grandma coulda made that play."

At the same time, concentration might lapse because despite the stakes, the young man has made this play countless times. Relaxing under pressure is good, unless, like tension, it passes a certain blissful point, what Aristotle called the Golden Mean.

Henry Daghlian and Louis Slotin died because they were careless about an exercise that each had performed many times. Once the blue light flashed and let them know the danger that was present, they each remained engaged and took the steps necessary to save others from disaster.

George Weil held in his hands the last cadmium rod between physics as it had always been practiced and a new age in which humanity would possess an unprecedented amount of energy and an unprecedented potential for destruction. Fermi's calculations could be right on the money, but if Weil lost his focus on the balance between confidence and carelessness, those calculations might have been utterly unimportant.

The squash court that morning was brutally cold. People, including Weil, were bundled against the temperature. Sweaters under sports coats under heavy overcoats with scarves about the necks. Gloves and maybe the hands in pockets as well. In the stands, maybe people had coffee, and we can imagine them tensing and shifting, bouncing slightly to stay as warm as possible. Huddling perhaps in tight bunches. But George Weil stood alone. The only one in the room with the responsibility to physically start the chain reaction.

Weil did have some backup for safety. Two other sets of control rods provided redundancy. One was a crude mechanism operated by Walter Zinn. If the reaction appeared to be speeding out of Fermi's and Weil's control, Zinn had the responsibility to swing an ax and sever a rope that held another set of control rods that would stop the experiment.

If these measures proved unreliable, a third set of control rods, called ZIP, could trigger automatically to shut down the chain reaction.

The last defense against disaster was the trio of graduate students described by Fermi as a "liquid control squad."[32] If their nerve held, in what would be an extremely chaotic situation, the young men were "to flood the pile with cadmium salt solution in case the control rods failed."[33] So, the experiment began.

Preparatory work on the pile had measured the activity of neutrons when all but the one control rod had been removed, so Fermi ordered that the pile be returned to that state. A single thirteen-foot cadmium rod was now the only barrier to the chain reaction. The instruments generated numbers that matched previous recordings when the pile had only a single cadmium rod. Fermi then told Weil to pull it halfway out.

The neutron activity accelerated, but it was well below the level required to generate the chain reaction. With no computer to help, Fermi calculated the mathematics of the experiment on a slide rule. From time to time, he told Weil to pull the control rod another six inches out.

The contrast was remarkable. Fermi, the Nobel-winning physicist, determined the activity within the pile through elaborate mathematics calculated with a slide rule, a device likely unknown to anyone younger than a baby boomer. By all accounts, he was calm throughout the morning as the intensity within the pile approached a point never before achieved. Richard Rhodes described the scene as more observers arrived at the squash court and took their places on the balcony: "The pile rising before them, faced with raw 4 by 6 inch pine timbers up to its equator, domed bare graphite above, looked like an ominous black beehive in a bright box. Neutrons were its bees, dancing and hot."[34]

Years before the Daghlian and Slotin tragedies, did anyone wonder about the construction of the beehive? Two physicists with experiential knowledge of the atomic effects on Hiroshima and Nagasaki were careless and paid with their lives. They had been working with a plutonium sphere the approximate size of a basketball. What were the potential casualties of an atomic pile of six tons of uranium metal and fifty tons of uranium oxide if it had been poorly constructed because of confusion between the physicists and craftsmen, both groups working without blueprints?

What of the Back of the Yards boys who built the beehive? Were they always sufficiently focused when placing the elements of the pile in their proper places? Anyone bored? Distracted? Anxious? Overserved the night before? Any factor that might have made the pile as lethal as the plutonium sphere that killed Harry Daghlian and Louis Slotin?

As it was, the fury of the dancing bees didn't fluster Enrico Fermi, but it was more than the automated safety system could bear. Late in the morning, a loud *BANG!* interrupted the experiment and likely sent heartbeats in the balcony into dances of their own. George Weil, of course, was standing next to the pile and would have felt the impact of all the control rods firing back into their original position with a startling crash.

The phlegmatic Fermi recalled the incident, "At 11:35 a.m. the counters were clicking rapidly. Then, with a loud clap, the automatic control rods slammed home. The safety point had been set too low. It seemed a good time to eat lunch."[35]

Was Weil as calm? Made of different stuff, might his nerves have been shaken? He'd been holding the critical control rod, and it would have fired from his hands to join its fellows in their initial state of engagement with the pile. When the experiment resumed, when once again he held the only control rod still preventing the chain reaction, what would be his emotional state?

At lunchtime in Central Standard Time on December 2, 1942, the key decisions that ran some risk of an unprecedented catastrophe were being made not by Franklin Roosevelt, nor the secretary of war, nor any other member of the Top Policy Group, nor the president of the University of Chicago, nor the mayor, nor the governor, nor anyone other than an Italian immigrant who had lived in America for only four years after emigrating from a nation with which the United States was at war.

Arthur Compton wrote of the "remarkable precision" between Fermi's projections and the actual results of the experiment.[36] Compton made no mention of a loud noise but concluded, "These preliminary tests were time-consuming and we adjourned for lunch."[37]

At two in the afternoon, the experiment resumed. Fermi directed that all but one of the cadmium rods be removed and that the remaining one be set at a point at which it had been measured earlier in the morning. He then had the control rod drawn to the same point that triggered the earlier shutdown; approximately seven feet of the rod had been drawn out.

Just before the pile achieved the chain reaction, Fermi ordered the ZIP safety device back in. As he choreographed the next steps, the single control rod was pulled another twelve inches out; then the ZIP control was removed. Compton remembered, "This we knew meant that the chain reaction should develop on an expanding scale."[38]

The historic experiment continued for over four minutes. The intensity is suggested by Compton's recollection of the time: "Finally after many minutes the meters showed a reading that meant the radiation reaching the balcony was beginning to be dangerous."[39]

At that point, Fermi ordered the safety controls back in. He summarized, "The event was not spectacular, no fuses burned, no lights flashed. But to us it meant that release of atomic energy on a large scale would be only a matter of time."[40]

Compton's recollection was more spirited, "Atomic power! It had been produced, kept under control, and stopped. The power liberated was less than that needed to light an electric lamp, but that power marked a new era in man's history."[41] He then gave his impressions of three men. He praised Fermi's calm command, especially his judgment that the people of the Metallurgical Laboratory were exhausted after such a historic achievement. Recognizing that blunders were now possible, Fermi took some time before determining the next steps.

Compton found a different reaction from Volney Wilson, one of the engineers on the balcony. "He was among those who had sincerely hoped that, even at the last moment, something might arise which would make it impossible to effect the chain reaction. The destruction it implied was a nightmare with which he was finding it hard to live."[42]

Crawford Greenwalt, an industrial engineer at DuPont who accompanied Compton after the experiment, offered a distinctly different impression. Greenwalt enthused about the world that nuclear power could bring about. Where Wilson had cringed at the prospect of a bomb, Greenwalt looked past the war to a revolutionary source of power that would result in changes beyond imagining.

Later that day, Compton reached James Conant. Their famous exchange seems somewhat awkward, two very smart fellows trying to sound cool. Compton said, "Jim, you'll be interested to know that the Italian navigator has just landed in the New World."[43] Conant replied, "Were the natives friendly?"[44] Compton assured him they were.

Some time later, at a dinner party, Laura Fermi was puzzled that each of the men arriving congratulated her husband. She asked why and was given innocuous answers: "Ask your husband." "Nothing special. He is a smart guy. That's all." "Don't get excited. You'll find out sometime."[45] Conventional sexism perhaps, but the only guest who was a woman and who knew the answer was no better.

Leona Woods worked in the Metallurgical Laboratory at the University of Chicago and helped her mother with a potato farm outside the city. Laura Fermi wrote of Leona, "Because I refused either to smash atoms or to dig potatoes, she looked down on me."[46]

Mrs. Fermi concluded, "Leona, I thought, owed me some friendliness."[47] She asked the potato-picking physicist what Enrico had done to earn the plaudits of the guests. "Leona bent her head, covered with short, deep-black hair, toward me, and from her lips came a whisper: 'He has sunk a Japanese admiral.' 'You are making fun of me,' I protested."[48]

She did no better with her husband: "'Enrico, did you really sink a Japanese admiral?' 'Did I?' Enrico would answer with a candid expression. 'So you did not sink a Japanese admiral!' 'Didn't I?' His expression would not change."[49]

Not until after the war did Laura Fermi get a truncated version of the truth. Enrico gave her a copy of the Smyth Report, officially known as *Atomic Energy for Military Purposes: A General Account of the Scientific Research and Technical Development That Went into the Making of Atomic Bombs*. Referring to the historic experiment, the report read, "The pile was first operated as a self-sustaining system on December 2, 1942."[50] Her husband's part in the work was summarized as, "This experiment had been performed under the general direction of E. Fermi, assisted principally by the groups headed by W. H. Zinn and H. L. Anderson. V. C. Wilson and his group had been largely responsible for developing the instruments and controls, and a great many others in the laboratory had contributed to the success of the enterprise."[51]

The nearly tedious language of the report masked an alarming prospect, one with which Laura Fermi had been made aware. After her family left New York and Columbia University so that Enrico could engage in the work at the University of Chicago, she and other new arrivals were invited to a party, one of a series that Arthur Compton and his wife arranged for the growing staff.

At each of the parties, Compton showed the British film *Next of Kin*: "It depicted in dark tones the consequences of negligence and carelessness. A briefcase laid down on the floor in a public place is stolen by a spy. English military plans become known to the enemy. Bombardments, destruction of civilian homes, an unnecessary high toll of lives on the fighting front are the result."[52]

Secrecy prevailed throughout the Manhattan Project. In Chicago the experiment in the squash court had worked almost exactly as Enrico

Fermi had predicted. Speculation of disasters had proved groundless, but no one who knew the science was entirely certain before the event that Chicago would be safe. *Critical mass* has become a common expression, but its origins lie in atomic fission, where it indicated an unknown state in which a steady progression could suddenly veer in a radical and dangerous direction.

Secrecy meant that people with requisite expertise would be separated into administrative compartments where exchanges of information, questions, and concerns would be impaired. The officials who supervised the entire Manhattan Project were too limited in their knowledge of the science or too distracted by other aspects of the war to control effectively the Arthur Comptons of the project.

The experiment in the squash court, historic as it was, remained one part of a vast and complex array of programs, all of which focused on winning the war. In its way, the bureaucratic mechanism mirrored the lattice of U-235, uranium oxide, graphite, and cadmium. Rivalries among and within science, the military, universities, were more than personal and professional jealousies. They were possible impediments to a project that seemed essential to victory over the Axis.

The reason why James Conant and Leslie Groves declined to stop Compton and Fermi from the experiment was that responsibility was divided among the various bureaucratic points. Each agency specialized in extremely esoteric aspects of research and development of an atomic bomb. Each official was distinguished, especially those with supervising authority, but no one knew enough about each aspect to presume to interfere with the exercise of responsibility by those with greater expertise.

Conant could have warned Bush, and Groves could have taken his concerns to Gen. George Marshall, the army chief of staff. But what would they have said? Their anxiety turned on questions of physics, and neither man could have been specific about the dangers he feared. Certainly, safety was a major concern of all the participants in the Manhattan Project, but building a bomb before the Germans could was an even more pressing matter.

Ultimately, Franklin Roosevelt bore responsibility for the chain reaction in Chicago. Whether or not he was aware of what was planned for December 2, 1942, is not clear, but the pattern in his wartime presidency was to trust his subordinates. He likely would have assumed that if Conant, Groves, and Bush trusted Compton and if Compton trusted Fermi, that would have been sufficient.

This new enterprise combined the authority of government with theoretical science and basic research. Among the consequences was a recalibration of various civic virtues, done with no serious democratic participation. Chicago emerged without harm, but whether the American civic culture fared as well is not so apparent.

[TWO]

FDR and the Einstein Letter

The path to the squash court began in 1939 with a letter written by several Hungarians, signed by a German, and read by a Russian to a patrician New Yorker who was the president of the United States.[1] The letter required a reading aloud because it buried the lede. Before getting to the third paragraph with its ominous reference to "extremely powerful bombs of a new type," Franklin Roosevelt might not have made it past "E. Fermi and L. Szilard" or "Joliot in France" or "a nuclear chain reaction in a large mass of uranium."

The letter was written on August 2 and presented to FDR on October 11, some weeks after Germany's invasion of Poland and the start of World War II. We can imagine Alexander Sachs, the reader, annotating the letter so that the very distracted president would understand that Albert Einstein thought that Nazi Germany had the means and the inclination to develop an atomic bomb, a device that, "carried by boat and exploded in a port, might very well destroy the whole port together with some of the surrounding territory." At least that.

Franklin Roosevelt replied to the presentation from Sachs, a trusted economics adviser, with a pithy summation: "Alex, what you are after is to see that the Nazis don't blow us up."[2] He then called in his de facto chief of staff Gen. Edwin "Pa" Watson. It was imperative that Watson, as the gatekeeper to the Oval Office, understood the importance of the new initiative; so referring to the Einstein letter, the president declared, "This requires action."[3]

It's a great line. Decisive in the face of crisis. Clear in its assessment of the urgency. It is the essential voice of a commander in chief, but it does generate questions of its own: Action of what kind? Action by whom? What other measures would have to be put on hold to keep track of uranium research in Germany? Should the United States start its own effort toward a nuclear bomb? What would all this cost? Could the effort accomplish its purpose in time to influence the war?

The answer to those questions in October of 1939 was that no one knew. The endeavor was unprecedented in both the nature of the science and the scope of the conflict, civilization's second cataclysmic war in twenty-five years.

When he heard about Einstein's concerns, Franklin Roosevelt was fifty-seven years old. He was nearing the end of his second term, but the crisis in Europe was enticing him to break the two-term limit that had prevailed since George Washington decided he'd had enough. A third term would mean both that Roosevelt had given Einstein's plea a green light and that he would be the president who would see his initial approval through to a conclusion.

If we think that FDR's reaction was the same that any president would have had, we might wonder how his immediate predecessors would have taken the news of the German threat. Would Woodrow Wilson have pondered the moral dimensions? Would Warren Harding have been overwhelmed? Would Calvin Coolidge have thought first about the costs? Would Herbert Hoover, the engineer, have been most intrigued by the science?

The questions are speculative, thus almost useless, but they do remind us that presidents matter. So for purposes of the Manhattan Project, who was *this* president? How would he go about answering the essential questions? What understanding of the American presidency had he acquired in his time in office? What of the executive's relationship with the other branches? What resources were available to realize his plans?

Franklin Roosevelt reacted to the Einstein letter as a pragmatic Progressive, a Hamiltonian, curious about power and its uses. He was especially committed to vigorous government led by an energetic executive. He certainly saw himself that way. In that position, he would tackle corporate or foreign threats to the nation. The country's interest, as he would put it, could be summarized as freedom of speech and religion plus freedom from want and fear not only for all Americans but also to people in every other nation. The New Deal had international dimensions.

The path from the Einstein letter to the squash court was relatively short and straight compared to the development of Roosevelt himself. That path was a long and tortured process, one that began with his being a Roosevelt.

We might see his public life emerging at his wedding to his cousin Eleanor on St. Patrick's Day in 1905. She was the niece of Theodore, who, at the time, was the president of the United States; as was often the case, Teddy was the star of the occasion, as he escorted his orphaned niece down the aisle.

TR seems to have been pleased by the marriage that united the Oyster Bay Roosevelts of Long Island with the branch of the clan up the Hudson River in Hyde Park, but the family merger had political limits. Franklin was fond of Theodore, but he joined the Democratic Party, a connection that he inherited through his parents. Further asserting his independence, FDR disdained Tammany Hall, the political engine of the Democratic Party in New York.

His first attempt at public office was in 1910 when he agreed to seek a New York State Assembly seat that appeared would become vacant. A last minute change of plans put the incumbent back in the race and left FDR with ambition but no place to channel it.

At that moment, a seat opened in the state senate—a harder task than the assembly, where the Democrats had a lock on the seat—but Roosevelt had the money, ran an energetic campaign, and won in a good year for Democrats. He had stumbled in his innocent run for the assembly and had fallen up into the senate.

His embrace of Progressive reform seems to have reflected both a sincere repugnance of Tammany's baser practices as well as a snobbish contempt for the urban machine. Tammany's corruption was so rich that George Washington Plunkitt famously organized it into the categories of "honest and dishonest graft."[4]

The lack of coherence in the Progressive movement was evident to one of its leading advocates who wrote, "In the beginning, it was spasmodic in its outbursts, innocent in its purposes, and narrow in its outlook. It sprang up almost spontaneously in a number of different places and in a number of different detached movements; its adherents did not look much beyond a victory at a particular election, or the passage of a few remedial laws."[5]

In distinct ways, Teddy Roosevelt, William Howard Taft, and

Woodrow Wilson were all Progressives, though the differences among them were sufficient to fashion a three-way battle for the presidency in 1912. In that contest, state senator Franklin Roosevelt supported Wilson, even though Cousin Teddy was running a quixotic campaign on the Progressive Party ticket; Wilson's victory led to Franklin's being appointed to Teddy's old post as assistant secretary of the navy.

Just a year into that job, Franklin impulsively jumped into a race in New York for a seat in the United States Senate. The move baffled his advisers and irritated Tammany Hall. The election was the first in New York after the passage of the Seventeenth Amendment, so FDR would appeal directly to the New York electorate . . . if he could get the nomination.

He could not. Tammany had no use for the fop from Hyde Park who had dismissed the wigwam as a haven for hacks. Roosevelt lost the Democratic nomination to James Gerard, the American ambassador to Germany, who did not even have to bother leaving Europe to get his party's nod. Defeated but still ambitious, arrogant, and dangerously naive, Roosevelt returned to Washington and the Navy Department, where he began a master class in politics and bureaucratic management.

Between 1913 and 1921, American government changed in ways more fundamental than at any period other than the Civil War. During the Wilson years, the Constitution was amended four times: the income tax was authorized; senators were popularly elected; the sale of alcohol was prohibited; and women were guaranteed the vote.

Tensions over the money supply, a battle in American politics since Alexander Hamilton crafted the first Bank of the United States, led to the creation of the Federal Reserve System in 1913. To this day, the Fed is a curious hybrid of national and regional parts as well as public and private authorities. It operates largely in secret, purporting to balance the interests of Wall Street financiers and Mississippi farmers, though no farmer has ever served on the Board of Governors.

Wilson also had two Supreme Court appointments during his tenure. The first was James McReynolds, who was perhaps a lunatic as evidenced by his undisguised loathing of women, Jews, and possibly anyone not named James McReynolds. His appeal to Wilson is all the more puzzling since the president later appointed Louis

Brandeis to join McReynolds. The court then had its first Jew and a justice so hate filled that he would refuse to have his picture taken in Brandeis's company.

Beginning when he was thirty years old, the assistant secretary of the navy had a prime spot to observe these historic decisions. The Navy Department was run by Josephus Daniels; showing again his considerable limitations, FDR's initial attitude about his boss was callow and rude. Daniels was a newspaper editor from North Carolina who was drawn to the pacifism and populism of William Jennings Bryan, who himself was a three-time loser in presidential elections and Wilson's secretary of state.

The navy was skeptical about Daniels because of his Bryan sympathies, and self-regarding sophisticates looked down their patrician noses at his lack of panache. We see the hypocrisy of the swells in the vulgar words of an associate of Senator Henry Cabot Lodge of Massachusetts who described Daniels as "a maggot in a putrid sore of the social organism."[6]

Behind Daniels's back, Roosevelt joined the snobbery. He mocked the secretary as "the funniest looking hillbilly."[7] As the younger man grew up a bit, he came to see that Daniels had political skills that Roosevelt himself had yet to acquire. Those skills would be honed against the backdrop of the Great War that began in Europe and spread throughout the world. America stayed out of the combat for nearly three years, but the nation could not remain unaffected by the economic and social forces of war.

War expands the state, and it does so permanently. In 1914, when the Great War began in Europe, the federal government of the United States spent $735 million on all its responsibilities.[8] In 1916, when British troops were slaughtered at the Somme and the French were "bled white" at Verdun, federal spending actually dropped to $734 million.[9] But in 1917, when German resumption of unrestricted submarine warfare sent Woodrow Wilson to Congress for a declaration of war, federal outlays nearly tripled to $1,977,681,751.[10]

While acknowledging the casualties as the most tragic cost of the conflict, money may indicate better the impact of war on the size of government. As stunning as the increase was in 1917, that was the last year ever that the federal government would spend less than

$2 billion. Expenditures jumped to $12.7 billion in 1918 and to $18.5 billion the following year before a peace dividend appeared.[11] Even with significant reductions, the lowest federal spending would ever be again was in 1927, when outlays were $2,974,000,000.[12] So by this measure, World War I caused the federal government to grow, in perpetuity, a minimum of four times its previous size.

During the war years, while Daniels concentrated on strategic-policy questions, Roosevelt carried the burden of administrative tasks. He handled contracts, inspected naval bases, and fought for more and better equipment. While honoring Wilson's position of neutrality in the Great War, Roosevelt had a more muscular view of protecting America's interests. In addition to more and better ships, he urged better housing and training for the sailors and marines. He had a very active view of his office, and he was operating in a culture of administration that was in the midst of phenomenal change.

The expansion of government exacerbated a fundamental issue of the Progressive Era. In an industrialized nation, one with massive corporate bureaucracies in the leading industries, what was the proper relationship between business and government? Should the large companies be broken up? Should they be allowed to grow but regulated against abuses? Should they be left alone but nationalized as state entities when they reached maturity? Few public figures argued for returning to laissez faire.

One aspect of the Progressive struggle to redefine the political economy was a split between capitalism and markets. Bernard Baruch, J. P. Morgan, and others were still committed to private ownership of property, but they concluded that markets were disruptive and wasteful. Baruch thought that markets made decisions in the rear-view mirror, figuring out the right course only after squandering resources on the wrong one. This view advocated planning instead of markets; that changed the question to: Whose plan?

Writing of the Great War, David Kennedy proposed, "The war forced both government and business to think and act on an unprecedentedly large and integrated scale, and the process was uniquely revealing of the character of the American economy and polity in the early 20th century."[13] Since government was one of the actors in this refashioning, politics inevitably came into the picture, and FDR became adept at its elements in a turbulent era.

Frederick Winslow Taylor developed a management strategy that became popular for its promise of efficient administration. His scientific management movement rested on time-and-motion studies that promoted the careers of efficiency experts and gave Spencer Tracy and Katherine Hepburn a chance to shine in their spoof *Desk Set*.

As the war dragged on, Roosevelt learned how Taylorism could give the navy greater returns on the taxpayers' money, but he also saw that pressing efficiency too hard in too limited a sense could create its own complications. Where Tracy's character, Richard Sumner, had to contend with his attraction to Hepburn's Bunny Watson, FDR was concerned about strikes in the shipyards if union workers were pushed beyond reason or if they feared the loss of their jobs. Roosevelt found a balance, described by James McGregor Burns: "The great lesson he learned during these years was that bureaucrats, workers, and sailors were human beings with human problems and failings."[14]

We may well miss the point if we think of FDR as a nice man who had a soft spot for the welder in the Washington Navy Yard. More likely, when he told a group of machinists, "I want you all to feel that you can come to me at any time in my office and we can talk matters over," he was thinking about the larger efficiency of labor peace.[15]

His eight years in Washington were extraordinary: constitutional amendments; controversial Supreme Court appointments; the most centralized monetary system in seventy-five years; senators chosen directly by the electorate and women joining that electorate, thus doubling its size; and Prohibition. Each was historic on its own, but all of them developed as Europe drew the world into the most destructive war ever fought to that point.

Early in this apprenticeship, Roosevelt was bruised by the rough politics of Tammany Hall; near its end, he saw the vain attempt of Woodrow Wilson to establish principles for permanent peace and an organization that would spare the world another cataclysm, an effort that broke Wilson's health. Roosevelt's mentors ranged from Wilson, the Puritan president, to Louis Howe, the president's closest adviser and a master of politics at close quarters. FDR had become a skilled bureaucratic politician, and the next presidential election would give him a chance to show that he could be a successful electoral politician as well.

In the campaign of 1920, Franklin Roosevelt was thirty-nine years old. He had not won a race for elective office since he was in his twenties. In political terms, he was also too young to be considered for the top of the ticket, but he was a contender for the vice presidential nomination because of the quality he assumed at birth: his name.

For his cousins in Oyster Bay, the presumption was another indication of Franklin's insufferable gall. Were he alive, Teddy would have been sixty-two, but he had died January 6, 1919. None of TR's sons was old enough in 1920 to run for the White House. Quentin, the youngest, had been killed in aerial combat a few months before the armistice at the age of twenty-three. The other sons had been physically or emotionally damaged after volunteering for a fight that Franklin had passed up.

Family ties broke as Teddy's children saw their cousin as a philanderer for his affair with his wife's secretary, a shirker for ducking military service and hiding behind President Wilson's insistence that he stay in the Navy Department, and a fraud for knowing more about high tea than survival in the Amazon. To see the Hyde Park dandy steal the legacy of Theodore Roosevelt was simply too much. All the Roosevelts were New York sophisticates, but when they brushed against one another in subsequent political tiffs, the tone of the contests might have shocked the toughest Tammany ward healer.

The 1920 race sent FDR across the country, covering more territory than any other candidate in the history of presidential tickets. The effort was not reflected in the election's outcome. The Republicans swept every state outside the South as Warren Harding and Calvin Coolidge won a crushing victory. Bad news for the Democrats, but Roosevelt was not damaged by the defeat. He was young, energetic, experienced, and a Roosevelt. He had made countless connections within the Democratic Party nationally, and he had campaigned with candidates in every part of the country. No doubt that he would have another chance at a national office.

At this point, a casual glance finds a man born to wealth and privilege who had done a reasonable job living up to expectations. We can see how he acquired the nickname "Featherduster" with its implications of frivolousness. Without academic distinction, he had been admitted to prep school at Groton, Harvard, and Columbia Law School, which he left after a single year. Without professional accomplishment, he had been elected to the New York State Senate. Unlike his famous cousin, he had not left his administrative post in the Navy Department to test himself in combat.

In fact, anything FDR accomplished seemed a lightweight version of TR's record. If Franklin bothered to examine his life after the 1920 defeat, he would have observed a breezy stroll that had combined public purpose with personal indulgence, such as his affair with his wife's secretary. In every way, he might have seemed unequipped for the trial that lay just ahead.

In 1921, to secure a future in politics, Roosevelt determined to remove a blot on his record. While assistant secretary of the navy, he had been accused of arranging to use enlisted men to entrap other sailors into homosexual acts as part of a strategy to clean up a naval base in Newport, Rhode Island. The charge had hung in the air during the 1920 campaign, and FDR wanted it resolved before trying again for the U.S. Senate or running for governor of New York.

He dashed to Washington DC in July 1921 to try to block a report by the Senate's Republican majority that would put the Newport business in a very bad light. Roosevelt failed to suppress the report, but it was so over the top that it did him little damage. Nonetheless, he was worn out from defending himself, and he looked forward to a vacation at a family home on Campobello Island.

The retreat was located in New Brunswick, Canada, just across from Lubec, Maine, the easternmost town in the United States. On his way there from Washington, Roosevelt paid a visit on July 28 to a Boy Scout camp at Palisades Interstate Park, along the Hudson River. He could expect that the scouts would be excited by his appearance and would pass their enthusiasm to the voting members of their families.

His mixing with the scouts, or some other exchange at that time, was catastrophic. Roosevelt picked up a virus whose full force became manifest at Campobello. Terrible fatigue combined with a high fever and great difficulty moving his legs. Within days, he was paralyzed from the waist down, with limited mobility in his arms and torso. A country doctor recommended deep massage for his legs, an excruciating ordeal that likely compounded the effects of the virus. A specialist was brought up from Harvard; he, perhaps mistakenly, diagnosed polio.[16] Over 90 percent of the victims of infantile paralysis recovered completely from the disease, but for the first time, FDR found himself a member of an unfortunate minority.

The physical trauma combined with an emotional horror that may be impossible to grasp. Months before, Roosevelt had been touring the country, traveling thousands of miles as the vice presidential candidate of the Democratic Party, seeking the office from which his cousin had ascended to the White House. A trip to London or Paris had been a routine experience for him; now, moving from his bed to the living room was beyond his capacity.

While he had never gone on safari or explored the Dakotas as Theodore had done, FDR was enthusiastic about sailing, swimming, golfing, and other active hobbies. In a few horrible days, he went from being a gentleman sportsman to being terrified at the thought of being trapped in a house fire. The cheerful dilettante descended into a bleak, emotional depression.

Over several years, Roosevelt remade himself through a brutal rehabilitation of body and spirit. He appeared to regain some ability to walk with human and mechanical assistance, but the sight was a ruse. FDR slung his useless legs forward while balancing his torso atop the braces and canes. An ebullient expression provided the distraction that let his audience believe that his paralysis was more an inconvenience than an incapacity.

Family, aides, and his indomitable will put Roosevelt back into the political picture in New York, but for some people who should have known better, he never entirely dispelled the reputation for being a lightweight. For instance, some of the old Tammany hands loyal to New York governor Al Smith remained dismissive of FDR.

This attitude became a lazy habit of people who refused to appreciate that Roosevelt's return to the public arena in the mid-1920s reflected a depth of character that prepared him for subsequent challenges. More to their peril, they missed that he had honed a determination that could make him a ruthless adversary.

FDR won the governorship in 1928 in a tough year for Democrats. When Smith, the Democratic nominee for president, lost New York to Hoover, Roosevelt seized the inside track as the most powerful politician in the state. He was reelected governor two years later and then won the Democratic presidential nomination after a very difficult fight in 1932. Along the way, Al Smith belatedly indicated an interest in a rematch with Hoover, and his supporters were shocked at the almost brutal treatment their man received from the Featherduster.

The nation was over three years into the Great Depression and desperate for leadership when FDR challenged the incumbent Herbert Hoover. The bad times had begun as a severe financial correction on Wall Street in October of 1929. By the following spring, banks were in trouble, and life savings were in jeopardy. The industrial and retail sectors of the economy that had enjoyed such a boom in the 1920s collapsed. Farmers, who had missed the prosperity of the Roaring Twenties, realized that the inadequate markets of recent years had fallen into substantially worse shape.

The hard economic times became a social disaster as the bonds of community broke. Unable to provide for their families, some men disappeared into America's vast interior or the anonymity of its great cities. A padlocked factory could mean bankruptcies and unemployment for the businesses that were sustained by the paychecks of that plant. John Steinbeck captured the rural tragedy of the Depression with one of the great American novels, *The Grapes of Wrath*, about an Oklahoma farm family losing its home.

The nation's trauma finally assumed a political dimension. For seventy years, the Republican Party had dominated American politics. Founded in opposition to slavery, the GOP remained identified with the martyred Abraham Lincoln. The Democrats had put together some strong urban machines, but its national constituency was limited to the South. In a notorious, and unsuccessful, slur, the Democrats were identified in 1884 as the party of "Rum, Romanism, and Rebellion."

The impact of the Depression was so deep and extensive that the Republican's Civil War coalition could not sustain itself. Herbert Hoover was a brilliant engineer, a humanitarian who had saved countless refugees from starvation, but also a prisoner of his limited conception of the American presidency when his own country needed the full use of his talents.

Roosevelt's campaign against Hoover offered nothing of programmatic substance to combat the Great Depression, but he certainly offered a change of personality from the increasingly dour Hoover. Avoiding specifics, Roosevelt promised energy, experimentation, and unrelenting action in contrast to a Hoover presidency that offered platitudes in the face of one of the great crises in the nation's history.

The campaign was one of those in which the challenger needs only to remind the voters that he is not the incumbent or, as John Nance Garner told his running mate when FDR asked what victory would require, "Stay alive 'til November."[17] He did indeed, although he narrowly survived an assassination attempt the following February.

His victory on November 8, 1932, was one of the greatest in the country's history. FDR won 57.4 percent of the popular vote and 472 of 531 electoral votes. Hoover carried Pennsylvania, Delaware, Connecticut, Vermont, New Hampshire, and Maine. Roosevelt won everything else, only the third Democrat since the Civil War to win the White House.

The inaugural address rested on a premise from a bible of the Progressive movement. Herbert Croly's *The Promise of American Life* was published in 1909, when FDR was preparing his run for the New York State Senate. While acknowledging the limitations of the approach, Croly examined American political history through the lenses of Thomas Jefferson and Alexander Hamilton. He further acknowledged that neither man got things entirely right, but he was emphatic that Hamilton had the better argument.

The nation's growth after the Civil War, the industrialization of the economy along with the rise of monopolies in finance and major industries, the impact on labor markets of millions of immigrants— all had presented challenges that the framers could not have anticipated. Abraham Lincoln had saved the American experiment by assuming unprecedented power, and Croly thought that something similar was necessary in the twentieth century.

Franklin Roosevelt needed no convincing. If the inaugural address were to tell his audience the truth about the economic roots of their misery, Roosevelt would have had to say that he had absolutely no idea. He suspected it had something to do with reckless spending by the Hoover administration, but he couldn't be sure. On his own watch, he would strive occasionally toward his preference for a balanced budget, usually with miserable results.

Clueless though he was about the economics of the matter, he had a brilliant grasp of the political aspects of the Great Depression. From the outset, he fired the executive branch with energy, the quality that Alexander Hamilton had described as, "a leading character in the definition of good government."[18] Hamilton had dismissed critics who worried that "a vigorous Executive is inconsistent with the genius of republican government," tracing bad government through a short, straight line to "a feeble Executive."[19] FDR could not have agreed more.

The country heard the Hamiltonian tones in Roosevelt's electrifying inaugural address. After the famous remarks about "fear itself," the new president reviewed the country's challenges in the starkest terms.[20] He listed the economic calamities that the nation faced and then concluded, "Only a foolish optimist can deny the dark realities of the moment." But he had also delimited "our common difficulties," describing them as, "thank God, only material things."

He had an explanation for the crisis, not in an abstract theory but in the persons responsible: "The rulers of the exchange of mankind's goods have failed, through their own stubbornness and their own incompetence, have admitted their failure, and abdicated." He excoriated the class that his cousin Teddy had called, "malefactors of great wealth." He said, "They know only the rules of a generation of self-seekers." He offered the moral proposition that "happiness lies not in the mere possession of money; it lies in the joy of achievement, in the thrill of creative effort. The joy and moral stimulation of work no longer must be forgotten in the mad chase of evanescent profits."

Roosevelt concluded his inaugural with his understanding of his constitutional responsibilities: "Our Constitution is so simple and practical that it is possible always to meet extraordinary needs by changes in emphasis and arrangement without loss of essential form." He elaborated, "It is to be hoped that the normal balance of executive and legislative authority may be wholly adequate to meet the unprecedented task before us. But it may be that an unprecedented demand and need for undelayed action may call for temporary departure from that normal balance of public procedure."

He considered "the measures" that he might need to propose or that Congress might fashion "out of its experience and wisdom." If these adjustments failed to curtail the crisis of the Great Depression, FDR pledged, "I shall ask the Congress for the one remaining instrument to meet the crisis—broad Executive power to wage a war against the emergency, as great as the power that would be given to me if we were in fact invaded by a foreign foe."

This closing section of the speech is an unambiguous statement of an important constitutional principle. FDR presented the Madisonian system of government, with its elaborate separation of power and checks and balances, as a dynamic system that required a recalibration from time to time. At the moment, as during the Civil War, Roosevelt proposed that the other branches defer to the executive as the branch that was equipped to take swift and decisive action and to adjust to rapidly changing circumstances.

His presidency began with a focus entirely on domestic matters. The famous one hundred days transformed the inaugural address into legislation. The banking system, agriculture, and the market economy itself were changed, sometimes radically so and in a matter of weeks. In this energetic and broad engagement with the crisis, we can see the experience that FDR gained during his time in the Wilson administrations. His relentlessness also reflects the tenacity that he displayed in his personal battle against paralysis.

Roosevelt had compared the Great Depression to an invasion by a foreign power; while he concentrated on reviving the American economy, an actual foreign power was itself reemerging in Germany. Five weeks before FDR was inaugurated, Adolph Hitler was appointed chancellor of Germany. Three weeks after the American president had assured his audience that fear itself was their only concern, the German Reichstag passed the Empowering Act, which turned legislative authority over to Hitler and his cabinet. Few checks remained on a sociopathic, racist regime atop the most powerful country in Europe.

Over the next few years, Hitler eliminated opposition within government, the military, media, universities, and any other source of authority. The few dissenters who remained were marginalized if they survived at all. Totalitarian government emerged in the Reich as it had in the Soviet Union and Italy. The system never promised respect for its opponents; rather, it claimed to be able to respond effectively to the crises of the day. In every case, those challenges meant the economic Depression; in Germany, Hitler's proposed remedy meant reversing the outcome of the Great War.

Realizing rather early the threat that the Nazis posed, FDR proposed new programs and policies that would show that an eighteenth-century government could function effectively in the twentieth century. America could remain a liberal constitutional republic and meet the challenges of the day. All that was required was the Hamiltonian adjustment in a Madisonian system. To Roosevelt's frustration, Madison fought back.

In *Federalist* No. 10, Madison rejected outright the remedy that Karl Marx would offer: the elimination of the unequal distribution of wealth, "the most common and durable source of factions."[21] Instead, Madison urged controlling the effects of faction; in *Federalist* No. 51, he explained how that would be done through a separation of governing power, its organization into checks and balances, and the tying of elected officials to distinct constituencies to provide an incentive against colluding. Power was fragmented, and it would remain so. Whenever a president or Congress pressed too far, their excess would trigger a reaction elsewhere in the system until balance was restored. By the time he absorbed the letter from Einstein, FDR was painfully aware that Madison's musings were much more than an elaborate theory.

His initial attack on the Great Depression had received the backing of a Congress that was little more than a rubber stamp. The National Industrial Recovery Act (NIRA) had been perhaps the most radical piece of domestic legislation in the history of the country. It replaced a market economy with a system something like Fascism (i.e., cartels organized in the major industries with the authority to establish "codes of fair competition"). The codes determined production levels, distribution of goods, their price, wages, and other elements that previously had been set by supply and demand.

This sweeping overhaul of the American economy was accomplished in a single month. The legislation was introduced on May 15, 1933, and it was signed into law on June 16. The pressure of unhappy interest groups that Madison directed into congressional districts and Senate seats were swept away by the crisis of the moment and the charm of the president. Two of the three branches had coalesced.

The third branch spoke two years after the NIRA became law. On May 27, 1935, in the case *A. L. A. Schechter Poultry Corporation v. United States*, the Supreme Court struck down the NIRA along with two other signature reforms of the New Deal, and it did so by unanimous votes.[22]

Charles Evans Hughes wrote the opinion in *Schechter* joined by the Progressives Louis Brandeis and Benjamin Cordozo and the misanthropic James McReynolds along with the remaining five justices. The members of the court agreed on little, but they were as one in their belief that the New Deal had gone too far. Hamilton had maintained in *Federalist* No. 78 that "the judiciary is beyond comparison the weakest of the three departments of power." He had explained that it lacked "influence over either the sword or the purse."[23] May 27, 1935, would not have been the day to explain that point to Franklin Roosevelt.

The NIRA had passed the House by a vote of 329 to 80 and the Senate by 61 to 26. The Supreme Court of the United States cared not at all. In theory, democracy in American government was limited precisely so that individual freedom would not be sacrificed on an impulse of the mob.

For the president, the court's actions defied the theory of government that the inaugural address had expressed. Chief Justice Hughes had attended the ceremony. He had, of course, administered the inaugural oath. Hadn't he been listening? Arguments to limit government were a staple of American political culture. Jefferson was famous for them even though he ignored them when he was president. The Whig Party formed in opposition to what they claimed was the imperial abuse of Andrew Jackson's presidency. The Whigs managed to win the presidency twice, but both of their unfortunate victors died in office. And their party followed a short time later. Their legacy was part of the emerging Republican Party, but the presidency of Abraham Lincoln was no example of limited government.

In the years after the Civil War, industrial and financial corporations represented an unprecedented challenge to the American political economy. The Progressive movement grew in opposition to the power of monopoly, and many Progressive reforms anticipated the fate of the NIRA (i.e., success in the elected branches before being ruled unconstitutional by federal courts).

One of the other cases decided on that May 27, *Humphrey's Executor v. United States*, challenged Roosevelt's control of administrative agencies.[24] FDR had fired William Humphrey, a commissioner of the Federal Trade Commission (FTC), one of the independent agencies, so called because the top officials do not serve at the pleasure of the president but for a number of years set by Congress. The FTC commissioners are determined by statute to hold their office for a term of seven years, during which the commissioner cannot be dismissed except for "inefficiency, neglect of duty or malfeasance."

Humphrey had been appointed by Herbert Hoover in 1931, so his term would not have expired until 1938. While alleging none of the causes in the FTC's enabling act, Roosevelt asked for Humphrey's resignation so that the president could appoint someone whose policy views supported the New Deal.

Humphrey refused to resign, and FDR fired him in October of 1933. Humphrey died a short time later, so the executor of his estate sued for back pay. The judgment of the Supreme Court rested on the status of the independent agencies, that they were not so much arms of the executive, constructed to carry out his will, but agents of Congress with legislative and judicial authority that no president could lawfully subordinate.

Roosevelt reacted to the *Schechter* and *Humphrey* rulings and other defeats by the court with a rage that drove out judgment. Any patience he might have had with the justices waned as he waited year after year for a resignation and the opportunity to appoint a modern thinker to the bench. Frustrated as the same collection of justices returned every year of his first term, he determined to get control of the court, bending it to his will as he had done with Congress.

His reelection in 1936 helped to increase the Democrats' control of Congress. The House of Representatives had 334 Democrats joined by 7 Progressives and 3 Farm Labor representatives against 88 Republicans. The Senate added 5 Democrats to bring that total to 76 against 16 Republicans, with 4 seats to the Progressive and Farm Labor Parties. Certainly this was the time to strike against a Supreme Court that, in FDR's phrase, had a horse-and-buggy interpretation of the Commerce Clause. It was not.

Democrats in Congress, more beholden to FDR than ever, recoiled at his attempt to bring the Supreme Court to heel. On February 5, 1937, Roosevelt presented Congress with his plan to fix the court. Clumsy and crude, the president proposed that justices retire from the court at the age of seventy with a full pension. If they declined to do so, they would be given an *assistant* who would also have a vote on the court. The Supreme Court could conceivably expand up to fifteen voting members.

This measure came a few weeks after another idea from the White House to give the president more control over the federal bureaucracy. Reacting to the *Humphrey* decision and to normal bureaucratic ennui, Roosevelt sought to assume greater control over administrative agencies. What appears to be a debate on a fine point of public administration became an opportunity to consider the most fundamental questions of governance in the American republic. Could a system of government designed in 1787 function effectively amid the challenges of the twentieth century? Could it embrace a Hamiltonian conception of the presidency without risking a drift to dictatorship as had happened in Europe?

The President's Committee on Administrative Management (PCAM) produced a study of the federal bureaucracy, known after their chairman as the Brownlow Report. Part of the report's focus was the independent agencies of the federal bureaucracies, the kind at issue in the *Humphrey* case. The PCAM proposed eliminating the independent agencies by transferring their responsibilities and authority to the cabinet department, where the president could control their leadership. The report also called for the establishment of an Executive Office of the President, pleading famously in its opening remark, "The President needs help."

Hearings on the Brownlow Report expressed a fundamental split in American politics. Skeptics in the Senate feared that diminishing the power of the Supreme Court and independent agencies signaled an unwise expansion of executive power. Would such steps not put us on a road something like the ones traveled in Berlin, Rome, and Moscow? No one suggested that Roosevelt should be thought of in the company of Hitler, Mussolini, or Stalin, but the totalitarian experiment in Europe made the proposals from the White House seem ominous.

The president's advocates countered that, unless the executive branch were strengthened, the country would be vulnerable to radical calls from erratic individuals. Demagogues abounded at the time. Huey Long had been assassinated in 1935, but Father Charles Coughlin remained on the radio. Communists offered relief from the economic misery through a redistribution of wealth. Dr. Charles Townsend proposed a pension system that would have given everyone over sixty a monthly check of $200.

Perhaps Madison prevailed. The Senate rejected what became known as the court-packing scheme in July by a vote of seventy to twenty-two, but the court itself expanded its thinking. A ruling in late March of 1937 in the case of *West Coast Hotel v. Parrish* sustained a minimum wage law on a set of facts that were nearly identical to those of a case a few decades before, a case in which the court ruled against the same type of law. Referring to the number of justices, the *West Coast* decision became known as the switch in time that saved nine.[25]

The Brownlow recommendations were rejected, but a version was passed in 1939. The independence of the regulatory agencies was preserved, in part because it meant that the agencies would be more susceptible to congressional influence. The Executive Office was established, two years after it was proposed, in acknowledgment that the arguments in favor of a more robust executive branch had some merit.

In the rivalry of totalitarian states and liberal democracies, Franklin Roosevelt operated in a most challenging governmental structure.

The dictators had to practice a particular kind of politics. Their word alone did not guarantee that action would follow, but defiance could trigger a lethal reaction. The parliamentary democracies of Europe linked the legislative branch with the executive and subordinated the courts to that union. Coalitions could collapse, and prime ministers had to be aware that insufficient political support could trigger elections. But neither the dictators nor the ministers had the kind of complications that Madison had fashioned.

FDR began his presidency with a subservient Congress. In stunningly swift fashion, he saw his major domestic reforms passed. Two years later, the Supreme Court nullified many of those efforts. Turning to his allies on Capitol Hill, he contrived to put the court in its place. As he saw it, the Supreme Court were the ones who were encroaching on the prerogatives of the other branches. His normally keen political sense having deserted him, Roosevelt found that his overreach caused a rebellion in Congress at the very point that the court had become more sympathetic. The intricacies of the Madisonian model are elaborate and powerful, and the Oval Office is a unique classroom to learn all of the implications. Hard lessons for the ambitious and determined Roosevelt.

With war returned to Europe, Roosevelt shifted a presidency that had been focused on economic reform to one engaged with international affairs. As the European crisis intensified with the Spanish Civil War from 1936–39, the German reoccupation of the Rhineland in 1936, the Anschluss in March 1938, and the Munich Conference that September, it became increasingly clear that no European country, nor any coalition of them, would be able to withstand the growing power of the Nazis.

American history is replete with examples of our interference in other countries, especially those of the Western Hemisphere. At the same time, a powerful isolationist sentiment counters the imperialist impulses. The nation of immigrants knew all too well the miseries of the old countries; having decided to escape them, many Americans were not inclined to send an army to reform the ways of Europe.

A tradition of neutrality traced to George Washington's Farewell Address, and the recent experience of the Great War reinforced the thinking that Europe should figure out its own mess. If we can sensibly think about an American mind, as it is laid out by Henry Steele Commager, we find that it clung tenaciously to isolationism even as the Nazis rose to power because Americans were repulsed in the 1930s by their reflections on the Great War.[26]

As it looked twenty years later, the conflict was triggered by the assassination of an inconsequential Austrian archduke, no doubt familiar only to Americans who knew of and cared about the difference between Hohenzollerns and Habsburgs. Not many such Americans. In the next four years, industrial production and modern management systems were employed to annihilate the youth of Europe for the sake of a family feud among cousins of the continent's inbred royalty.

In 1914 the youth of the belligerents cheered the start of the Great War. They were, in Wilfred Owen's phrase, "children ardent for some desperate glory."[27] By the spring of 1917, when Wilson asked Congress to make the world safe for democracy, millions of a generation had been slaughtered on the western front.

American neutrality increasingly tilted in the direction of England and France before Woodrow Wilson went to Congress on April 2, 1917, to secure a declaration of war that Congress provided four days later. Adequate preparation of American forces took nearly another year, during which Wilson steadfastly refused to send Americans to fight under the unimpressive command of the Allied general staff.

When the American forces arrived in Europe in 1918, their impact was decisive, but in less than a year of fighting, they paid a terrible price. Over 53,000 were killed in combat. Another 63,000 died in accidents or from disease, and more than 204,000 were injured. The war was also almost certainly a factor in the Great Influenza, which killed over 675,000 Americans in 1918 and 1919.[28]

To rally Americans to abandon neutrality and enter the carnage, President Wilson appealed to the highest values of American culture. So inspired, the country's enthusiasm for the effort collapsed when the Treaty of Versailles proved to be anything but a foundation for peace, freedom, and prosperity.

Disappointment turned to disgust and outrage when the U.S. Senate created the Nye Committee, officially the Special Committee on Investigation of the Munitions Industry. Over more than a year, beginning in September of 1934, the hearings produced evidence that were persuasive to many Americans that the nation's sacrifice had been for the profits of munitions makers and bankers. Sons had died, and others had returned too damaged in body or mind to take over a family farm or small business. The natural transition in which a younger generation cares for its aging parents changed, in too many cases, to one in which those parents desperately tried to comfort a child who could not function independently.

Germany had been seen as a brutal aggressor in the Great War, and one led by the especially ridiculous Kaiser Wilhelm II. In 1939 Germany was back and led by an incarnation of evil that threatened Western civilization itself. Despite the incontrovertible horror of the regime, not even the Nazi threat could move the American people to a willingness to join the conflict that raged again across Europe.

As it had done during World War I, the United States would stay out of the European war until provoked directly. FDR knew that an American entry was all but certain, but again, he did not have the authority within Madison's model to commit the nation to war on his own volition. As deftly as possible, he needed to use that time of isolation to aid the Allies in their heroic defense and to ready America for the inevitable engagement.

Presented with a challenge from Albert Einstein, Franklin Roosevelt reacted as a member of a family that had distinguished itself in public service but also as a member who had maintained an independence that could be maddening to his cousins. He was a Progressive who saw excessive reverence for the separation of powers and checks and balances as dangerous romanticism. From his years in the Wilson administrations, he knew that war in the twentieth century was a challenge that would require massing the entire resources of the nation.

To secure that degree of cooperation, the country would have to rally to some transcendent principle. Lincoln had elevated *union*. Wilson had called for making the world *safe for democracy*. The call to battle was dangerous. Union had degenerated into Jim Crow and the apartheid of the American South. Wilson failed to persuade

European nations that democratic cooperation should replace historic rivalries.

In fact, democracy took a beating within the United States as civil liberties were suppressed in the Sedition Act and as racial and labor protests triggered violent reactions. Nor could Wilson persuade the American Senate to agree to the country's joining a League of Nations where disputes might be peacefully resolved, but he broke his health in the attempt.

Roosevelt had seen that Progressive ideals were not self-implementing. Complications would abound, and appealing to sentiment risked losing valuable reforms to unreasonable disappointment. At the same time, even if the balance between democracy and an efficient government could be recalibrated, the other responsibilities of state would have to be met. War or no war, judges would have to be appointed and confirmed; money, raised and spent prudently; agencies, trusted with authority but supervised to stay consistent with general purposes.

What did Roosevelt's "This requires action" mean? It meant that the German threat of an atomic bomb would have to be investigated and that a proper response would have to be determined and executed. It meant that this effort would be his task, requiring the cooperation of Congress and administrative agencies that simply must comply with the decisions he would make. It meant that he would face a challenge that Woodrow Wilson could not have imagined, but unlike Wilson, he would find the ways to bring all the facets of government behind him to lead the nation.

[THREE]

A Bungled Start

Franklin Roosevelt's remark on October 11, 1939, about Nazis blowing us up expressed an urgency that was followed in his administration by eight months of futility.

After hearing the account of the Einstein letter, FDR wrapped up his meeting with Alexander Sachs and Pa Watson by telling Sachs to pass along the information about the German threat to Lyman Briggs, the head of the Bureau of Standards in the Department of Commerce. Within a week, FDR created the Advisory Committee on Uranium and put Briggs in charge of it. The president filled out the committee with Col. Keith Adamson from Army Ordnance and Cdr. Gilbert Hoover from the Navy Bureau of Ordnance.

From that point until June of 1940, the Uranium Committee met formally only twice, although the members communicated regularly, outside the meetings, with assorted advisers. Gradually, two camps emerged: *Do more now* and *Wait for the results of serious experiments on atomic fission*. These factions advanced incompatible recommendations in a kind of bureaucratic tennis match that precluded decisive action.

The winter of 1939–40 and the subsequent spring were the months of the Phoney War, *Sitzkrieg*, a period in which the conflict in Europe was confined to naval engagements and skirmishes in Scandinavia. Nothing phony about those battles to the people who fought them, and certainly any delusion about the looming catastrophe should have been dispelled by Germany's conquest of the Low Countries in the spring of 1940. The surrender of Belgium on May 28 became an especially urgent matter since King Leopold's order to his troops to stand down meant that the uranium resources in the Belgian Congo might be accessible to the Reich, a prospect about which the Einstein letter had warned.

The German military also used those months to prepare the next phase of its conquest of Europe: crushing France and unleashing its air war against England. All the while, the Uranium Committee had managed to scrape together $6,000 from the army and navy budgets.[1] At the time, it was enough money to buy a house in the Hamptons but not enough to counter the nuclear threat from Berlin. By the time the Roosevelt administration realized that the committee was inadequate for its mission, German troops were standing in Paris, and the Luftwaffe was selecting targets in Britain.

In certain quarters, Lyman Briggs became something of a scapegoat for the bumbling beginning. The Bureau of Standards' own history proposed, "A younger man might have seized on the adventure into the unknown promised by nuclear fission, but Dr. Briggs had learned to be cautious."[2] This assessment was shared by some of the leading figures in nuclear physics. Ernest Lawrence and Karl Compton (Arthur's brother) were especially vocal. Compton complained that Briggs was "by nature slow, conservative, methodical and accustomed to operate at peacetime government bureau tempo."[3] A fair charge?

Briggs had been trained as a soil physicist, and he began his public service in 1896, six years before the Bureau of Standards had been established. Why then did FDR think he was he the man for the job? The bureau's history claims that "Roosevelt said he must have the advice of Dr. Briggs, his principal counselor in the official family on scientific matters."[4]

Alexander Sachs offered a different explanation. Having in mind the two ordnance officers who joined the chairman on the committee, Sachs thought that Briggs and the Bureau of Standards would be able to evaluate atomic fission free from the biases of the army and navy. A history of the Atomic Energy Commission (AEC) dismisses that explanation: "This may have been the case, but there was a more obvious explanation for appointing Briggs. This, after all, was a problem in physics. Why not have it investigated by the Government's physics laboratory?"[5]

The unfortunate answer to that question is that Lyman Briggs and the Bureau of Standards were not up to the task, though not through particular faults of their own. An effective reply to the Einstein letter would require thousands of people—from theoretical physicists and engineers to craftsmen in the building trades; contractors; suppliers; and the people to feed, house, and clean up after them. All these efforts would have to have been organized and managed by an administrative apparatus of uncertain nature and elements. That administrative agency would have to guide and promote scientific research into fission while maintaining the tightest security, including controls on collaboration among the scientists.

Congress would have to authorize and appropriate staggering amounts of money and would likely have to do so with few members knowing what they were approving. All of this would have to be done quickly if the German threat were to be blocked or countered, and this unprecedented challenge would have to be met by a system of government whose fundamental qualities remained the same as they had been in the first decade of the nineteenth century when a trade embargo nearly broke the constitutional framework.

It's no disgrace that Lyman Briggs was not entirely equipped for this challenge. As it was, he called the initial meeting of the Uranium Committee for October 21, 1939, just ten days after his initial contact with Alexander Sachs. He invited Sachs to join the meeting along with physicists Fred Mohler from the Bureau of Standards and Richard Roberts from the Carnegie Institution. Sachs, in turn, took it upon himself to invite three of the Hungarians who had been at the forefront of alerting the administration to the German threat: Leo Szilard, Eugene Wigner, and Edward Teller.

This first meeting of the Uranium Committee produced the request for the $6,000 research funds. The figure came from Teller in reply to a question from Commander Hoover, the navy's ordnance officer, who had asked how much money would be needed to purchase enough graphite to test the substance's effect in slowing down the neutrons that would generate nuclear fission.[6] Controlling the speed of the neutrons would determine whether fission could be achieved at all and, if so, whether it would be used as a power plant or a bomb.

Teller's fellow Hungarians thought immediately that his answer was about one-sixth of what actually would be needed. The meeting also reflected some tension that would be expected when alpha males from government, the military, and science gather to hash out a common purpose.

At the meeting, in Richard Rhodes's account, "Briggs spoke up to defend his committee. He argued vigorously that any assessment of the possibilities of fission at a time when Europe was at war had to include more than physics; it had to include the potential impact of the development on national defense."[7] Briggs was reacting to others at the meeting whose estimates of a timetable for fission research seemed to treat the question from the tranquil perspective of peacetime science. That was the very complaint that Karl Compton had made about the chairman. But Briggs understood that the committee's responsibility was to disrupt or counter a Nazi atomic bomb, and that task was urgent. There was no indication here that Briggs was a lethargic chairman.

A short time after the meeting, Leo Szilard sent Sachs an encouraging assessment of Briggs: "I expected Briggs to enlarge his committee by including men like you, [Karl] K. T. Compton or [George] G. B. Pegram. It was a surprise for me to hear that he wanted to include younger physicists who are themselves actively engaged in doing research on uranium, namely Fermi, [Merle] Tuve and [Jesse] Beams."[8]

Briggs seems to have been aggressive in finding capable people to advise the three members of the Uranium Committee, but he also reflected the complaint about him that his pace could be somewhat languid. The Uranium Committee issued a report of this first meeting and sent it to FDR on November 1. Watson wrote to Briggs on November 17 that the president had the report and would hold on to it. He certainly did.

Thanksgiving, Christmas, New Year's, and Groundhog Day passed with no word from the White House about the Uranium Committee's report. Finally, on February 8, 1940, Watson informed Briggs that he planned to remind the president about the report. He asked the chairman for any additional thoughts that might be useful for Roosevelt to hear. Briggs replied on February 20 that the army and navy had provided the $6,000 that Teller had requested back at the October 21 meeting, four months earlier.

If Briggs was satisfied with the progress of the Uranium Committee, Alexander Sachs was not. Sachs was a leader of the *Do more now* faction; on his own initiative early in February, he had obtained from Watson a copy of the November 1 report. Knowing the president as he did, Sachs thought the paper was too academic. Whatever limitations this economist had regarding atomic fission, he was extremely perceptive about how to make a point to a public official who was swamped, "punch drunk with printer's ink," as Sachs put it.[9]

That understanding is why Sachs had waited nearly two months for the opportunity to present the Einstein letter to FDR along with his own assessment of the German threat. Even when German tanks rolled into Poland, Sachs remained disciplined until the right moment presented itself. But waiting for the right moment was one thing—getting lost in a bureaucratic maze quite another.

The October 11 meeting with Roosevelt had been successful in getting the president to initiate action based on the danger that Sachs had presented. Call Briggs. Form a committee. Put ordnance officers from the army and navy on it. Have them meet, and issue a report. Put the report in a file, and plan on getting back to it at a later point. Get distracted by a string of matters so urgent that they prevent returning to the initial concern. It's a classic bureaucratic dance, but Alexander Sachs knew that it would not produce the action that Roosevelt had ordered.

Sachs took another initiative, putting himself in the middle of things, grasping as best he could the emerging breakthroughs in nuclear physics. In the middle of March, he informed the White House of progress related to graphite as a medium for atomic fission. He asked FDR to call another meeting to determine the next stage of activity.

Two weeks later, at the end of March, the reply came from Watson, who counseled waiting for experiments at Columbia University on graphite. Early in April the tone changed when the president contacted Sachs directly, suggesting what, in effect, was a second formal meeting of the Uranium Committee.

By this time, Briggs had become convinced that U-235 needed to be separated in kilogram quantities for purposes of a chain reaction, and the centrifuge seemed to be the device best suited for that separation. At this point, two questions needed to be answered by the physicists: How could significant quantities of the very rare isotope U-235 be acquired? And was graphite the best material through which neutrons could pass before shattering the U-235 nucleus?

On the twenty-eighth of April, the Uranium Committee met, joined by Sachs, Pegram, Fermi, Szilard, and Wigner. Adm. Harold Bowen also attended. Sachs seemed most eager for action. He was described as, "impatient with Fermi's conservative position."[10] Sachs may have had the least understanding of the scientific obstacles of anyone at the meeting. If so, it might explain the belief that he thought, "If the United States would plunge ahead . . . the difficulties experienced in the laboratory would tend to disappear."[11]

The meeting should not be thought of as divided between the timid and the bold. We do well to remind ourselves that those attending who wanted more vigorous action (Szilard was another) risked bringing the atomic endeavor to ruin if they exhausted limited resources in a mistaken strategy for achieving the nuclear chain reaction.

Briggs's insistence on testing ideas before acting on them was entirely reasonable in the circumstances, and he seems to have carried the meeting. As described in the AEC history, "The Advisory Committee agreed on the need for investigation, but it was ready to proceed on only a small scale and a step or two at a time. As Briggs reported to Watson on May 9, the committee did not care to recommend a large-scale try for a chain reaction until it knew the results of the graphite measurements at Columbia."[12]

The meeting also considered alarming news about a substantial part of the Kaiser Wilhelm Institute in Berlin being devoted to the study of uranium. That warning had been included in the Einstein letter, and it appeared to be coming to pass while the American response stumbled along. The German threat was determined in the summer of 1939 but not presented to FDR until that October. Thereafter, the administration had taken several steps in response to that warning, but at a minimum, weeks passed between those steps: a report in November; an update in February about a nominal fiscal decision; conversations in March and April about pending experiments in physics laboratories; and then the news that the Germans seemed to have been proceeding apace.

Even after learning about the research in Berlin, another week or two was expected before the committee received the Columbia University results about graphite. No charging ahead with graphite despite Sachs's confidence that all would be well.

On the other major scientific question of accumulating enough of the isotope to warrant a massive program to generate atomic fission, Briggs was told by his advisers that "they favored tests on a laboratory scale to determine which method appeared best for concentrating substantial amounts of U-235."[13] Again, the *Wait for serious experiments* faction had prevailed.

In mid-May the results from Columbia confirmed that graphite was a very promising medium. A special advisory group was called to meet on June 15, 1940. Its composition was little different from previous gatherings of the Uranium Committee, but some critical steps were about to be taken.

By the end of May 1940, two problems in the American response to the Einstein letter were becoming more evident. First, the only agency established for the purpose of investigating atomic research was the Uranium Committee headed by Lyman Briggs, and it had no control over any other organization's personnel, despite the urgency of its charge. In describing the laboratory tests that would find the best way to acquire U-235, the AEC's history mentions that the physicists who recommended lab tests "proposed to enlist the principal isotope-separation specialists and launch the work in June, when the academicians among them could escape their teaching duties."[14] The implication is stunning when we think about it. At the time, the Roosevelt administration saw itself in a race to prevent Nazi Germany from acquiring an atomic bomb. That task was becoming ever more urgent through the spring of 1940, yet no one seemed to think it possible to turn the grading of final exams over to teaching assistants so that America's best talent could focus on the nation's survival.

Money was the second indication of how unprepared the country was for the challenge it faced. Back in the April meetings, where Sachs was increasingly restless about the lack of urgency he sensed in some of the scientists, he realized that significant funds would be necessary if fission were to be pursued at the pace he desired. Sensing that government money might be hard to secure, he floated the idea of financing the research privately.

Some weeks later, Sachs considered securing a presidential aegis for a nonprofit corporation to direct the atomic research. In June of 1940, Vannevar Bush, the president of the Carnegie Institution, a private scientific research center, informed Briggs that, if the government failed to come up with sufficient funds to perform the necessary research, his shop might be able to fill the gap.

Certainly, Lyman Briggs was no firebrand as an administrator, but the more fundamental problem for a vigorous response to the Einstein letter was the place of science in American government. The administrative structure in which Briggs had to operate had no serious authority. Its purpose was to investigate and to advise. When some of those advisers thought Briggs's leadership to be uninspired, the chairman had little in the way of leverage to prove them wrong or to pull them back in line.

As to the financing of uranium research, Briggs had to determine his budget as he went along. He had no assurance that Congress would provide the necessary funds for the several avenues of research. Conceivably, he would be in the position of a middle school trying to retain sports programs and art classes. Bake sales for fission? If so, the fault was not Lyman Briggs's.

Government and science in America have had a peculiar relationship from the nation's beginnings. The complications in that association had been manageable for roughly 150 years, but they were becoming ominous as the threat from Germany became more apparent.

The Uranium Committee couldn't keep pace with the Nazi conquest of Europe; neither could it control the advancement of nuclear physics in America. At research universities across the country, scientists were beginning to take the first steps to figure out how to put the theory of nuclear fission to some practical purpose. The exact purpose was still undetermined: a new source of energy to power existing machines or, in Einstein's phrase, "extremely powerful bombs of a new type."

In the tradition of scientific research, the people working on atomic fission shared their findings with one another. They invited colleagues to check their results in order to confirm the experimental results. The direction of research would be determined by the questions generated by those experiments, not by a directive from any government agency. The Uranium Committee struggled simply to stay current with the research on fission and could not focus that research in any way consistent with the president's command for action.

Roosevelt himself, desperate to help Winston Churchill, the new British prime minister, was in no position to direct nuclear physicists. For the president, the matter at hand was figuring out ways to aid the European democracies despite the constraints of three neutrality acts that Congress had passed over the previous five years.

The legislation reflected the powerful isolationist sentiment that continued to grip the United States even as the German army advanced. Roosevelt was certain that America would eventually enter the war, and he was just as sure that early and effective assistance to England and France would benefit America by degrading the enemy that the nation would ultimately face. His attention focused on finding loopholes in the neutrality acts as well as helping future allies through creative strategies that those laws had not anticipated.

Amid those pressures, imagine a presidential aide trying to explain to FDR the limitations of the abundant uranium-238 isotope and the promising characteristics of the extremely rare uranium-235; the different results whether using fast or slow neutrons to trigger the fission of those atomic nuclei; the current thinking about whether graphite or heavy water was a better medium through which the neutrons would pass; and the discovery of a transuranic element called plutonium, which might be as fissionable as U-235 and would be far easier to acquire.

The aide might sum up by asking the boss if the product he preferred was an almost limitless source of nuclear power that could be used, for example, to fuel a submarine indefinitely or if he wanted a bomb that could blow up a city. The administration had no such aide, so there would be no such briefing.

The performance of Lyman Briggs and the Uranium Committee from October of 1939 to June of the following year is easy to criticize, but such criticism is easy to the point of being unfair. The history of the Atomic Energy Commission makes a point about another science organization affiliated with government, arguing that the National Resources Committee "never gained the administrative position or the support from scientists that were essential for it to become an adequate instrument for mobilizing the nation's scientific strength."[15]

For the administration, the history continues, "Roosevelt's thinking must have been conditioned by the rather uneasy relations that had existed between the Administration and the scientific community. There was little basis for sentiments of mutual confidence. No adequate machinery was at hand."[16] Not then, and not before.

The reason why "no adequate machinery" was available to Franklin Roosevelt is evident in the history of Lyman Briggs's agency. The Bureau of Standards was a long time coming. Congress didn't establish the agency until 1903 despite its being proposed over a century earlier by Washington, Jefferson, and other framers.

Article 1, section 8, of the Constitution authorizes Congress to "Fix the Standard of Weights and Measures," language drawn from the Articles of Confederation. Congress then declined to do so for well over a century. The Louisiana Purchase doubled the size of the United States in 1803. Lewis and Clark explored the vast territory without any nationally established determination of length. How far from one point to another in an expanse of 828,000 square miles? Hard to say exactly, since we had no precise agreement on the length of a mile.

The rest of the nineteenth century included technological revolutions in transportation and communications. These breakthroughs, in turn, permitted a westward expansion that turned America from a regional power into a transcontinental nation with a dose of imperial appetite for overseas territory. We subjugated Native people, conquered and annexed the northern half of Mexico, fought the Civil War to keep the nascent superpower under a single flag, absorbed the arrival of millions of immigrants from Europe and Asia, and facilitated the emergence of an industrialized economy. We did all this with a haphazard set of standards for length, weight, mass, volume, and other traditional measurements and with no standards for the emerging industries in electronics, radio, and telephones.

This chaotic history is a puzzle, in light of America's roots in the Enlightenment. George Washington boasted, "The foundation of our Empire was not laid in the gloomy age of Ignorance and Suspicion, but at an Epoch when the rights of Mankind were better understood and more clearly defined, than at any former period."[17] Thomas Jefferson and Benjamin Franklin are the founders we most associate with the Enlightenment, but Washington's observation applies as well to John Adams, James Madison, and others who thought their way through to the Constitution.[18]

The values of the day were not confined to an elite. Bernard Bailyn has noted that the popular press reflected the same attachment: "In pamphlet after pamphlet the American writers cited Locke on natural rights and on the social and governmental contract, Montesquieu and later Delolme on the character of British liberty and on the institutional requirements for its attainment, Voltaire on the evils of clerical oppression, Beccaria on the reform of criminal law, Grotius, Pufendorf, Bulamaqui, and Vattel on the laws of nature and of nations, and on the principles of civil government."[19]

Pamphlets and coffee houses were the democratic means for spreading the new ideas. We would not be surprised to learn that Locke and Montesquieu were being discussed at Harvard, Princeton, and William and Mary, but Beccaria, Pufendorf, and Bulamaqui are today likely to be mentioned only in graduate seminars. To think that they were part of popular conversations about public affairs is remarkable. The graduate seminars in the eighteenth century were not confined to universities. The Starbucks of the times were places where people could learn and argue about new ways of thinking about their place in a polity.

With such deep and thoughtful considerations by masses and elites, why did we delay so long in establishing standards fundamental to scientific progress? The official history of the Bureau of Standards proposes, "Federal reluctance to enter scientific fields and congressional agreement to keep in bounds those it perforce established grew out of the nature of the Constitution, which reserved to the individual and to the States the greatest possible freedom and the maximum opportunity for private enterprise consistent with the public good."[20]

Perhaps, but elevating individual freedom to a paramount place in our civic culture requires us to overlook some of the most significant events of our history. In certain respects, we had more freedom under the Articles of Confederation, which we replaced with the Constitution. Certainly, Patrick Henry, George Mason, Mercy Otis Warren, and other anti-Federalists thought so, thinking that the Constitution betrayed the values for which the American Revolution had been fought.

The Civil War established that the freedom of states did not extend to their leaving the Union. The sovereignty of the individual states had limits. Even in a federal system, the authority of the national government reduced the states to a subordinate status.

In another area of uncertain federalism, we began the nineteenth century with a Bank of the United States. We let it expire. We reauthorized it. We let it expire again. We fought the Civil War with a jerry-rigged financial system fashioned by Treasury Secretary Salmon P. Chase, who later, as Chief Justice of the United States, declared his creation unconstitutional.[21] We then fought furious political battles in the late nineteenth century among advocates for gold, silver, and paper currencies; from time to time, we found ourselves at the mercy of millionaires to right the fiscal ship of state.

The Enlightenment foundation that Washington celebrated might have been impressive and popular, but it quickly ran into resistance that traces to fundamental qualities of American political culture. The scientific pursuit of truth is a problem for some people. Specifically, scientific truth is true for everyone; so for example, if smoking cigarettes is associated with pulmonary disease, that's universally the case. It doesn't mean that every individual who smokes cigarettes will suffer emphysema or lung cancer, but as more people are persuaded of the risks, including the dangers of secondhand smoke, it does mean that cigarette smokers find ever-fewer places to indulge the habit. The individual's right to smoke becomes subordinated to the right of others to breathe more-healthful air.

Scientific findings thus obtain a kind of power. In the culture of science, experimental results are less a matter of personal belief or preference than is the case for religious doctrine, artistic taste, or the attachments of sports fans. While any of us can choose a particular religious tradition, opera over country, or Cardinals rather than Cubs, we cannot choose our own boiling point of water or unique laws of motion. Those findings may also be inherent in nature, but they are presented to us by people who have the knowledge and wherewithal to investigate the natural world. This capacity to understand science means that some of us can tell the rest of us about the truth of things, and that can be a problem.

The agreement on weights and measures was not the same kind of issue as discovering the cause of yellow fever, but it did mean that individuals would lose their freedom to determine what constituted a pound or a foot or a quart. Weights and measures would have more in common with the formula for gravity than whether Beethoven was better than Mozart. Individual preference in fundamental factors of commerce would be subordinated to the legal determinations of others. Since the Constitution authorized Congress to set those standards, this aspect of science and commerce became political. If political, then individual preference was back in play; America had enough people who did not want to be told by Washington DC the definitions of various measurements that the exercise of that constitutional authority was delayed for 113 years.

This political dispute about standards was another aspect of federalism. For purposes of measurement, are we the *unum* with one national system or the *pluribus* with an array of systems with each fashioned to the preferences of particular regions? The resolution of that question emerged in the late nineteenth century with new industries that required greater precision in measuring than what had been acceptable in established commerce. Our earlier question about the distance between two places in the Louisiana Territory could be answered satisfactorily with "about a day and a half's ride." Electricity, telephones, steel manufacturing, and petroleum required much more exact information.

Many of these new industries were monopolies, meaning that an authority, the monopolist, could impose standards across state lines even if the government remained stuck in the old political dispute. Add the development of legally enforceable standards in European countries, and we have a competitive threat from abroad that encouraged action at home.

Our emergence as a world power at the turn of the twentieth century was a compelling factor in Congress's establishing the Bureau of Standards in 1903. The agency's influence expanded significantly during World War I. The industrial aspect of the conflict was unprecedented, and the bureau was an essential part of America's decisive entry into the war.

The task for the bureau anticipated the challenge presented in the Einstein letter: "Artillery, ammunition, communication equipment, aircraft, and armored plate, all of Allied design, had to be adapted to American raw materials and American methods and machines."[22] And the bureau itself was affected by its mission: "The scientific resources of the country were to be utilized principally in developing new sources and substitutes for war-scarce materials, devising new instruments and equipment for the Armed Forces, and accelerating standardization and mass production techniques in industry."[23]

Specialists emerged in roles as important, if not as heroic, as those of valiant warriors: "The demand for weapons, armor, engines, rails, trucks, and other heavy duty equipment was to make it a metallurgists' war; the need for substitute materials, for nitrates, for the agents and materials of gas warfare made it a chemists' war."[24]

Like other areas where government directed the American economy, peace meant that centralized control over standards would abate. Direction of research in universities and corporate laboratories would return to the people who ran those institutions. Consumer goods became a focus of production as research into the next generation of armaments slowed dramatically.

Lyman Briggs spent World War I at the bureau, working on a wind tunnel for aviation research. The experience informed him of the dynamics of an agency that has to function as a kind of administrative drag racer, getting to maximum acceleration from a standing start as fast as possible. The urgency of the Great War would have prepared him to reject, as he did, suggestions at the Uranium Committee that a leisurely pace was advisable in fission research.

At the same time, Briggs seems not to have had the administrative skills to drive his agency independent of a very distracted president. Blaming him for the stumbling start to the atomic bomb is inaccurate and unfair, but order and energy were nonetheless required. And they were about to be provided.

FOUR

The President's Man and the Liberal State

The tragedy of World War II offers compelling characters leading the combatants in a conflict that Milton might have included in *Paradise Lost*, right after Satan's being tossed from heaven. For Americans, the dominant theme might be their disabled president's using every trick in his Machiavellian brain to help his friend the British prime minister rally his nation against an onslaught from the incarnation of evil in Berlin.

Josef Stalin is inconvenient in this tale. The leader of the Soviet Union was a sociopath himself, but he was *our* sociopath, for the moment at least. His country carried the military burden against Germany, but at a theoretical level, their battle was between rival totalitarian systems. Which oppressor do you prefer?

Until the attack on Pearl Harbor, Japan was a secondary player in the Western mind, an ominous threat to other Asian states but not, as we saw it, to civilization itself. Fascist Italy and its preposterous *Duce* might have been *opera buffa* in peacetime, but this was war. And the slaughter of innocents in Ethiopia from 1935 anticipated the fate of Europe.

In the summer of 1940, with the uranium project foundering, Franklin Roosevelt was presenting the story of this war to the American people with as much skill as Homer, Thucydides, or Shakespeare. If he were too vague about the threat, the lingering economic challenges would continue to consume the public's attention. On the other hand, if he were too explicit about the misery endured by conquered people, the isolationist urge might be irresistible. Telling the tale was a drama in itself, because the setting was the first campaign in which an American president was seeking a third term.

For the sake of winning that election, FDR equivocated with the voters. As he put it, "I have said this before, but I shall say it again and again and again: Your boys are not going to be sent into any foreign wars."[1] The president could have passed a polygraph, because the word *foreign* gave him his way out. He would not have to send the country to war, because he knew full well that the war would come to us.

Almost lost in the drama of the conflict was the theoretical essence of the argument that lay beneath the horrors of combat. The proposition from totalitarian states was that democracies could discuss problems but not solve them. The challenges of the twentieth century were of a nature that made this argument critical rather than academic. The carnage of the Great War had coincided with extraordinary economic and cultural changes from the Armory Show and the *Rite of Spring* riot, to labor and racial violence, to revolutions that brought down teetering European monarchies. The war was also a factor in the pandemic of 1918, another monumental issue for any modern state.

The apparent tranquility and prosperity in America during the 1920s gave way to the Great Depression. Every modern state faced the challenges of economic collapse as well as the social effects that roiled families, villages, farms, and great cities. If times had ever been this bad before, the experience of poverty and fear would not have been so widely known as they would be in the 1930s through radio, the tabloid press, and movie newsreels.

Decisions would have to be made in Western nations, and the madman of Germany insisted that the debating societies could not make them. For the totalitarians, dissent and opposition could not be tolerated, because they would lead to delay and confusion. The promised efficiency of the Nazis would mean that, if the Einstein letter conveyed the truth, the renewal of a European war threatened not just civilization but the survival of any nation that resisted Berlin.

For Franklin Roosevelt, the threats from the dictators could be met, but not without some reasonable adjustments in American government. As he had learned in the Wilson administration and experienced in his first two terms, the impediments designed into the American Constitution by James Madison could defeat the purposes that the document's Preamble promised to insure. How could he "provide for the common defense" if Congress and the courts could meddle as they had done with the New Deal?

Advancing the cause of liberal constitutional democracy would require the government to move in the direction of Alexander Hamilton and his energetic executive. Further, the president's argument would need to incorporate the Progressive ideal of an active state, one that anticipates and precludes challenges rather than one that suffers from and reacts to them. He would need to convince the American people that Hamiltonian adjustment was a necessary theoretical refinement that would need to be converted into effective action.

In the summer of 1940, Congress was locked into isolationism. Franklin Roosevelt was consumed with crafting his reelection strategy, the uranium program was in the hands of administrators with few resources and less authority, and Germany was determining the government of France and threatening the future of England. The nonaggression pact with the Soviet Union, signed a week before the German invasion of Poland that started World War II, gave Hitler the opportunity to fashion a war of his choosing. If that war included Germany's having weapons of nuclear fission, no force in Europe nor, at the moment, any countering move by the United States would prevent it.

But at that dire point, an electrical engineer showed up.

In 1940 Vannevar Bush had been in Washington for a couple of years.[2] He had left MIT after weathering some turbulent academic politics, determined to develop a significant place for science in America's defense against the war that he saw as inevitable. At the university, he had ultimately developed a confident association with MIT's president Karl Compton. In 1938 this experience in Cambridge was useful preparation for his new job as head of the Carnegie Institution, where he faced serious financial and personnel issues. Both are classic headaches in organization theory, but when managing very smart people who purport to seek the truth, cutting budgets and reining in mavericks is particularly difficult.

One of Bush's first tasks at the Carnegie Institution was getting rid of Harry Laughlin, a leading figure in the eugenics movement.[3] The idea of improving society through judicious breeding practices was enormously popular in America, especially among those who were convinced they belonged in the elite that was being encouraged to have more children. As to the rabble whose offspring were the cause of crime, poverty, disease, and other afflictions, Laughlin had another idea: They shouldn't be allowed to reproduce. The state should protect society by preventing the unfit from reproducing.

In one of the lowest moments in American law, Justice Oliver Wendell Holmes dismissed an appeal from Carrie Buck, who was trying to block a forced sterilization by the state of Virginia. Holmes and the majority rejected Buck's argument in a two-page decision that—referring to Carrie, her mother, and her daughter—included the notorious phrase, "Three generations of imbeciles are enough."[4]

Having Laughlin on the roster was a source of pride at one point, but that point had passed. Now he was an embarrassment and had to go. Bush displayed the administrative skills to persuade his board to go along with severing Laughlin from Carnegie despite the intervention of important figures who sought to protect him. After this success, Bush was able to rename Laughlin's old eugenics shop and cut its budget drastically.

A few months after arriving at Carnegie, Bush also assumed a senior position at the National Advisory Committee for Aeronautics (NACA). His responsibilities increased significantly when Joseph Ames, NACA's chairman, became ill. Bush had to appear before the Senate Appropriations Committee to argue for federal money to create a research lab in Sunnyvale, California. He had something of a tantrum in this first engagement with the legislative branch. Madison might have chuckled. Having the capacity to see a threat, even knowing the way to meet it, guaranteed nothing in a system in which the power of the state was divided and organized against itself.

The army and navy were planning on spending over $200 million on new aircraft, and the lab would be helpful in developing the best possible planes both because of the science that the facility would promote and also because its location in California would put it near the manufacturers who would be building the aircraft. The logic of the proposal was evident to Bush, but the logic did not incorporate political factors central to the thinking of the Senators.

G. Pascal Zachary describes Bush's attempt to get money for the lab as a fairly good example of a meltdown: "It was the first time Bush had ever asked Congress for anything, and his inexperience showed. He was scared, lost his temper and generally acted like a 'rank amateur.'"[5] Then it got worse: "The senators interrupted him repeatedly. Finally, Bush smashed the table with his fists, insisting on an audience."[6]

Demanding that senators pay attention is not usually a wise approach, as Bush found out when his petition was denied. Months later, the money was secured after John Victory, NACA's executive director, observed the proper rituals of congressional courtship. The lesson was painful to Bush's ego but useful in preparing him for subsequent engagements with the legislative branch. In keeping with the Hamiltonian tilt of the Roosevelt administration, Bush preferred to pursue his aims without any engagement with the legislative branch.

The man and the moment combined in the summer of 1940 when the supremely organized and systematic Vannevar Bush presented an idea to Franklin Roosevelt, whose uranium project was a collection of intriguing possibilities haphazardly organized. Like the president, Bush saw war coming to America, but where FDR needed to juggle an assortment of crises, Bush was able to focus on bringing coherence to the nation's scientific resources. Specifically, he had an idea for an organization that could coordinate the disparate parts of American science and direct them with efficiency rarely found in government.

To approach the president with his plan, he sought the assistance of Frederic Delano, Roosevelt's uncle, who in turn drafted Harry Hopkins to get Bush a meeting with the boss. Bush and the president did not know each personally, but that misses a critical point. Both were men of Cambridge, Massachusetts. FDR was a Harvard graduate, and Bush a former professor at MIT. They were comfortable in a certain crowd, that of very intelligent men who were raised to travel in elite company. This background gave Bush any confidence he might otherwise have lacked to ask the support of the president.

On June 12, 1940, Bush went to the White House to tell Franklin Roosevelt about his idea for the National Defense Research Committee (NDRC). The agency would be "a coordinating committee, responsible to the president, that would contract with universities and industrial labs to perform research at the behest of the Army and the Navy."[7]

After a few brief pleasantries, Roosevelt approved the plan and promised Bush perhaps more than he could have hoped: "a direct line to the White House, virtual immunity from congressional oversight and his own line of funds."[8] All of this was accomplished in about twenty minutes. Bush had taken more time that day to eat lunch.

The meeting between Bush and Roosevelt was one of the supreme moments for the legendary Eastern Establishment. FDR contacted the secretary of war and the secretary of the navy, urging their cooperation with the NDRC. Roosevelt also brought the National Academy of Sciences on board. Bush drafted Cambridge. James Conant, president of Harvard, and Karl Compton, president of MIT, joined the NDRC; in an example of diversity for that time, Richard Tolman, president of Caltech, completed the academic triumvirate.

The official history of the Atomic Energy Commission mentions that the NDRC did not include any foreign-born scientists to placate the security concerns of the army and navy and in part because the committee had "one eye on future encounters with Congress."[9] Despite the contributions of Enrico Fermi, Leo Szilard, Albert Einstein, and others born abroad and despite the urgency of being as prepared as possible for a cataclysmic war, the old prejudices that date to the Alien and Sedition Acts of the 1790s were able to assert themselves.

The frustrations with the Uranium Committee were being tackled with great focus and energy. After the Vietnam War, David Halberstam tagged the architects of that conflict "the best and the brightest," a jab at their Ivy League backgrounds.[10] Even if the officials of the Kennedy and Johnson administrations were guilty of the hubris that was Halberstam's charge, they could have come by it honestly. Many of the architects of Vietnam had the same pedigree as the men that Vannevar Bush recruited, and that background did not encourage self-doubt.

Bush's men had the training, talent, personalities, and character that subsequently would be so criticized as the reasons for the tragedy of Vietnam, but in the 1940s the grounds for the academics' confidence were plainly evident as they organized American science and prepared it for the ordeal ahead.

At first the NDRC might have been a grave threat to the entire enterprise of developing nuclear fission. Under Lyman Briggs's nominal leadership, research proceeded albeit in an uncoordinated way. The new agency meant that academic and industrial research could be organized into an effective tandem, with both then applied to a military purpose. But Vannevar Bush had serious reservations about fission research. He hoped that the chain reaction would prove impossible because he feared that pursuing an atomic bomb would divert resources from weapons that could be decisive in the war.

Bush was certainly aware of the developments in nuclear physics. The Carnegie Institution was a cosponsor of the conference in Washington DC on January 26, 1939, months after Bush had arrived. That was the gathering at which the breakthrough of Otto Hahn and Fritz Strassmann was disclosed to physicists, including the newly arrived Enrico Fermi and the visiting Niels Bohr. Newspaper coverage of the conference generated a popular fascination with the promise of fission as a source of electric power.

For all the excitement among the scientists and the bubbling curiosity among laypeople, Bush was skeptical. He found the idea of a fission bomb implausible, and his elitist sensibilities were put off by the opinions of people who had read something in a newspaper that they couldn't begin to understand.

More important, Bush was very interested in weaponry that could be decisive in a war that he thought inevitable for the United States to engage. As Pascal Zachary writes, "In late 1940, his highest priorities were radar, submarine detection and the proximity fuze [sic]. Each of these areas promised advances that would reach the battlefield in time to affect the current war. Atomic enthusiasts, on the other hand, did not know how to build an atomic bomb, when one might be ready or what it would cost."[11]

The issue was not an idle one. A crash program to build an atomic bomb risked diverting resources that could be essential in defense of the democracies. The concern was expressed by James Conant who wrote, "To me, the defense of the free world was in such a dangerous state that only efforts which were likely to yield results within a matter of months or, at most, a year or two were worthy of serious consideration."[12]

Even in the first few months of World War II, it was clear that the conflict would not play out as the Great War had. The slaughter in the trenches had been replaced by the blitzkrieg that put German troops in Paris in the first summer of the new war. The superior administrative efficiency of the NDRC might mean a faster route to an unfortunate end (i.e., a poor choice in selecting research targets could lure the Allies from an effective defense to a fanciful one and with greater speed). Radar would mean seeing beyond eyesight. Sonar would mean finding the U-boats that threatened the American lifeline to Europe. The proximity fuse would mean that bombs would explode at a point that could deliver the most lethal force. The military benefits of these weapons could have been lost if the fission bomb proved to be a chimera.

Vannevar Bush was in a position that was unavailable to Lyman Briggs. By leading the NDRC, he could direct the enormous power of American science and industry. Had it not been for the terrifying prospect of a German bomb, Bush might well have shut down the uranium project. As it was, he adopted the Uranium Committee, bringing it under the supervision of his NDRC. The committee was renamed the Uranium Section or the S-1 Section of the NDRC, and Lyman Briggs continued to be its head.

For the rest of 1940, grants were secured that allowed research to proceed into the major scientific questions relating to nuclear fission. The administrative stagnation that had preceded the NDRC was not immediately overcome. The old complication is clear from the lag in granting the first contracts. Columbia University secured the first grant in November of 1940, five months after the NDRC was established.

The amount was $40,000, and it was drawn from the budgets of the army and navy, as had been the case with the initial funding of $6,000. The contract with Columbia ran for a year; at its conclusion in the fall of 1941, the NDRC had awarded $300,000 to sixteen projects operated in major universities, government agencies, corporations, and private research institutions.

The progress that the NDRC realized in uranium research is impressive, but it remained a minor part of the total scientific effort that was attending to national defense. As the Smyth Report put it, "Scale of

expenditure is at least a rough index of activity. It is therefore interesting to compare this figure [the $300,000] with those in other
branches of war research. By November 1941 the total budget approved
by NDRC for the Radiation Laboratory at the Massachusetts Institute
of Technology was several million dollars."[13] Bush and Conant may
have made sure that their concerns about more promising technology being delayed because of fission research would not be realized.

Early in 1941 the essential questions of uranium research rose again,
this time at a critical point. If a weapon could be developed from
splitting an atomic nucleus, it would have to be developed quickly
to be of use in the present war. If uranium or plutonium were a
fuel to supply electricity, the normal pace of scientific investigation
would be fine. While nuclear energy remained an interesting and
important possibility, the urgent matter was a bomb, and pursuing a
bomb required decisions from the top of American government. As
is often the case with the most important issues, those critical decisions would have to be made on the basis of incomplete information.

Complicating our understanding of how those determinations were
made, the key actors are unclear. According to the Smyth Report,
Lyman Briggs initiated the decisive moment for the program: "In the
spring of 1941, Briggs, feeling that an impartial review of the problem
was desirable, requested Bush to appoint a reviewing committee."[14]

Bush appointed Frank Jewett, president of the National Academy of Sciences, to set up the group; Jewett named Arthur Compton, Karl's brother, its president, with Ernest Lawrence among others
as members with the task to determine "the military importance of
the uranium problem and to recommend the level of expenditure at
which the problem should be investigated."[15] It was a fish or cut bait
moment in which Lyman Briggs appears to have played a critical role.

Pascal Zachary offers a different account: "In March 1941 Bush
finally began to face the flaws in Lyman Briggs's handling of fission.
Ernest Lawrence, a Nobel Laureate in physics and strident critic
of Briggs, forced the issue into the open."[16] As we have seen, Lawrence's criticism focused on the pace of Briggs's management and
the assumption that the years at the Bureau of Standards had turned
Briggs into a lethargic bureaucrat.

Lawrence also pressed James Conant and Karl Compton, the Harvard and MIT presidents, to make clear to Briggs the urgency of getting answers about fission as quickly as possible. The pressure then moved to Bush. Compton, Bush's former boss at MIT, softened the attack by acknowledging the enormous responsibilities that Bush bore, and noted that fission understandably had lacked the attention it needed. He extended the same excuse to Briggs and implied that Bush had little leverage over Briggs since the latter was Roosevelt's first call after learning of the Einstein letter.

The uranium program, adrift a few months earlier, had become a real mess. Bush's preference for the NDRC was for the agency to pursue research that was further along, but now he had a near rebellion in the ranks. He certainly had seen egos flare while at MIT, but the adage that academic politics are the most vicious kind because the stakes are so low did not apply here. Bush's initial move in restoring order was to set Ernest Lawrence straight.

They met in the middle of March, and Bush issued an ultimatum: if Lawrence were to remain a part of the NDRC, he would either go along as directed or keep his concerns within channels. As Zachary describes it, Bush followed a very delicate balancing act. He needed to let Lawrence know who was running things, but he also realized that Lawrence, the inventor of the cyclotron, had extraordinary gifts that would be hard to find in anyone else. Bush's strategy was to bring Lawrence further inside the tent. He asked the Nobel to "act temporarily as Briggs's personal adviser."[17] Faced with a possible exile from the most important work going on in physics, Lawrence agreed.

Near the end of March, in this telling of the tale, Lawrence was the one who suggested a review committee to Bush. Lawrence had paid for college by selling kitchenware, and here he was again marketing a product by explaining its benefits to the consumer. A review committee could keep Bush, the engineer, up to speed with what were sure to be rapidly developing breakthroughs in nuclear physics. They would, in the course of that instruction, be able to offer essential advice to Bush.

The ultimate consumer of the uranium research was Franklin Roosevelt, and Bush understood that the better he grasped the intricacies of fission research, the better he could explain them to the president. By assuming a somewhat dependent role with the physicists, Bush's influence with the president would grow.

During the summer of 1941, Bush and Lawrence swapped letters aimed at smoothing any lingering tension. Each praised the other's performance, and in so doing, they cleared the way for further ventures. What those ventures would be was still to be determined as the review committee that Frank Jewett set up delivered a series of reports.

Bush was slowly grasping the physics of nuclear fission, and he also saw that his own field of engineering would play a vital role in the construction of any atomic bomb. Engineers would be the ones to turn the findings of the physicists into instruments of war. In addition to the issues of science and technology, Bush also faced the inevitable politics from the old factions of *Do more now* and *Wait for more research*. His hopes that Jewett's committee would resolve the conflicts were unmet, perhaps because Jewett was in the camp that wanted to move with considerable deliberation.

The review committee reported in May of 1941 that, for another $350,000 and six months, they could probably have a recommendation about atomic research. Bush rejected the proposal as too leisurely and asked for an assessment of the shortest timetable with an emphasis on the engineering aspects, how long it would likely take to build an atomic bomb.

Jewett came back with a second report in July, and its primary effect was to cause Bush to lose his remaining confidence in the review committee. The timing here is fascinating. The issue in the spring of 1941 regarding uranium research was a classic: fish or cut bait. To determine the correct choice, Bush set up a committee of very smart men who, more or less, shared his bias that full-scale commitment to a bomb was probably a reckless move.

They operated on the entirely reasonable premise that issues like feasibility of atomic fission require extensive and deliberate investigation, with any findings replicated over and again. No surprise then that their reports, while not saying "no," did say "not yet."

While Jewett's official investigating committee pursued its mission, Bush was starting to find the determination peculiar to the converted. From sources outside of Jewett, Bush was becoming persuaded that a bomb was feasible, and he was coming to appreciate the real obstacles in producing the weapon.

One barrier was that, though the war proceeded, it did so without American participation. Our absence of involvement was an affirmative decision to stay out of the conflict. The Nazi-Soviet Non-aggression Pact ended on June 22 that summer, with the German invasion of the Soviet Union. On August 12 the House of Representatives extended by one vote the time of service for men drafted into the armed forces. In another reflection of Congress's determination to steer clear of the foreign war, the budget of the NDRC was cut, as were emergency funds that had been paying for the uranium research going on about the country.

Another factor was this mindset of the academics. The realities of the conflict meant that the practice of action after the most thorough investigation would have to be abandoned. As we've seen, Lyman Briggs understood that adjustment, even though Ernest Lawrence charged that he was guilty of that very tendency. In short, asking the academics to make a thoughtful review and recommendation between fishing and cutting bait had been a mistake.

While increasingly frustrated with Jewett, Bush was coming to believe that research on a bomb held more promise than he had previously believed. Part of his confidence came from Europe. He had evidence that the British bomb project was moving ahead expeditiously. Specifically, the physics questions were being answered in a positive way. A bomb was possible if the necessary resources could be applied.

At the same time, Bush had no clear idea what was going on in Germany. The threat alone, however, added to his growing sense that atomic research should be a higher priority than it had been when the NDRC was established the previous fall. The German prospect was always the ultimate drive to the American bomb. Whatever the odds that the Nazis would have an atomic bomb, no one could doubt what they would do if they were successful in producing one.

In an intriguing organizational development, the greater importance of uranium research caused it to require a new home. On June 28, 1941, Franklin Roosevelt established the Office of Scientific Research and Development (OSRD) by executive order. The AEC history describes the NDRC as "a great step forward, but a year's experience had revealed certain imperfections."[18] The history specified two problems. First, the NDRC could drive research with more purpose than the original Uranium Committee, but it had little to offer in terms of development. The engineering of a bomb, perhaps the aspect most central in Bush's thinking, was not well served by the agency.

Second, the NDRC had more authority and support than the Uranium Committee, but it had no authorization to compel cooperation from military laboratories and those of other agencies. Bush announced to the NDRC at a meeting in late November of 1941 that the S-1 Section was being transferred to the OSRD. James Conant was Bush's liaison to the S-1 Section, which would continue to be chaired by Lyman Briggs although in an administrative structure that bore little resemblance to the Uranium Committee that FDR set up late in 1939.

On October 9, 1941, the fish or cut bait question of the previous spring received almost an answer from the source that mattered ultimately. During the summer, Bush had met several times with Henry Wallace, Roosevelt's vice president and the only member of the administration with serious training in science who had also run for elected office as FDR's running mate. Bush brought the president up to date with the various developments of the summer: "He outlined the British conclusions, mentioning the amount of uranium necessary for a bomb, the cost of a production plant, and the time needed to achieve a weapon."[19] Bush stressed that he could not guarantee the successful production of a bomb, but he indicated that he had moved past the grave doubts that he held just a few months before. He then got his marching orders that were pure Roosevelt. Bush should floor the accelerator while being ready at all times to slam on the brakes.

From the AEC history, "Bush was to expedite the work in every possible way. He was not, however, to proceed with any definite steps on an 'expanded plan'—on construction as opposed to research and planning—until he had further instructions from the President."[20] The distinction is mentioned in an almost breezy fashion: "Bush now had the authority, not to make a bomb, but to discover if a bomb could be made and at what price. When this investigation should point the way to a production program, he would need further Presidential sanction. Until then he had virtually a free hand."[21]

If Bush were building a house, he would have been authorized to assess the land, review zoning and code regulations, hire an architect, get blueprints with an estimate of the ultimate cost. He would not have been authorized to hire a contractor. Fission research was not a house. Finding out how to make an atomic bomb and the cost of the effort would require some testing that may or may not fall clearly within the brief that Roosevelt gave Bush.

An example of this ambiguity was the chain reaction in the squash court at the University of Chicago in December of 1942. As we saw in chapter 1, a physical or mental error in the building of the atomic pile could have imperiled a city of over 3 million people, and that fear is what alarmed Conant and Gen. Leslie Groves when they heard about the experiment from Arthur Compton. Where does research end and development begin? Sometimes an exercise might not conform to that neat division.

The October 9 meeting did clarify who held responsibility for the policy aspects of any fission project. Roosevelt made clear that he alone held final authority on proceeding with work on a bomb, but he recognized a need to delegate to advisors who could keep the program secret. Known as the Top Policy Group, this collection was limited to FDR, Vice President Wallace, Bush, Conant, Secretary of War Henry Stimson, and Army Chief of Staff George C. Marshall.

One effect of this organization was to define more clearly what other researchers were to do. The researchers most emphatically were not needed to express their views on whether or not to proceed with work on a bomb. Their purview was confined to scientific questions of fuel separation, U-235 or plutonium, quantities needed to fashion a bomb, and the engineering requirements of proceeding. Go or no go; securing the necessary funding; the extent of cooperation with the British—these were policy questions that would be handled by Roosevelt and the five men he trusted with the responsibility.

Among the most daunting challenges was money. As an atomic bomb moved from being a theoretical possibility to a tangible program, the staggering sums that would be necessary were ever more apparent. Not only was the enormous expense a complication, but the pursuit itself could jeopardize success. In government, money means Congress, and Congress normally means public hearings. It certainly means a lot of people knowing what's up, not only the members of the House and Senate but people on their staffs and perhaps anyone who feeds, clothes, or houses any one of them. In short, Congress means exposure, like it or not.

The Roosevelt administration, like every administration before and since, preferred secrecy, a quality that increasingly has become associated with national security, at least among those employed in the executive branch. If the normal budgetary process were followed, separate hearings before different committees would be necessary to authorize uranium research as a legally sanctioned policy; then an appropriations process would follow, to determine the exact amount that would be allocated each year. Bush, Conant, and other members of the Top Policy Group had been dubious about the merits of pursuing an atomic bomb, and they could assume that any number of House and Senate members would have those same doubts. The elected officials would also be more than willing to air their concerns in public.

As the administration saw it, an end run was in order. Zachary writes of Roosevelt's men and the financing puzzle, "They solved it, not by seeking congressional approval, but by creating the first 'black,' or secret, weapons budget in the nation's history. First coming from 'a special source' under Roosevelt's control, funding for the bomb later was buried in the yearly budget of the Army Corps of Engineers."[22] Over $2 billion requires quite a burial, and a first-year House member would notice that amount of money going to an agency with a record of having to explain cost overruns dating to the early nineteenth century. As we will see at a later point, a small number of congressional leaders were brought into the atomic secret, and they were charged with getting their colleagues to go along without questions. They succeeded well enough to keep Harry Truman in the dark even while he chaired a Senate committee that was investigating waste in the military.

As the American uranium program developed, it increasingly challenged an understanding of a fundamental balance in our constitutional system. James Madison famously described the trick in *Federalist* No. 51. After dismissing the fantasy of angelic rulers, he wrote, "In framing a government which is to be administered by men over men, the great difficulty lies in this: you must first enable the government to control the governed; and in the next place oblige it to control itself."[23]

Anticipating Madison, John Locke had described the state as a night watchman, a protector of property but not a device to fix all of society's ills; few in eighteenth-century America would have disagreed with that notion. But even in that time, this attitude about government could not stop intrusions on liberty, such as the Alien and Sedition Acts of the Adams administration.

These were some of the complications of controlling the governed in the midtwentieth century, a challenge that has become only more acute in the years since. As to controlling the state, Madison relied on the elaborate system of checks and balances in which, he insisted, the legislative branch would be dominant, thus requiring its division into two houses with very different terms of office and methods for selecting the members.

Occasionally, Madison gave a nod to the benefit of public officials of sterling character, but he didn't pin the prospects for the republic on the integrity of its office holders. "Ambition must be made to counteract ambition," he proposed.[24] Energy in pursuing one's own interests would be the most reliable dynamic on which to fuel the engine of state. At the Constitutional Convention in 1787 and in the subsequent process of ratification, Madison engaged allies and adversaries, and he doubtless saw saints and rogues in both camps. Vice, in a curious way, was as unreliable as virtue, so this experiment in governing would rely on mechanisms arranged in a way that permitted public action when a preponderance of factions favored a particular course and when the judiciary, insulated from popular opinion, found no threat to civil liberties or the rule of law.

Through Franklin Roosevelt's cunning, the Manhattan Project was substantially insulated from Madison's remedy of separated powers and checks and balances. Impossible to escape was the problem that *Federalist* No. 51 addressed. That was the notorious problem of faction, identified and examined by Madison in *Federalist* No. 10. He began that essay with an alarm about "the violence of faction," a reference perhaps to Shay's Rebellion, the event that exposed the limitations of the Articles of Confederation and that helped trigger the Constitutional Convention.[25]

Factions, Madison explained, were caused by people's attachment to different public figures, to various causes in religion and government, also to their personal economic interests: "Those who hold and those who are without property have ever formed distinct interests in society. Those who are creditors, and those who are debtors, fall under a like discrimination. A landed interest, a manufacturing interest, a mercantile interest, a moneyed interest, with many lesser interests, grow up of necessity in civilized nations, and divide them into different classes, actuated by different sentiments and views."[26]

To this roster of divisions, Madison noted that the unequal distribution of property was the most significant cause of faction. Recognizing that all these factors are serious, Madison suggested that people will choose up sides and put on different uniforms even if nothing important is at stake: "So strong is this propensity of mankind to fall into mutual animosities that where no substantial occasion presents itself the most frivolous and fanciful distinctions have been sufficient to kindle their unfriendly passions and excite their most violent conflicts."[27]

Franklin Roosevelt found ways around *Federalist* No. 51, but he could not keep factional strife out of the Manhattan Project. If the system of government could not be trusted to control those forces, some other solution would have to be created. It fell to FDR's administrators to devise remedies of their own. Academics, manufacturers, real estate dealers, the military, and all kinds of providers of goods and services participated in the development of the atomic weapon, many without realizing it at all. We saw in Chicago that a labor dispute sent the first controlled chain reaction to the university campus instead of a site farther away from the heart of the city. If the inevitable strife among interests could not be contained better than that one battle between unions and management, the success of the Manhattan Project would be in jeopardy.

This theory and structure of government had survived for nearly a century and a half. Sometimes the theory approached mythology, while realities imposed adjustments in the operation of government. These accommodations doubled the size of the United States with the acquisition of the Louisiana Territory in 1803. They fashioned a doomed scheme to balance free and slave states in the Senate through the Missouri Compromise of 1820. The nation's imperial expansion into Mexico produced, as Emerson put it, a meal that we could not digest. The Civil War forced a radical expansion of the freedom the framers had embraced while limiting its benefits to a segment of the population. This same structure and culture then permitted a retreat from the promise of Lincoln's second inaugural address, allowing an American apartheid to rule the South for a century. How the modern corporation fit into our political economy is an issue that we have yet to figure out; by the time of FDR's presidency, we were finding ourselves forced to engage other nations who were wrestling with many of these same issues, wrestling in ways that might well threaten our own survival. So it was in June of 1940, when the uranium program finally received serious attention.

Leaving to one side the cautions of Madison and the other framers, the Roosevelt administration determined in effect in the summer of 1940 that pursuing the constitutional guarantees of providing for the common defense and promoting the general welfare required focus and sustained commitments on very specific goals. When, as was true of the Manhattan Project, too little was known to establish goals to pursue, focus and energy had to be brought to bear to determine those objectives as quickly as possible.

At this point, the development of an atomic bomb had acquired two new aspects. One was an organizational structure, and the other was the recruitment of the right people to handle the tasks that kept arising. For Madison, structure meant the engagement of the three branches in an intricate dance that prevented any one of them from accumulating too much power. For Franklin Roosevelt, preserving the essence of Madisonian values against the threats from foreign powers meant developing an efficient organization entirely within the executive branch free from interference from Congress or the courts. Money would be required, and that meant engaging the legislative branch. Engaging was not the same as giving House members and Senators access to meddle with a presidential prerogative.

An important instrument in Roosevelt's securing control of the research and development of the atomic bomb was the executive order. The various agencies that were central to organizing resources and directing them effectively were created by presidential fiat. Controversial in our own time, the executive order has been with us for a while.

It is hard to chart the executive orders because the term wasn't in use until the twentieth century, but their equivalent was the means of Abraham Lincoln's Emancipation Proclamation as well as his extremely controversial suspension of habeas corpus. The latter move was challenged in the case *Ex parte Merryman*, and Chief Justice Taney, author of the execrable Dred Scot decision, excoriated Lincoln for what Taney claimed was an abuse of power.[28] The chief justice ordered Lincoln to rescind the suspension, and Lincoln ignored him.

Franklin Roosevelt had used executive orders from the start with his declaration of a bank holiday after his first inauguration. He then engaged the practice more than 3,500 times for matters ranging from ceremonial observances to the notorious Executive Order 9066, which permitted the internment of American citizens of Japanese heritage. Nothing in 9066 mentioned Japan, but the order delegated authority to officials whose hysteria and bigotry targeted people with that heritage, even if they were born in the United States, didn't speak Japanese, and never visited the home of their ancestors.

Executive Order 9066 was challenged in court in *Korematsu v. United States*.[29] The Supreme Court upheld the order, with three dissenting votes. The justification was the exigencies of war and subsequent deference to the executive branch.

On the face of it, establishing administrative agencies is a step that is fairly tame, even uninteresting, to most people. But the Advisory Committee on Uranium, the National Defense Research Committee, and the Office of Scientific Research and Development made decisions with enormous implications for the success of the war effort and for the safety of Americans living near facilities for fission research and also the health of those people as substances like plutonium were examined for their potential use in a bomb.

The executive order bypasses the Madisonian structure, so it should always be carefully considered when used for anything beyond the mundane. Harry Truman used it to integrate the armed forces and also to seize control of the steel mills when a strike threatened production during the Korean War. The Supreme Court found that the seizure was unconstitutional, and Truman complied with their judgment.

Vannevar Bush had extensive experience in administration. We have seen that he came out of the academic wars at MIT to run an important research institute where a leading figure was a eugenicist with congressional protection. Bush was also a cofounder of Raytheon, so he could add commercial management to his sources of knowledge in the historic task of getting others to do what, in the eyes of the manager, they should be doing.

Having put some administrative definition into uranium research, Bush prepared to let go of the implementation. The NRDC had become the OSRD, with the original Uranium Committee defined as the S-1 Section and shifted from one agency to the other. By the summer of 1942, physicists remained unclear about key aspects of atomic fission. The best fuel for that purpose, the best way to collect that fuel, the cost of so doing, and the relationships among the key actors were still in dispute, but it was time to act. That had been FDR's initial reaction to the Einstein letter three years before, but now the urgency of the war, the promise of the British researchers, and the terror of an atomic bomb in the hands of the Nazis meant that the action would proceed with purpose and resources despite the uncertainties.

The actual building of an atomic bomb would still require the resolution of all sorts of organizational puzzles, but the president of the United States had decided that those puzzles would be the responsibility of the army. An army officer would be given charge of seeing that a bomb was produced in time to have an impact on the war. Perhaps based on his experience as the assistant secretary of the navy in the Wilson administration, FDR made it clear that the navy had no significant role to play in the endeavor.

The army established the Manhattan Engineering District (MED) of the Army Corps of Engineers in New York City on August 13, 1942. Leslie Groves was put in charge of building an atomic bomb, subject to his promotion to brigadier general, which was done on September 23. Like Bush, Conant, and others, Groves was almost annoyed with the assignment, thinking that the fission bomb was likely to prove impossible; as a fighting man, his preference was to be overseas in the middle of the action. Groves, however, had shown just the qualities needed for the vast and complex project with his management of the construction of the Pentagon.

Groves moved his office from New York to Washington and selected Oak Ridge, Tennessee, for the location of one of the major plants of the operation. Oak Ridge was near a dam that was part of the Tennessee Valley Authority (TVA); thus it had a sufficient source of electric power for the unprecedented work ahead. It was also reasonably close to Washington and visits from General Groves, and it didn't hurt that Tennessee was the home state of Senator Kenneth McKeller, a senior member of the Senate Appropriations Committee.

The other major locations for the Manhattan Project were in Hanford, Washington, and Los Alamos, New Mexico. Hanford would be responsible for the production of the plutonium, which was a transuranic element that had been discovered to be more easily fissionable than even U-235. And Los Alamos was picked as the laboratory for figuring out how to turn all this research into a bomb.

Groves, dropped into the middle of things, tackled theory by pressing experiments. He would have been told that U-235 was the best fuel for a bomb, unless plutonium was, but that gathering U-235 from U-238 was a difficult proposition. Brilliant people, each of whom insisted that their way was best, offered four different techniques for the separation.

Alfred Nier of the University of Minnesota proposed using a mass spectrometer "to send a stream of charged particles through a magnetic field."[30] He might have downplayed the twenty-seven thousand years that would be needed to separate a single gram of U-235.

John Dunning of Columbia University advocated gaseous diffusion, a method that would have passed uranium atoms through a porous filter, with the lighter U-235 isotope negotiating the barrier more easily than its atomic cousin.[31] The technique was more effective than the electromagnetic method of Nier, but it still was prohibitively expensive.

A promising alternative was the use of a centrifuge that would have spun the isotopes in a cylinder in which again the lighter U-235 would have separated. Jesse Beams of the University of Virginia led this research.[32]

Liquid thermal diffusion was the choice of Philip Abelson of the Carnegie Institution, Vannevar Bush's official shop even while he directed scientific research for the administration on a salary of a dollar a year. As described in a report from the U.S. Department of Energy, "Into the space between two concentric vertical pipes Abelson placed pressurized liquid uranium hexafluoride. With the outer wall cooled by a circulating water jacket and the inner heated by high-pressure steam, the lighter isotope tended to concentrate near the hot wall and the heavier near the cold."[33]

These four methods of isotope separation were pursued in various academic labs with funding from private sources. At the same time, Fermi and Szilard worked on the engineering of a chain reaction whenever and however sufficient fuel were made available. At the outset in 1939, Fermi quickly concluded that fission was a promising method of producing nuclear power, but whether it could yield an explosion was not so apparent. If it could, Fermi had serious doubts that the apparatus could be small enough to be effective as a bomb.

Work in the labs of Ernest Lawrence at Berkeley led to two new chemical elements, transuranic for being man-made and heavier than uranium. The new elements were named neptunium and plutonium. The latter, in particular, was much more promising as an explosive agent than U-235, and its production would be simpler, more effective, and cheaper than any of the isotope separation methods. Nonetheless, advocates for U-235 were able to keep that fuel in play along with the methods for extraction.

The Oak Ridge facility grew quickly to become the fifth-largest city in the state of Tennessee. It included the Clinton Engineering Works, whose efforts at the time consumed one-seventh of all the electricity produced in the United States. In the initial programs of the New Deal, designed to battle the Great Depression, FDR was not shy about an approach of "try everything because we need only one plan to work." The same attitude directed the Manhattan Project.

At Oak Ridge, the Y-12 plant was dedicated to the electromagnetic separation that Ernest Lawrence favored. Lawrence and his crew tinkered at length with "shims, sources and collectors" to figure out the most promising design.[34] By January of 1943, a month after the squash court, the operation of the Y-12 plant was in the hands of the Tennessee Eastman Corporation. It in turn would contract for "equipment to be manufactured by the Westinghouse Electric and Manufacturing Company, the Allis-Chalmers Manufacturing Company, and the Chapman Valve Manufacturing Company. General Electric agreed to provide electrical equipment."[35]

The more companies that were brought into the production process, the more workers hired for construction—whether of wooden barracks or cyclotrons—the greater the problem of keeping the enterprise secret. Oak Ridge was expected to employ about thirteen thousand people when first designed. In short order, more than forty thousand were engaged. How would it be possible to purchase 38 million board feet of lumber without attracting attention? What would be the story for the U.S. Treasury and all who pay attention to it, when asking for fifteen thousand tons of silver bullion to use as a substitute for copper?

Again and again, the answer to design and engineering challenges was to expand. In time, racetrack configurations were determined to be the best way to separate U-235, and racetracks were added to the original estimate so that the ultimate goal of getting a bomb quickly might be met. Eventually, work on two of the racetracks had to be abandoned lest a more promising approach starve for lack of resources.

Elsewhere near Oak Ridge, a K-25 gaseous diffusion plant was built. This had been the method of isotope separation that had been given the highest priority by yet another review committee that Groves had established in 1942. The Lewis Committee, unlike others of its type, consisted of officials from DuPont who may have had a perspective different from that of the academics. Their preference for gaseous diffusion was shared by the British researchers whose findings were so critical in changing the minds of Bush and Conant in the summer of 1941. In time, the K-25 plant was subordinated to the Y-12 facility, which simply seemed to be more likely to achieve the promised separation of U-235.

Thousands of miles away, in the state of Washington, an elaborate set of plutonium plants were constructed miles apart from one another in and near the town of Hanford. Among the apparent complications, "Hanford became the Manhattan Project's newest atomic boomtown. Thousands of workers poured into the town, many of them to leave in discontent. Well situated from a logistical point of view, Hanford was a sea of tents and barracks where workers had little to do and nowhere to go."[36]

Workers became bored and left their jobs to scatter across the country, having seen in detail the work being done on the bomb. Again, we see the human factor emerge in this dazzling exercise in atomic physics. General Groves was well aware of the needs of the workers. Years later, after discussing various administrative challenges, he wrote, "Added to all these problems was the very urgent one of providing adequate living accommodations and the essential community services for all the Hanford workers." He went on, "Among other things, we had to build laboratories, storehouses, shops, change houses, fences, electric, steam and water lines, sewers and storage tanks, as well as hundreds of miles of roads, railroads and distribution lines."[37]

This review gives us an idea of the security nightmare in the actual construction of the bomb. When the uranium project was confined to physicists discovering the mysteries of nuclear fission, relatively few people had the intellectual capacity to understand anything specific. As noted, it would have been impossible not to realize that all the lumber and other materials transported to the squash court at the University of Chicago meant that a major event was underway. At the same time, very few people would have understood the details about that event, and Fermi and his associates would not have gossiped about daily activities.

In the construction phase, however, thousands of people were expected to provide the grunt work in less than ideal conditions. Writing of the challenges the workers faced at each of the plants of the Manhattan Project, Groves realized, "Life in each had its own unique aspects but certain factors were common to them all—isolation, security restrictions, Spartan living conditions, monotony."[38]

He speculated that women had it worse than the men. He described a long, cross-country trek to Hanford, followed by a forty-five-mile bus trip to the plants, after which came the first night's sleep in a reception area without personal effects. They had been drawn to the work, in part, because the pay was good, but the women may also have been intrigued by the adventure of leaving home for some place entirely new. Certainly, for many of them, the chance to contribute to the war effort while a loved one was overseas would have been compelling. But Groves recognized that, coming to Washington, they might have imagined forests of pines, realizing on arrival that Hanford is in a desert.

He mentioned details such as the damage to shoes caused by the women having to walk on gravel paths complicated by mud and dust. Shoes were rationed, so damage to a pair could be a serious matter.

Groves acknowledged, "Admittedly, our concern for morale was not entirely altruistic, for a stable clerical force was essential. We simply could not afford a constant turnover. The trouble was the employees found it easy to get jobs in Yakima, Seattle and other near-by cities where living conditions were far pleasanter."[39]

He concluded that dealing with reactor design, the risk of radiation affecting fish in the Columbia River, and the shoes provided quite a range of issues, all of which could have grown into a threat to the success of the venture if not managed effectively.

The Top Policy Group was supplemented on September 23, 1942, with the creation of the Military Policy Committee. Their purpose was to take some of the pressure off Groves by giving people engaged in the project someplace else to go in addition to the newly minted general. The Manhattan Project developed an extensive organization chart that reflected the various sets of experts who were needed to complete the bomb. Academic administrators supervised scientists in an uneasy relationship, since the knowledge of the bureaucratic subordinates gave them a degree of autonomy that others might not have enjoyed. Gathering the materials necessary to build a bomb required the participation of corporations, contractors, and other businesses.

The military had a unique role because they would be delivering the bomb and also because they could impose the secrecy that the project demanded. Putting academics under the control of military brass would have given Mozart countless opportunities for comic operas, but some way had to be found to get cooperation from parties who, by personality and training, were inclined to go their own way.

Tip O'Neill famously professed that all politics are local. The Roosevelt men were learning that all politics are also personal. The various administrative arrangements—from the Advisory Committee on Uranium to the NDRC to the OSRD and the Top Group—were significant to a degree, but the Manhattan Project's success depended even more on the interplay among the key officials.

Madison put great stock in organizational structure and process, and he certainly is the figure who laid out a field on which politics and policymaking are conducted. At the same time, if we look more closely at Vannevar Bush's treatment of his fellows, we can appreciate that organizational structure is insufficient to bring success to a venture. The character and behavior of the actors in the organization are the critical elements.

We have seen the elaborate care that Bush took to resolve Ernest Lawrence's concerns about Lyman Briggs. He could have barked some orders—and maybe, in fact, he did—but the larger message was that he needed both men. And he needed them to realize that.

Another opportunity for a bureaucratic train wreck arrived with Bush's introduction to Leslie Groves. The two met after Groves was put in charge of the army's end of the Manhattan Project. As Groves remembered the meeting, "Through some oversight, he had not been informed [of the appointment] and, consequently, was quite mystified about just where I fitted into the picture and what right I had to be asking the questions I was asking. I was equally puzzled by his reluctance to answer them."[40] Bush made a call and was finally informed about Grove's new responsibility. Being informed did not mean that he was happy.

Bush sent a note to a War Department official, expressing doubt that Groves "had sufficient tact for such a job."[41] He acknowledged that he had been told that Groves is "blunt," but Bush concluded, "Regarding Groves, I fear we are in the soup."[42] After relaying the incident in his memoirs, Groves wrote, "Despite this inauspicious beginning, my relations with Bush, from that day on, were always most pleasant and we soon became, and remain, fast friends. We have often laughed about 'the soup.' Never once throughout the whole project were we in disagreement. He was a pillar of strength upon whom I could always rely."[43]

Bush showed a remarkable capacity to avoid some classic bureaucratic traps that bait egos and send projects to their doom. A memo written later in the war indicates that this skill was less a happy quirk of personality than a thoughtful strategy for accomplishing an important purpose. Writing to four of his closest aides a month after the D-day invasion, Bush mentioned, "In the heat of trying to work out a matter I made a remark which injured deeply one of the men in this outfit for whom we all have enormous regard. Fortunately, he brought it up a few days later, I realized what I had done, and I made amends as far as I could. But it caused me to wonder."[44]

He elaborated that the OSRD was under great stress related to the invasion. Where final exams had frozen uranium research in the spring of 1940, Bush acknowledged, "We are at the end of a winter when academic men normally look forward to respite, and there is no respite in sight."[45] He went on to praise the four men and the agency for which they all labored, noting the civil manner in which they operated despite the stakes.

He concluded, "I write this memorandum because the incident, that I do not need to go into in detail, rests heavily on my mind. I urge that all of us watch the organization with care, take every step possible to untangle amicably the little incidents and frictions that are bound to arise, seek out the man who badly needs respite before he cracks, and see that he gets it, and in general attempt to hold the line and come through the present intense period in harmony. I will certainly attempt to do my part in this if any of you will tell me where you think I could head in to advantage."[46]

By November of 1942 the Roosevelt administration committed to a full-scale program to produce an atomic bomb. Questions that had not been answered in the research to date would have to be answered as part of the production process. One such set of questions was answered the following month in the squash court at the University of Chicago.

By the end of 1942, Bush, Conant, even Lyman Briggs were still central to the Manhattan Project, but the bomb was acquiring its own momentum. As we saw in chapter 1, when Conant and Groves learned about the fission experiment in Chicago that December, they were taken aback. But neither thought that they were in a position to stop Enrico Fermi and Arthur Compton. Interesting that Fermi was not eligible to join formally the National Defense Research Committee because he had been born in Italy. The military feared that the foreign-born scientists might be security risks, but as the top administrative units learned of the plan for a controlled chain reaction, the Italian-born physicist had more actual influence than even Gen. Leslie Groves.

By the time of the squash court, the only factors that could have stopped the production of an atomic bomb would have been if it had not been scientifically feasible or if the Axis powers surrendered before a bomb had been tested. Absent those two factors and absent Congress being fully aware of the expense, the risks, and the diversion of resources—absent all of that, the United States would possess an atomic bomb.

[FIVE]

MAUD—Working with the British

The Manhattan Project was secured in the executive branch, meaning that it was secured ultimately in the person of Franklin Roosevelt—safe from the meddling of Congress but not safe from factions and the difficulties they bring. The word *faction* itself has a negative connotation, as does its modern equivalent *special interest group*. No one brags of being a proud member of special interest groups. They are always made up of "the other," for the reason Madison indicated in his definition in *Federalist* No. 10: "By a faction I understand a number of citizens, whether amounting to a majority or minority of the whole, who are united and actuated by some common impulse of passion, or of interest, adverse to the rights of other citizens, or to the permanent and aggregate interests of the community."[1]

He may have been overly harsh. People also organize out of powerful commitments to their own understanding of "the permanent and aggregate interests of the community." The most difficult conflicts may result not because people are focused on their narrowest gain but because they see truth and good at the heart of some issues. Their opponents may then be mistaken, obtuse, or venal, with mistaken being the mildest explanation for the subsequent obstruction.

In the Manhattan Project, the swirl of factions included physicists, academic administrators, elected officials, agency officials, military brass of the army and the navy, contractors, building supply companies, people in skilled trades, real estate agents, cooks, clothing suppliers, janitors, and any other endeavor germane to the daily needs of tens of thousands of people at sites across the land.

These factions contended over how to split the atomic nucleus; the element whose nucleus would be split; the best way to obtain whatever element it might be; the amount of the element needed for testing and ultimately for a bomb, as opposed to a source of nuclear energy; a bomb or nuclear energy for this war or the future; whether to share information with anyone who might have a useful idea or to promote security by keeping things on a need to know basis; and making sure that the housing, food, and shoes are adequate so that people don't leave for parts unknown with marvelous stories to tell about a supersecret project.

Then the Americans started talking with the British, and these challenges grew exponentially.

The alliance between the United States and Great Britain came to be expressed in the relationship between FDR and Winston Churchill, the British prime minister.[2] They proved to be friends of a sort, but that qualifier reflects an array of complications beyond their dueling, domineering personalities.

Given their competitive characters, Franklin Roosevelt and Winston Churchill developed something remarkably close to complete trust in each other. When pressed by subordinates for decisions that would give direction to resolving factional disputes, both men urged cooperation. The lines that define nations would be ignored in a common cause against Nazi Germany with a complete interchange of ideas and information.

The bond was welcome news to the British, but the Americans were left sputtering. Patents? Trade secrets? Licenses? What of the postwar nuclear power industry or the numerous American firms vitally interested in those matters? For FDR and Churchill, these were issues that could wait, because the central question for both men was how to defeat Germany in the shortest span of time. For the people with the task of actually producing a bomb, that question was inextricably linked to all the questions over which they contended with one another.

For the Americans, their president could be maddening. He would seem to say one thing to Churchill and then back off when an aide explained a complexity that hadn't yet occurred to the boss. In the past, when Roosevelt would indicate, for example, to the Departments of Agriculture and the Interior that each had responsibility for the nation's forests, the impacts were relatively low. In the race to build an atomic bomb, the stakes could not have been higher, and the president's seemingly breezy way of dealing with fundamental questions could be utterly frustrating. No reason to think that anyone involved was acting out of selfish or sinister motives, but the lack of a clear and consistent direction compounded a job that was enormously difficult in the best of circumstances.

Franklin Roosevelt and Winston Churchill learned of the potential of an atomic bomb at roughly the same time. Churchill was advised of the progress in nuclear fission from his friend Frederick Lindemann, Lord Cherwell to those who were not his friend. The timing was propitious. In August of 1939 Churchill was brought into Neville Chamberlain's cabinet to his old post as first lord of the admiralty, the position from which he resigned during the Great War after the disaster in the Dardanelles. This news from Lindemann came just before World War II began and about two months before Roosevelt received the Einstein letter.

Lord Lothian (Philip Kerr to his parents) was the British ambassador to the United States when the war began. Early in 1940 he proposed that America and Britain develop a scientific exchange. Introducing a complication that would trouble the Americans in a few years, "at first, the London authorities hesitated. They thought they had more to give than receive and doubted the ability of neutral Americans to keep secrets."[3] More than once, the British would have those concerns read back to them.

By the summer of 1940, scientific advantage and concerns about leaks were marginal issues. The collapse of military resistance to the Nazis on the continent had forced Chamberlain's resignation in May and his replacement by Winston Churchill, who informed his countrymen that they faced unremitting sacrifice. Any help that could come from the United States at that point would be especially useful.

The first meeting to determine the specifics of a cooperative venture in wartime science was in September. A British and Canadian delegation, led by Sir Henry Tizard, arrived in Washington to meet with officials from the American armed forces and the National Defense Research Committee (NDRC). Factions again. The army favored a complete and open exchange of information, but the navy had some programs that were off limits.

Vannevar Bush appealed to Gen. George Marshall and Adm. Harold Stark to resolve the difference. They took the matter to Secretary of War Henry Stimson and Secretary of the Navy Frank Knox. "On October 24, they informed Bush that they would make information available on all devices in use or under development except the Army bomb ballistic tables and the Navy bombsight and two-way-firing antenna mine."[4] Referring to the devices that would be new to the British, Marshall and Stark added, "Should the British Government want to put these in production, it would have to make appropriate arrangements with the patentees or original manufacturers."[5]

In March of 1941 James Conant visited London to advance the cooperation in science, especially the establishment of scientific offices by each country in the other's capital. He was well received since he had been very determined in urging the American government to prepare for the German threat. His testimony in favor of the recently passed Lend Lease Act won him the regard of the beleaguered British. Perhaps relying on Conant's reputation, Lord Cherwell brought up atomic power one day over lunch. Conant expressed the doubts he held at that time about its feasibility, and Cherwell indicated that a bomb might be possible. Conant thought the remarks to be musings between colleagues and not important enough to mention in his report when he returned to Washington in April.

The summer of 1941 was the time of conversion for Bush and Conant. As mentioned, the American review committee, headed by Frank Jewett, which was supposed to reach a conclusion about the wisdom of a crash program to build an atomic bomb, was spinning its wheels to Bush's great frustration. At the same time, a report from the British atomic committee accomplished what Jewett's group had not. The MAUD Report indicated that fission was sufficiently promising to warrant a vigorous effort to build a bomb. (MAUD is either an acronym standing for Military Application of Uranium Detonation or a code word standing for nothing at all. The British atomic program was also camouflaged with the name Tube Alloys.)

The MAUD Report also impressed Churchill, and he created a unit within the Department of Scientific and Industrial Research to work on an atomic bomb. A key figure in the British effort was

Wallace Akers, an engineer with the Imperial Chemical Industries (ICI) who was assigned to the project, an assignment that eventually complicated the exchange of information with the Americans.

Before Pearl Harbor, Franklin Roosevelt and Winston Churchill met in August of 1941 on ships off the coast of Newfoundland and worked to establish such additional American assistance as was legally possible. Roosevelt was probably more candid with his counterpart than he was with members of Congress, who required more subtle treatment. The meeting was their first, aside from a brief encounter at a dinner in England in 1918 during the Great War after which FDR remembered Churchill poorly and the prime minister remembered the president not at all.

They next saw each other near the end of December of 1941, when Roosevelt could drop the pretense of neutrality. Even though the American entry into the war was due to the attack from Japan, the two leaders agreed that they would focus on Germany as the priority. As had been the case in the Wilson administration, the United States had to get to a war footing as quickly as possible.

England was two years into the war, while Roosevelt had to figure out how to build a military force with the proper resources going to the various branches of the armed services. Millions of American men would have to be housed, fed, clothed, and equipped; to do so, government would have to direct the economy to military ends. The army, navy, marines, and airmen also would have to be trained for a horror unfamiliar to the great majority of them. They would then have to be integrated into a multinational force to pursue a strategy for victory that had yet to be determined.

The urgency of their common cause and the burden of their shared responsibility did not guarantee that Roosevelt and Churchill would cooperate, let alone find mutual trust and confidence. As it was, each charmed the other from the first. Each understood how the world looked to the other as perhaps no one else could. Meetings with military officers, industrialists, diplomats, journalists, legislators, and others essential to the effort consumed their public lives. In contrast, when Roosevelt and Churchill met, they could pick up from their last gathering. From time to time, one would try to play the other, but they seemed to appreciate that the person who best understood the burdens and even the exhilaration of the challenges was the chief executive of another country.

As both countries made progress on the bomb, the general agreement on complete cooperation required refinement. On June 19, 1942, Churchill arrived at Hyde Park, the president's boyhood home, where they enjoyed a rest from the pressures in their respective capitals, drank copious amounts of alcohol, discussed the progress of the war, and reiterated their determination that work on an atomic bomb would be a common effort.

As Churchill remembered the arrangement later in February of 1943, "The partners were to be equal; they were to share fully in the results."[6] The AEC history identifies the problem that remained unresolved: "There was no written agreement and no effort to spell out the details of the joint effort. The discussion was in general terms, partly because neither leader was in a position to conceive of the complications that would arise in practice. Partly, no doubt, the lack of precision reflected Roosevelt's habit of avoiding inflexible commitments."[7]

Even when information was exchanged, differences could arise about the best course of action consistent with that information. Sir John Anderson was another key member of Churchill's cabinet with an imposing title and an equally impressive manner. He was the Lord President of the Council, described as, "not a man to be taken lightly."[8] He initiated a discussion about one of the issues that seemed lost in the happy union of Roosevelt and Churchill.

British scientists had put great stock in the gaseous diffusion method of isotope separation. Not long after Churchill had left Hyde Park, Anderson reported that the prototype plants for that approach were delayed and might not be ready for use for several years. Sir John saw an opportunity in some information sent by Vannevar Bush: Might gaseous diffusion be incorporated into American plants being built to test methods for building a bomb?

In a separate letter, Sir John proposed a foundation for the postwar control of nuclear power. His ideas included a common policy on patent law in Britain and the United States and control by the respective governments of discoveries in the field so that commercial interests would not confound international agreements.

Bush was not ready for either overture. He replied that the American program had its own issues to resolve that precluded any immediate commitments. He reaffirmed the general notion that cooperation was a good idea and that some postwar plans to impose rational order on a nuclear industry was a sound notion, but both would have to wait.

In September of 1942 Leslie Groves was put in charge of the Manhattan Project and promoted to brigadier general. The appointment was more than a symbolic shift. The United States was going to figure out how to build an atomic bomb and develop the theory along the way. As to their principal ally, "When cooperation with the United Kingdom came up for discussion, the premium on speed made the complications of an international venture seem unattractive, especially since the United States was doing ten times as much work as Britain."[9]

On October 1 Bush conveyed the American position to Sir John Anderson. In various forms, the point would recur through the war: We remain committed in principle to a full exchange of information with you, but we will not be held back if you can't keep up. Nor will we depart from promising avenues to test methods that you favor but that our own experts have considered and dismissed. Nor will we help you build a postwar nuclear power industry as a byproduct of our research into how best to blow up the Axis.

This argument shows the limits of the authorities at the top, Roosevelt and Churchill. In a paternalistic sense, they might ask their charges if they were getting along. The Americans could say yes, and FDR would have no way to grasp what Bush meant by *keeping up* or *promising avenues* or *methods that experts rejected*. Officially, of course, Franklin Roosevelt was in charge, but whether he could impose his will on his subordinates depended on his understanding of what they were doing. Since they would be the ones who would have to explain their actions and the issues that precipitated them, there was little chance that he could change their decisions.

British officials could complain to Churchill that the Americans were not honoring the agreement made that summer at Hyde Park. Churchill was in no better position than Roosevelt to contest the narrow choices that the Americans made; unable to make that challenge, the British found themselves increasingly pushed to the margin by the Americans.

Stimson brought the president up to date on the Manhattan Project after a cabinet meeting on October 29. He explained that the Americans were doing the lion's share of the work, and he wanted to know what commitments FDR had made to Churchill. Another classic response, "Roosevelt replied that he had talked with no one but Churchill and with him only in a general way."[10] Stimson, splitting hairs himself, suggested that the full exchange of information continue, but only the information that was necessary. Since the Americans would define necessity, the weakness of the British position was evident.

Further undermining the British were memories from the Great War that were still fresh in the minds of Roosevelt, Bush, and Stimson, all of whom had held important jobs in that conflict. As much as they admired Churchill, the Americans had not forgotten his earlier performance. Among the array of issues that Roosevelt and Churchill discussed was the invasion of Europe. The Americans favored a cross channel expedition as soon as possible.

Churchill countered by urging a campaign in North Africa, followed by an invasion through the Balkans, which "reminded Stimson of 'the fatal decision to go half-baked to the Dardanelles' more than a quarter-century earlier. In the end, the United States went along on North Africa, but the dispute left a legacy of resentment."[11] Churchill had earned the admiration of millions with his brave and prescient stance against the Nazis, but his character could be admired while his judgment was questioned.

At this unpromising time, Wallace Akers was coming to town. The ICI executive arrived in Washington to meet with Conant and Bush. The two Americans were in accord on the vital specifics. The principle of a full exchange was sound, but the particulars confounded the principle. On one issue, "Since, among the production processes the British had done significant work only on diffusion and the heavy-water pile, Bush and Conant were reluctant to admit them to the centrifuge, the electromagnetic method, and the graphite pile, all strictly American in origin and development."[12]

The Americans also concluded that, as they progressed in the production phase of the bomb, prudence required that access be increasingly restricted. Leaving American scientists and their work and ideas open to the British was no longer sensible. "Need to know" would direct who was told what. On the American end, these limitations were sensible in the circumstances. The interchange of ideas and information that had been agreed to at Hyde Park surely wasn't absolute; rather, it meant that the exchange would proceed up to the point that it endangered or delayed the program. And then Wallace Akers arrived.

Three meetings with Conant in November were increasingly difficult. The American argued for the United States giving the British only the information that they could put to a military purpose in the current war. He ruled out anything that might be used postwar either commercially or militarily or for anything that did not bear on the prime goal: the defeat of Germany as soon as possible.

Akers countered that without fuller access to other information, the British could not know if information was germane to the common purpose of defeating Germany. He added that Conant's position was inconsistent with the agreement between Roosevelt and Churchill.

Time once again for clarification from the president. Conant summarized three options to present to FDR. He could stop all exchange of information with the British; he could open the floodgates to total exchange; or he could restrict the flow as Conant had suggested to Akers.

Bush took Conant's options to Roosevelt along with supporting materials that included a letter from Akers laying out the British position. The president chose the Goldilocks position of continued interchange with limitations. Again, these were scientific restrictions that he would not have been able to fully understand, though he may have sensed that they would not please his friend the prime minister.

On February 16, 1943, Churchill sent a note to Harry Hopkins routed through FDR. It read, "Do you remember our conversation about that very secret matter we called 'Tube Alloys' which you told me would be put right as soon as the President got home? I should be very grateful for some news about this, as at present the American

War Department is asking us to keep them informed of our experiments while refusing altogether any information about theirs."[13] The frustrated Churchill signed the note, "Prime."

Hopkins replied a week later, asking Churchill for a memorandum of particulars from Sir John Anderson "of what he considers to be the basis of the present misunderstanding, particularly the copies of the original memoranda or any references or conversations which form the bases of the misunderstanding."[14] He added that he had done some checking and found that the Americans "feel that there has been no breech of agreement."[15]

A couple of days after Hopkins wrote to Churchill, the prime minister received a memo from Vannevar Bush on the matter of interchange with the British. Bush wrote that he had collected information pertinent to the issue but that he doubted it would clear up the disagreement. As he saw it, the material fell into three categories: scientific research, military application, and manufacturing processes. Bush claimed that the OSRD focused only on the science, that the military now had charge of the other two categories.

Bush added that he didn't think the dispute with the British would be resolved by looking at notes and memos because they were all rather general. The question of interchange could be settled by looking at practice, and he offered a case in which the British declined to share information about a "Whittle engine device" on grounds of security.[16] Playing the trump card, Bush concluded, "This particular case, where interchange has been interpreted by them in a restricted fashion, seems to me to be parallel in many respects with the case which we considered."[17]

A day after receiving the memo from Bush, on February 27, 1943, Prime sent two memos to Hopkins. They are strong evidence that the problem between the two countries was that, in essence, the issues of interchange had split into two levels. All involved, especially Roosevelt and Churchill, agreed that cooperation was essential if a bomb were to be developed as quickly as possible. Repeatedly, however, the details confounded that cooperation.

Prime began the first memo with the assurance, "There is no question of breech of agreement."[18] He mentioned "complete mutual confidence" and then brought up the meeting that he thought settled the matter: "When the President and I talked of this matter at Hyde Park in June 1942, my whole understanding was that everything was on the basis of fully sharing the results as equal partners. I have no record, but I shall be very much surprised if the President's recollection does not square with this."[19]

Without going into the specifics at the heart of the dispute, Churchill asked Hopkins "to review the position and restore the original policy."[20] He referred to the accompanying memo as providing the grounds "that, if I had to justify my case on grounds of fair play, I should have little difficulty in doing so."[21]

This second memo is a review of atomic research in both countries, beginning with the Hahn-Strassman research in November of 1938. Then in the middle of 1940 when Americans visited England and British scientists came here, "information was freely exchanged both in written documents and verbally."[22] On October 11, 1941, FDR wrote to Churchill that the two of them should be in regular communication, "in order that any extended efforts may be coordinated or even jointly conducted."[23] Churchill replied in the month of Pearl Harbor, "I need not assure you of our readiness to collaborate with the US administration in this matter."[24] There were more meetings in the spring of 1942, culminating in July of that year with the Hyde Park agreement, in which it was "the Prime Minister's clear recollection that the whole basis of the conversation was that there was to be complete cooperation and sharing of results."[25]

Subsequently, Vannevar Bush and Sir John Anderson, the Lord President, discussed the execution of the Hyde Park agreement, and they focused on a joint venture of building a plant in North America to proceed with the production of a bomb. Sir John, Churchill stated, "emphasized his conviction that the closest cooperation and exchange of technical information was essential and should be safeguarded by an agreement between the two governments for joint execution of the project and joint wartime and post war control."[26] Wallace Akers then arrived in Washington for further discussions, and that may have complicated matters.

After conversations with Akers, James Conant gave him a memo stating, "That interchange on design and construction of new weapons and equipment is to be carried out only to the extent that the recipient of the information is in a position to take advantage of this information in this war."[27] Herein lies the problem. Churchill ended the memo with the complaint about Conant's position that "it limits drastically interchange of technical information and entirely destroys the original conception of 'A coordinated or even jointly conducted effort between the two countries.'"[28]

Almost a month later, Churchill still had not heard back from Hopkins, and he was getting somewhat anxious. In a memo of March 20, 1943, he wrote, "I am hoping to receive a reply to my telegram to you of February 27 about tube alloys. Time is passing and collaboration appears to be at a standstill."[29] Hopkins wrote back immediately, "I am working on tube alloys and will let you know as soon as I know something definite."[30]

The personal tie between Roosevelt and Churchill seems at times to have set them apart even from their own administrations. When the two leaders would meet, cooperation between their countries was as logical as cooperation between the two of them. By the spring of 1943 FDR's key aides concluded that it was time to rein in their president. If Harry Hopkins needed something definite from his American colleagues, he was about to get it.

James Conant sent a letter to Vannevar Bush on March 25, and it began, "It seems to me of the greatest importance to be sure that the President understands the basic issue. The question is whether or not British representatives shall have full access to plans for the design and construction of the manufacturing plants which we are now building and full knowledge of their operation."[31] He explained that, in effect, making the British full partners of General Groves was a mistake.

In his numerous conversations with the British, Conant had concluded that they would not be building manufacturing plants for an atomic bomb during the present war. A small country subject to constant bombing was no place for such a venture. Far better to put a plant in the United States or Canada.

Stressing security considerations, Conant suggested, "From the point of view of the security of the United States, knowledge of the design, construction and operation of these plants is a military secret

Albert Einstein
Old Grove Rd.
Nassau Point
Peconic, Long Island

August 2nd, 1939

F.D. Roosevelt,
President of the United States,
White House
Washington, D.C.

Sir:

Some recent work by E.Fermi and L. Szilard, which has been communicated to me in manuscript, leads me to expect that the element uranium may be turned into a new and important source of energy in the immediate future. Certain aspects of the situation which has arisen seem
to call for watchfulness and, if necessary, quick action on the part
of the Administration. I believe therefore that it is my duty to bring
to your attention the following facts and recommendations:

In the course of the last four months it has been made probable -
through the work of Joliot in France as well as Fermi and Szilard in
America - that it may become possible to set up a nuclear chain reaction
in a large mass of uranium,by which vast amounts of power and large quantities of new radium-like elements would be generated. Now it appears
almost certain that this could be achieved in the immediate future.

This new phenomenon would also lead to the construction of bombs,
and it is conceivable - though much less certain - that extremely powerful bombs of a new type may thus be constructed. A single bomb of this
type, carried by boat and exploded in a port, might very well destroy
the whole port together with some of the surrounding territory. However,
such bombs might very well prove to be too heavy for transportation by
air.

1. The Einstein-Szilard letter.
(Continued on following page)

The United States has only very poor ores of uranium in moderate
quantities. There is some good ore in Canada and the former Czechoslovakia,
while the most important source of uranium is Belgian Congo.

In view of this situation you may think it desirable to have some
permanent contact maintained between the Administration and the group
of physicists working on chain reactions in America. One possible way
of achieving this might be for you to entrust with this task a person
who has your confidence and who could perhaps serve in an inofficial
capacity. His task might comprise the following:

a) to approach Government Departments, keep them informed of the
further development, and put forward recommendations for Government action,
giving particular attention to the problem of securing a supply of uranium ore for the United States;

b) to speed up the experimental work, which is at present being carried on within the limits of the budgets of University laboratories, by
providing funds, if such funds be required, through his contacts with
private persons who are willing to make contributions for this cause,
and perhaps also by obtaining the co-operation of industrial laboratories
which have the necessary equipment.

I understand that Germany has actually stopped the sale of uranium
from the Czechoslovakian mines which she has taken over. That she should
have taken such early action might perhaps be understood on the ground
that the son of the German Under-Secretary of State, von Weizsäcker, is
attached to the Kaiser-Wilhelm-Institut in Berlin where some of the
American work on uranium is now being repeated.

Yours very truly,

A. Einstein

(Albert Einstein)

2. Albert Einstein and
Niels Bohr, 1930.

3. FDR, assistant
secretary of the navy.

4. Enrico Fermi.

5. FDR signing the
Declaration of War
against Japan.

6. Enrico and Laura Fermi.

7. Leona Woods of the
Chicago team.

8. The experiment in the squash court.

9. Members of the s-1 Committee (*left to right*): Ernest Lawrence, Arthur Compton, Vannevar Bush, James Bryant Conant, Karl Compton, Alfred Loomis.

10. J. Robert Oppenheimer and Gen. Leslie Groves.

11. Gen. Leslie Groves
and Enrico Fermi.

12. Klaus Fuchs.

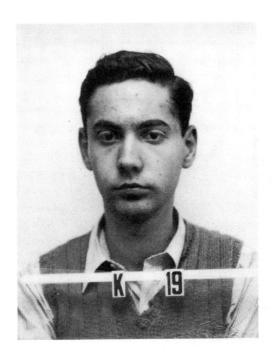

13. Theodore Hall.

14. Werner Heisenberg.

15. FDR and Fala.

16. The Trinity test at 0.025 seconds.

17. Henry Stimson, secretary of war.

18. Vannevar Bush, Harry Truman, and James Conant.

19. Crew of the *Enola Gay.*

20. Little Boy—the Hiroshima bomb.

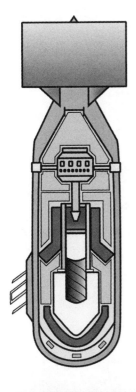

21. Schematic of Little Boy.

22. Mushroom cloud over Hiroshima.

23. *Bock's Car.*

24. Fat Man—the Nagasaki bomb.

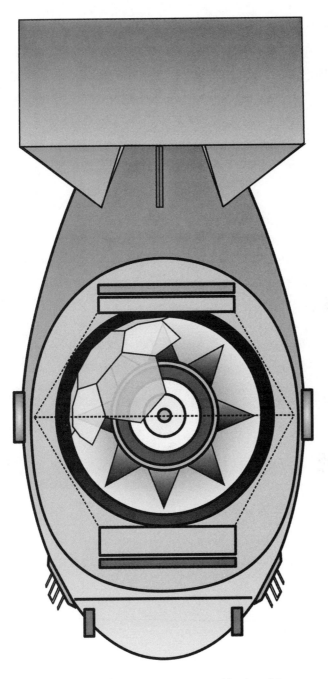

25. Schematic of Fat Man. Image created by AnonMoos.

26. Mushroom cloud over Nagasaki.

which is in a totally different class from anything the world has ever seen if the potentialities of this project are realized."[32] These categories of knowledge were, of course, precisely the kinds of things that workers of the plants would learn. While Conant was trying to keep this information from the United States' closest ally, General Groves was trying to keep his clerical and maintenance workers from quitting and then scattering about the country while possessing vital information about the development of a bomb.

Security risks alone left Conant unable to see any advantage to letting the British have all the information about the bomb, when their connection was long-term and commercial, whereas ours was immediate and tied to national security.

Conant then brought up commercial considerations. He described the British Imperial Chemical Industries (ICI) as a "chemical trust" and "very nearly a monopoly."[33] His letter to Bush pointed out that the British sent industrialists to hammer out a common policy with the Americans, who were represented by scientists. Those industrialists had an interest in nuclear power once the war was over. Conant then sang the early promise of nuclear power: "The use of nuclear energy for power production is being studied in many countries. If this problem is solved, it will lead to new sources of power which will affect the distribution of industry over the world, because this source of energy will be so easily transportable compared with coal, oil or electricity."[34]

As Conant fully appreciated, the American economy tilts, at least theoretically, strongly in the direction of markets. A number of competing firms have a self-interest in providing the best product or service at the lowest price to capture market share and make money. The idea is Adam Smith's invisible hand. To help the community, focus on your own welfare.

In England, monopoly might be more tolerated, as it was in the case of ICI. Conant's letter to Bush noted that "in this country, in contrast to Great Britain, there are a number of powerful competing chemical companies and public opinion would demand that licenses be granted to all of them for the development of these matters in a commercial way."[35] He indicated that, like the president, he was not terribly interested in the commercial prospects of the post-war nuclear power industry. He was concerned about national security, and commercial considerations might complicate that goal.

He was also troubled that, when working with the British, the Americans sometimes had to deal with business executives. Wallace Akers, a top official of ICI, was the person he had in mind. American officials thought Akers's questions and objections were best explained by understanding them in the context of ICI and post-war nuclear power.

Conant concluded that he feared Akers and others had undue influence on British policy: "Indeed, in my opinion, this whole controversy might never had arisen if the negotiations had been in the hands of British scientists comparable to yourself [Bush] and if those British scientists had had the same voice in determining policy in Great Britain as you have had here in the United States."[36]

At the end of the month, on March 31, Vannevar Bush, on instructions from FDR, sent a five-page memo to Hopkins outlining the complex American position on interchange. Bush added more subtlety to the American argument, a move not likely to facilitate an accord. The five pages can be summarized as proposing that the British must be objecting either to the policy of restricting access to certain scientific programs or to the way in which the Americans were carrying out that policy.

Intentionally or not, Bush had laid a trap for the British. If they objected to the policy, they would have to explain why they themselves had limited access to some of their own programs. He went on to defend the policy of restricting interchange to matters directly related to building weapons for this war. Such a policy went beyond the atomic bomb. Both the Americans and the British had followed it for other devices. The primary benefit of the restriction was to facilitate security. No one without a need to know should be aware of these scientific breakthroughs. He repeated that the British had insisted on this restriction throughout the war.

Bush then went right at Churchill himself. He quoted the prime minister's memo alleging that the American practice "destroys" the Hyde Park understanding. Pressing his point, Bush insisted that deviating from the limitation the Americans have been exercising would mean "giving information to those who could use it, not for the best prosecution of the war effort, but rather for other purposes, such as after-the-war commercial advantages."[37]

Bush pounded home the problem of giving away "the fruits of our development as a part of post-war planning except on the basis of some over-all agreement on that subject, which agreement does not now exist."[38]

The argument resumed in May with different characters assuming the familiar roles. This time Bush went to Harry Hopkins's office to meet with Lord Cherwell, who opened by asking Bush why American policy on full exchange had apparently been rescinded. Bush countered that, while it had been modified, it was the progress in the Manhattan Project that had dictated the adjustment.

Turning the project over to the army meant that new considerations would dominate the decision making. Security, Bush explained, would be chief among them. He added that the tight restrictions extended within the American camp itself, that the British were being treated no differently than we were treating our own.

Bush wrote a memo that May 25 in which he summarized a conversation at the White House with Harry Hopkins and Lord Cherwell. They had covered the familiar ground again with Cherwell acknowledging that the British did indeed have postwar interests at play in the negotiations.

Hopkins told Bush after the meeting that, for the first time, he felt he understood the problems that had been confounding the cooperation between the two countries. Bush assumed Hopkins's insight would go to Roosevelt, writing at the end of his memo, "He evidently intends to talk to the President about it, although he did not say so."[39] Bush indicated that he "would sit tight and do nothing unless and until I heard from him further on the matter."[40]

In July 1943 the conversation resumed in London with Bush having to make his case to Churchill himself in the presence of Henry Stimson. The prime minister was bristling at what he thought was near insubordination by the American officials. He had a deal with the president, who "had given him his word of honor that the two nations would share equally in the effort, but every time he got an agreement to modify the present arrangements, somebody in the American organization knocked it out."[41]

Churchill reached a point at which he contacted Roosevelt directly. On July 9 he wrote a memo identifying himself as "Former Naval person." In it he wrote, "Since Harry's telegram of 17th June I have been anxiously awaiting further news about Tube Alloys. My experts are standing by and I find it increasingly difficult to explain delay. If difficulties have arisen, I beg you to let me know at once what they are in case we may be able to help in solving them."[42]

Roosevelt was in a state himself. Conant and Bush had persuaded him that limitations on the exchange were sound, but he also appreciated Churchill's predicament.

Hopkins advised FDR to stand with Churchill, and the president sent instructions to Bush in London to "renew, in an inclusive manner, the full exchange of information with the British Government regarding tube alloys."[43]

The issue then took a turn within the American camp. Bush knew that Churchill would appeal to Stimson, and he wanted the secretary of war fully briefed on the merits. To do so, he sought the help of Harvey Bundy, Stimson's aide. Bundy was especially concerned about the constitutional aspects of a postwar agreement on nuclear power: "For Roosevelt's own protection as well as a matter of principle, [Bundy] wanted [FDR] to stay within his war powers. It was not proper that the President encourage by executive action the creation of a great new British industry with unforeseeable economic and commercial implications."[44] Stimson had another take.

The secretary came down on Churchill's side. He thought that good relations between the two countries would be more important during and after the war than even the concerns that Bush had raised. With the matter seemingly settled, fortune stirred the pot.

FDR's message to Bush to *renew* the full exchange agreement had been botched in the decoding. Bush read that he was to *review* the agreement. Churchill had made some concessions to the Americans, and Bush feared that any whiff of bad faith might make a complicated and strained situation perhaps impossible. The negotiations had been framed by the broad personal understanding of the British and American leaders, but that agreement continued to be strained in the application. Details had undercut the bond between powerful friends, and now chance risked making matters far worse. As it happened, Bush discovered the error before any complications materialized.

Sir John Anderson travelled to Washington to work on the details of the clarification just reached. Five points had been identified in London. As Churchill proposed, "First, the enterprise would be completely joint with free interchange; second, neither government would employ the invention against the other; third, neither would pass information to other powers without consent of its partner; fourth, use in war required common assent; and fifth, the President might limit the commercial or industrial uses of Great Britain in such manner as he considered fair and equitable in view of the large additional expense incurred by the United States."[45]

The fifth point in particular appears to be a sweeping statement, but it may have been as void of substance as the agreements on full exchange had been. Perhaps Churchill could not imagine a president of the United States other than Franklin Roosevelt, nor could he have predicted how British commercial interests would react to any policy established solely by an American president. The concession may have eased the tensions of the moment, but it could not remove all the difficulties that tested the alliance.

In fact, strains remained within the American administration. Informed at a distance about the tug of war for FDR's position on limiting the exchange with the British, Leslie Groves offered a cheeky observation that the president "once again (through his close personal relationship with the Prime Minister) . . . had been precipitated into a matter on which he was not fully informed."[46] Groves's pique suggests that the British prime minister had captivated the president, that their friendship was jeopardizing sound decisions in the American interest.

Before a meeting in Quebec in August of 1943, Vannevar Bush may have had his own concerns about Roosevelt's determination. The AEC history mentions, "Bush was worried lest Roosevelt weaken under the influence of the persuasive Churchill and throw away the commitments he had wrested from the British."[47]

Pascal Zachary writes that Bush had his own frustrations with

FDR: "Bush was alarmed by the president's tendency to casually strike deals with the British on weighty issues such as whether to tell the Russians about the bomb."[48] Zachary also mentions, "Bush was offended by Roosevelt's clubby relations with Churchill. He wanted the president to lean more heavily on him. He also thought the president's seat-of-the-pants decisions on atomic matters might actually stimulate an arms race."[49] Was FDR as dreamy and easily led as Bush and Groves feared? A contrary interpretation is that the Roosevelt charm was a defense that the president used to keep Churchill where he wanted him.

In Jon Meacham's masterful account of the relationship, we read about a Franklin Roosevelt who had no sentimentality that could be manipulated. The Teheran Conference in November of 1943 was the first meeting of Roosevelt, Churchill, and Stalin. As Meacham sets the scene, "The chill between Roosevelt and Churchill came from the east, and it settled in slowly. 'No lover,' Churchill said after the war, 'ever studied the whims of his mistress as I did those of President Roosevelt.' In Teheran, the bill for Churchill's seduction of Roosevelt came due."[50] After reviewing the various ways that America had sustained the British during the war, including their joint work on an atomic bomb, Meacham sees Roosevelt turning on Churchill in a calculated effort to charm Stalin.

From this perspective, Roosevelt applied a genial manner to make it easier for others to accept that the United States was the dominant military and economic power in the world. After Stalin had concluded his nefarious nonaggression pact with Hitler and after France's capitulation, Roosevelt understood and respected Britain's standing alone. He also was aware that the Soviet Union bore the major burden of the German military. He may even have grasped that Stalin might have interpreted the collapse of France as a strategy to shift the German war machine to the east, where it would pound Soviet forces. If so, the famous Roosevelt grace and the ghastly martinis would bring Uncle Joe around.

The concerns that Churchill could manipulate Roosevelt are wrong. Where did the British wind up in any seduction the prime minister tried of the American president? They received some warships that Roosevelt understood were no longer needed for American defense.

Before the United States entered the conflict, war production sent Americans back to work, further strengthening the economy and the country's leverage over other nations. The United States did not enter the war one day before it chose to. Roosevelt's homey sermons, in which you lend your neighbor a hose so that the fire that would consume his house won't threaten your own, were more than clever metaphors. It let the British fight alone with American weapons, while the United States was spared the casualties.

Not long after Roosevelt and Churchill met at the White House in December of 1941, Singapore fell to the Japanese, a devastating blow to British imperial morale. An exchange between Roosevelt and Churchill indicated that each understood the balance of power between their two countries. FDR sent an encouraging note that scorned critics as "back seat drivers" and counseled, "I hope you will be of good heart in these trying weeks because I am very sure that you have the great confidence of the masses of the British people. I want you to know that I think of you often and I know you will not hesitate to ask me if there is anything you think I can do."[51]

Churchill responded warmly, "When I reflect how I have longed and prayed for the entry of the United States into the war, I find it difficult to realize how gravely our British affairs have deteriorated by what has happened since December seven."[52]

Summer seemed to be the season of Anglo-American accord, followed by winters of tension over the particulars. In August of 1943 Roosevelt and Churchill signed the formal resolution of months of difficult negotiations between the allies in formal sessions and informal conversations in London and Washington. The AEC history makes an interesting argument about a factor helpful in settling the issues: "The Quebec Agreement was an effort to resolve a basic conflict of interest, a conflict as intricate and divisive as any in the long annals of Anglo-American discord. Fortunately, the dispute took place behind the ironbound doors of wartime secrecy, and popular passions were not a factor."[53]

If the history suggests that elegant diplomats could work through matters that would send untidy masses into paroxysms of incoherence, it has missed its own point. While scientific, military, and commercial details were too sophisticated even for Roosevelt and Churchill to grasp fully, the negotiations on the Quebec Agreement were difficult primarily because of the doubts that each side had about the motives of the other.

Akers seems to have thought that the Americans, having acquired the early British research on fission, had decided to freeze out their ally from the products of that research. Certainly, they were being presumptuous in reserving for themselves the authority to decide what to reveal and what to keep to themselves.

For Conant, the most plausible interpretation of the British position was that it was aimed at stealing a march on a postwar commercial gain. Akers was more than a tough negotiator. He was a businessman looking out for the long-term interests of ICI while German hegemony over at least a substantial part of Europe was still a possibility.

No doubt that, if the negotiations were presented to the American and British people, a resolution would have been considerably more difficult, if not impossible, since it would have reflected the additional numbers of interests that would have been involved, even more factions to pursue advantage and deflect costs.

A Combined Policy Committee met in Washington a couple of weeks after the signing in Quebec. Henry Stimson was sandbagged, finding out that he was chairing the committee just as it was about to have its inaugural session. He pressed FDR and Churchill later, insisting that he could not do justice to the task, given his competing responsibilities; so they appointed an aide who would carry the bulk of the administrative burdens. One of those burdens popped up immediately: the apparently immortal matter of translating general agreements into specifics.

The American Military Policy Committee authorized the release of information about everything except the electromagnetic method and the graphite pile. Those matters were too far along in production to pause while the British caught up. Such a delay would frustrate the primary goal of getting a bomb as soon as possible.

Visits to Los Alamos were another tough issue. Few Americans had the run of the place, and certainly any foreign official would have to agree to significant limits on access if it were possible to set foot in the facility at all. Another layer of advisers to and liaisons between this committee and that, and the interchange could proceed.

The AEC history mentions that some exchange of information was already underway while the formal administrative apparatus was forming: "Akers had arrived in New York with his fifteen experts, a team that included not only theoreticians Rudolph Peierls and Klaus Fuchs and experimentalist Franz Simon but also specialists on instruments, corrosion, pumps, and barriers."[54]

The history's only other reference to Klaus Fuchs describes him as one of "many able men of less renown."[55] That low profile served Fuchs well since he served as a Soviet spy from the beginning of his participation in the Manhattan Project. For all the filters and restrictions to catch spies and saboteurs, Klaus Fuchs managed a post at Los Alamos, mingled with the better-known geniuses, and passed secrets to the Soviets from 1942 until 1949 when his treachery was finally uncovered.

Mischief and self-inflicted damage have emerged since World War II from an insistence on secrecy in the name of national security. It becomes easy to be skeptical about claims of secrecy and national security. They may even become a target for ridicule. So the Fuchs case becomes a cautionary tale.

Additional layers of review and scrutiny may simply commit ever-more resources to a system that can be penetrated. New layers of complexity may plug some gaps, but they also come with their own flaws. Checking the luggage over and again may introduce some complacency because every agent will know that colleagues will review the same object of examination. Will I be quite so vigilant if I know that others will check my work?

The damage from Klaus Fuchs's treachery did not interfere with the development of a bomb to be used in World War II. It did prove to be an element in the early days of the Cold War, lending some credence to the ranting of Senator Joe McCarthy and the vicious smears of his minion Roy Cohn. To this point, the worst fears about the rivalry between the United States and the Soviet Union—both armed to the teeth with nuclear weapons—have not come to pass, but the reality of spies among us may well have contributed to a kind of hysteria in our political culture that the framers associated with unconstrained democracy.

The difficulties between the Americans and the British traced to the chemistry among the two leaders and the officials who tried to transform an almost sentimental bond between Roosevelt and Churchill into a program that would produce an atomic bomb. Personalities were one factor in the Manhattan Project, but other considerations applied as well.

The Roosevelt-Churchill connection relied on their similarities of class, outlook, and prejudices, but they also came to their jobs with distinct differences. For example, their war aims perhaps varied, with FDR seeking a world in which his Four Freedoms thrived, a world in which everyone could express ideas and worship according to personal lights. They would also be safe from the oppression of poverty and despotism, not because it satisfied an abstract ethical principle, but because it offered the best chance of lasting peace and the security that would bring.

Churchill might have preferred a return to the empire of Victoria and Kipling, but he seemed to know that its sun had in fact set. If the *Pax Britannica* could not be restored, it may have remained his reference point to guide the Allied deliberations as the war proceeded.

The second international conflict of the century had become the most complex project of human engineering ever undertaken. On the face of it, Allies and Axis, freedom and tyranny, good and evil, life and death. The smoothest component of what became known as the United Nations should have been America and England, and in many ways, that was true. They were also *two countries separated by a common language* Churchill might have said, maybe quoting George Bernard Shaw, who may have been quoting Oscar Wilde. Language would indeed be a complication, and there would be no translator to blame.

Comparing the two countries in terms of their political cultures, we find it's the monarchical state that is the more democratic system and the one that lines up popular choice throughout the several branches of government. Churchill could expect that Parliament would follow his lead, but Roosevelt could rarely take for granted congressional support despite the powerful effect his coattails provided. Madison again. The system of separated powers with checks and balances could complicate the exercise of governing, even in wartime.

Each held his office after very different challenges. Roosevelt had to break the tradition of no more than two terms. The constitutional impediment of the Twenty-Second Amendment was not yet in place, but the informal constraint that the third term simply wasn't done was formidable. Wendell Willkie, the Republican nominee, attacked Roosevelt for the conceit of thinking that only he could lead the nation, but 55 percent of the nation agreed in 1940. FDR won 449 electoral votes by carrying thirty-eight states, while Willkie won 82 electoral votes and ten states.

Defined terms of office, an electoral college that has put four people in the White House despite their losing the popular vote, a judicial branch subject only very indirectly to the will of the electorate—all of these and more are examples of the limits the framers imposed on democracy. They did not equivocate in explaining their reasons.

Skepticism about the value of public participation in policy making was captured in *Federalist* No. 55, in which Madison wrote, "If every Athenian citizen were a Socrates, every Athenian assembly would still be a mob."[56] An Englishman born in London would be a *subject* of the British crown. The title of *citizen*, a supreme status in classical Rome, was not his to enjoy; yet the authority of the British state was not fragmented in the way that the American Constitution provided. In the complicated partnership between Churchill and Roosevelt, we do well to appreciate that they did not assume the leadership of their countries through the same circumstances.

To lead his country into war, Franklin Roosevelt had no alternative to running for reelection. Winston Churchill faced a different path. Elections in the United Kingdom had been suspended due to the war, and the electoral hiatus would last from 1935–45. A coalition of the major parties had been in place since 1935, with Stanley Baldwin serving as its first prime minister. Neville Chamberlain, who brought Churchill into the cabinet as First Lord of the Admiralty when World War II began, succeeded Baldwin in May of 1937. That position was the one Churchill had held in the Great War until the disaster in the Dardanelles forced his resignation. With the failure of the policy of appeasement and the German surge in the spring of 1940, Chamberlain resigned in favor of Churchill's becoming prime minister.

The president and the prime minister took two very different routes to their respective offices. Roosevelt had to make his case to the American electorate, and Churchill had to navigate the opposition of numerous government officials who saw him as overly ambitious and too eager for war. Perhaps the skills they honed in gaining their positions helped them to handle the enormously complex set of issues ahead, or perhaps nothing could have prepared them for what awaited.

Expectations of their governments also differed significantly. A more powerful labor movement in England promised jobs, health care, public control of major industries, and other policies that were well beyond what was politically palatable in the United States. For all the impact of the New Deal, that collection of programs hit its limits in both the legislative and judicial branches.

If we take a brief detour through some domestic policies of the New Deal, we can see in some detail how awkward it was to fit the Manhattan Project into our constitutional framework and our political culture. The Madisonian balance—limit individual freedom where necessary but tie the institutions of government in a knot to prevent unreasonable restrictions on liberty—was presented as a bedrock principle of American political culture in one of the 1935 court cases that so vexed Franklin Roosevelt. FDR might have been especially galled that this limited role of government was proposed by one of the nation's leading Progressives.

Benjamin Cardozo was a sole dissenter in the 1935 case *Panama Refining Co. v. Ryan.* The case challenged a section of the National Industrial Recovery Act (NIRA) that we considered in chapter 2. The contested section authorized the president to block the shipment of petroleum in interstate commerce if the oil were produced in excess of limits designed to reduce the supply of that product. The price of domestic oil during the Great Depression sometimes dropped to less than a nickel per barrel, and the NIRA was intended to hold the inventory of oil in check until demand could drive the price back up to a profitable level.

Cardozo was satisfied that by limiting the authority to one industry and restricting the executive function to one act, that of banning the shipment of excess oil across state lines, the delegation by Congress to the president was permissible. Several months later, the entire NIRA was challenged on a range of grounds, and Cardozo joined a unanimous court in striking the delegation from Congress to the National Recovery Administration (NRA), an executive agency whose responsibility would include setting codes of fair competition.

This delegation troubled Cardozo because it was not confined to one industry, "canalized" as he put it.[57] He added, "Here, in the case before us, is an attempted delegation not confined to any single act nor to any class or group of acts identified or described by reference to a standard. Here, in effect, is a roving commission to inquire into evils and, upon discovery, correct them."[58]

Cardozo was not exhibiting knee-jerk hostility to the New Deal. He had a clear theory about the role of government in America, and he could not square the NIRA with that theory. The problem was less the authority of the law to extend to all of interstate commerce; rather, it was the expectation that the government was assuming a role well beyond Locke's concept of a night watchman.

The codes of fair competition became the target for Cardozo's judgment. Considering the Federal Trade Commission (FTC) for comparison, the justice found that the agency had the authority to eliminate *unfair* methods of doing business. Fine by Cardozo, but he objected to another approach to government regulation of business, "one that is struggling now for recognition and acceptance."[59] He made the distinction between the two approaches as positive and negative, and the positive responsibility, "the planning of improvements as well as the extirpation of abuses," was new and unwise.[60] He went on, "What is fair, as thus conceived, is not something to be contrasted with what is unfair or fraudulent or tricky."[61] He concluded, "This is delegation run riot."[62]

Cardozo was working off Madison's distinction between controlling the governed and controlling government itself. Using Cardozo's framework, the Federal Communications Act of 1934 would have been within bounds because it brought order to the use of the nation's airwaves, replacing the collision of audio signals from the new technology of radio. The Securities and Exchange Act of the same year would be fine because it simply outlawed swindling in the sale of stocks and bonds. The National Labor Relations Act of the following year gave workers a statutory right to organize unions and bargain collectively. It outlawed coercion in the nation's labor market, so it too targeted bad practices for elimination.

Where Cardozo's template breaks down is a program like Social Security. Is poverty among the elderly the product of an unfair commercial practice? It would be if a miscreant targeted a retired person's life savings, but if an octogenarian were destitute as a result of market forces that conformed to the law, it's not clear if government's intrusion into the insurance and pension businesses would be proper.

If Social Security and other assistance programs could pass Cardozo's test, what about the Apollo program? Would we have gone to the moon without the spur of a fifty-year rivalry with the Soviet Union to persuade the rest of the world to sign on with capitalism, markets, and liberal constitutional democracy? Does the outlook of Madison and Cardozo allow for a state that tries to anticipate challenges and tackle them when they are more manageable through preemptive action?

America was not simply a laggard in its social and economic policies. It genuinely held distinct views from the democracies of Europe, and those perspectives influenced the country's modification of its government. In 1887 Woodrow Wilson wrote one of the foundation articles in the emerging field of public administration. At the time, he was a thirty-year-old assistant professor at Bryn Mawr, but he still should have known better. Wilson's article was titled "The Study of Administration," and it was published in *Political Science Quarterly*.[63] His point was that we could make a distinction between politics and administration. Politics should concern itself with the making of policy decisions, while administration should focus on the execution of those decisions. Tell it to Vannevar Bush.

Wilson proposed that it was safe to discover public administration in other countries because "when we study the administrative systems of France and Germany, knowing that we are not in search of *political* principles, we need not care a peppercorn for the constitutional or political reasons which Frenchmen or Germans give for their practices when explaining them to us."[64]

If we doubted the insignificance of any corruption that learning from Europeans might pose, Wilson continued, "If I see a murderous fellow sharpening a knife cleverly, I can borrow his way of sharpening the knife without borrowing his probable intention to commit murder with it; and so, if I see a monarchist dyed in the wool managing a public bureau well, I can learn his business methods without changing one of my republican spots."[65]

Decades of experience, especially the prosecution of the Great War, clarified that the neat distinction between making a decision and carrying it out was never so neat as when it was in the mind of Woodrow Wilson. Practice and reality muddled the theoretical camps. One could perhaps conclude that the tasks of deciding and implementing were distinct, but the players confounded things by switching uniforms, often at the worst possible times.

The American experience with transforming atomic theory into a bomb included elaborate tensions between factions that believed in a deliberate and thorough approach to complex questions of science and those that were almost frantic to build a bomb to drop on the Germans and win the war. That wrinkle in the American program appeared any number of times and in almost every part of the elaborate administrative apparatus that moved the Manhattan Project.

Those same issues contended in England, but with bombs falling on London, the British made a firm commitment to build a bomb as quickly as possible. As they worked through the balance between analyzing theory and building a weapon, they made great strides in determining the science. Something like getting the notes from a gifted fellow student, when the Americans got the results of MAUD research in that critical summer of 1941, the information convinced Vannevar Bush and James Conant that their doubts about fission research were unfounded.

In another example of the importance of the personal in public policy, Roosevelt and Churchill seem to have been persuaded by their personal engagement to a point that they forgot about the serious and difficult issues that occupied their staffs. The friendship between the two is one of the most interesting and important features of the Second World War, but Madison understood that friendship is an unreliable foundation for governing. As it was, the bond between Franklin and Winston frayed as the war went on. They never completely lost their respect and affection for each other, but the friendship was founded in public responsibilities. Whatever they thought of each other, they put their nations first.

Before the war ended, Roosevelt died suddenly if not unexpectedly, and a British electorate that had tired of the burden of war bounced Churchill.

In the category of strong, capable leaders, few would be in the conversation with Franklin Roosevelt and Winston Churchill. Theirs was a personal alliance that overcame all kinds of obstacles to confront and defeat Nazi Germany. They did all of that with an eye to the peace that followed; when their totalitarian partner mobilized the Soviet Union against the West, the foundations of that peace endured through the fifty years of the Cold War. The principles at stake in the 1940s were again defended successfully and, most remarkably, without the need for total war.

At the same time, a close look at their leadership in the Manhattan Project reveals profound weaknesses that could plague any public official faced with the burden of directing a course of science. A command of detail is a source of power for an executive staff. The matters over which the British and Americans contended were not entirely beyond the comprehension of Roosevelt and Churchill. After listening to the discussion between Vannevar Bush and Lord Cherwell, Harry Hopkins said he got it. He understood for the first time what the argument concerned: Does the United States give information only to those who can help manufacture an atomic bomb for use against the Axis, or should the interchange be more comprehensive with the British having a chance to get at least an idea of the material being withheld?

No one expected the American president or the British prime minister to decide gaseous diffusion versus electromagnetism versus a centrifuge versus liquid thermal diffusion. Those methods for isotope separation were inherent in the back-and-forth between the two allies, but the essential issue was the extent to which the Americans trusted the British not to use the wartime research for postwar commercial gain.

In the future, we may need leaders who are sufficiently familiar with the language, questions, players, and methods in an array of scientific issues so that they can be honest participants in the making and execution of policy. Whether or not the challenges in the future have the drama of the Second World War, the issues we face may be every bit as fundamental to our survival, peace, and opportunities.

To assume the seats of power, the men and women who would hold civic authority will have to be able to navigate a nominating and election process that sometimes keeps buffoons in the game long enough to distract from candidates who take a serious approach to governing.

Roosevelt and Churchill appointed talented people to key positions in the Manhattan Project. They then trusted those aides to press the public interest, as they understood it. A head of government might be limited to setting a broad policy and resolving disputes as they arise. Over and again, Roosevelt and Churchill insisted that they wanted cooperation between their respective countries. When brought closer to the specifics of the differences between the two countries, FDR acknowledged that his sweeping calls for partnership failed to match the particulars of the case.

This quality of leadership is rare, and events and staff controlled Roosevelt and Churchill as much as they determined the course of the atomic research. If having capable leaders and trusted aides is not enough to guarantee policy that is made in the public interest, we shall have to find additional means of protecting ourselves from the next beguiling idea.

SIX

The German Bomb

At some point, sooner or later, somebody somewhere was going to build an atomic bomb. If not the United States in the 1940s, then another country at another time.

America built the bomb near the midpoint of the twentieth century not to avenge Pearl Harbor nor to intimidate the Soviet Union nor even to shorten World War II. The unprecedented commitment of resources were poured into the Manhattan Project because the key actors were terrified at the prospect of Nazi Germany building an atomic bomb first.

As we have seen, the Einstein letter began the American effort to build the bomb, and a careful reading of the text gives us an additional insight into matters we have considered to this point. The syntax itself makes the essential point: The possibility of building an atomic bomb was uncertain, but Germany was in a prime position to build a bomb if it could be built. And if they did so, the consequences would have been devastating.

The letter opens with a reference to work by Enrico Fermi and Leo Szilard indicating that uranium could become "an important source of energy in the immediate future." It then counsels "watchfulness and, if necessary, quick action on the part of the administration."

Referring again to the efforts of Fermi and Szilard, the letter adds the work of Frederic Joliet-Curie in France to the breakthroughs in nuclear physics. The authors then torture the King's English with, "It has been made probable . . . that it may become possible" to trigger a chain reaction that would generate tremendous power. What kind of power?

"This new phenomenon would also lead to the construction of bombs, and it is conceivable—though much less certain—that extremely powerful bombs of a new type may thus be constructed." Something very important in physics is likely to happen in the very near future. Will it be the worst possible case? Probably not, but the worst possible case would be very bad indeed. So, what should the United States do?

"In view of this situation you may think it desirable to have some permanent contact maintained between the Administration and the group of physicists working on chain reactions in America." You, meaning Franklin Delano Roosevelt, might want to "entrust with this task a person who has your confidence and who could perhaps serve in an unofficial capacity." Enter Lyman Briggs.

Briggs, it was suggested, should keep the administration informed of developments in this field as well as monitor the lack of uranium fuel in the United States. He should also "speed up the experimental work." The work was being done primarily in universities, but their budgets are too limited. So additional money might be secured by the Briggs person, "through his contacts with private persons who are willing to make a contribution for this cause" and perhaps also by engaging industrial laboratories.

The letter concludes with the news that Germany has stopped the sale of uranium from Czechoslovakia perhaps because the son of the Nazi undersecretary of state gained a position at the Kaiser Wilhelm Institute, where fission research was underway.

The Einstein letter reads as the product of a committee. Szilard and Edward Teller wrote it, and perhaps Einstein had some suggestions about the content. We can imagine one of the authors pressing hard for urgent steps while another cautioned against seeming strident. We might ascribe the mixed signals to English not being the first language of any of the writers, but too much American legislation is written exactly in the same fashion of balancing contending positions to believe that the structure of the letter reflects a lack of linguistic sophistication.

The letter never goes beyond suggesting what the American president might want to do. This modesty fits the case since the authors may not have had much of an understanding of the president's responsibility. They proposed that the Briggs person serve in an unofficial capacity, that he ask for money through voluntary contributions and perhaps for the use of industrial laboratories if the heads of those corporations were inclined to lend their support.

While the letter indicates that the United States faced a possible lethal threat from Germany, it does not call for a response commensurate with the risk to national security. Perhaps Szilard, Teller, and Einstein thought it was not their place to make a bold charge to the president. Perhaps they assumed that Roosevelt would know what to do. He did indeed call for "action," but, as we have seen, the ambiguity of the letter anticipates the stumbling beginning of the Manhattan Project. When the pursuit of an atomic bomb might have stopped completely, the dread of a German bomb spurred the effort forward.

Before risk assessment was turned into a science, humans had been balancing pain against reward since we calculated the best course to get to the next bounty of hunting and gathering. Mapped on a graph, we estimate the likelihood of an event occurring and then determine the gain or loss if the event indeed comes to pass. So it was with the German bomb.

The American atomic bomb began with Franklin Roosevelt's declaration, "This requires action," the antecedent being the contents of the Einstein letter. Since Otto Hahn and Fritz Strassman split the uranium nucleus, releasing energy in the form of the strong nuclear force that holds protons and neutrons together, physicists in several countries were making stunning progress seemingly by the month.

Many of those physicists were German, and although those of Jewish heritage were fleeing Germany and Austria, a number of them remained to serve the fatherland. Would they have the talent to figure out what to do with the emerging knowledge of atomic fission and the uranium resources available to the Reich in Czechoslovakia and conceivably in the Belgian Congo?

Otto Hahn stayed in Germany. Having figured out the mechanics of fission, he might well also figure out how to turn his discovery into a weapon. Unbeknownst to the Allies, Hahn, it would turn out, did not participate in the German atomic bomb project. In fact, when in British captivity he learned of Hiroshima, he considered suicide so keen was his grief and despair.[1] But even more ominous than the possibility of Hahn's involvement, Germany retained a physicist perhaps brighter than any other star in the field and younger than most as well.

Werner Heisenberg was thirty-eight years old when the war began. He had won the Nobel Prize for 1932 based on his pioneering work in quantum mechanics. He had studied with Niels Bohr, battled with Irwin Schrodinger, and left his mark on popular culture with his uncertainty principle. On a tour of America in 1939, he was urged to stay in the United States, where he might have found an academic position at any university in the country. He declined.

Heisenberg's commitments are one of the great mysteries of the war. Was he tolerant of Nazism for the sake of some larger purpose he saw for Germany? Was he obtuse about the evil of Hitler's regime? How did he so infuriate his friend and mentor Niels Bohr in a visit to Copenhagen? Did he sacrifice his reputation and risk his life in order to sabotage the German atomic bomb project?

When World War II began, Werner Heisenberg was more than one of a number of brilliant scientists who were grasping the meaning of quantum physics. He might have been the most brilliant of them all. He was the one who developed quantum mechanics, a breakthrough that solved a problem that had baffled Bohr, Einstein, and other luminaries.

His proposal of the uncertainty principle has given him a broader reputation than the other geniuses acquired. His famous proposition is that we can know either one of two qualities of an electron—its location or its momentum—but we cannot know both at the same time. The concept was expropriated by other scientists and presented as, "Observation affects the behavior being observed."

An anthropologist, for example, must be extremely careful in observing a community, lest the presence alters the behavior of the members being watched. More particularly, when a supervisor shows up, the performance of the subordinates changes. If you want to know how your charges are performing on the odd Tuesday, you need to evaluate them unobtrusively.

Physicists themselves may think that the value of Heisenberg's insight may have been overblown. They may also, with considerable justification, find themselves frustrated by those of us who are curious about their work but without the intellectual capacity to understand it. When we interpret what they're doing as it makes sense to us, we can hope for a patient reply. As to the significance of the uncertainty principle when applied elsewhere, David Lindley has written that the notion that observation alters behavior would be known by anyone taking home movies at a family reunion.[2]

Since the threat of a German bomb was essential to triggering the Manhattan Project, why was that threat not seriously defined before the United States committed such enormous resources to countering it? The answer may be that determining whether or not the threat was credible would have required a major intelligence operation plus significant time. If the answer confirmed that a German bomb was on the way, it would have been too late for the Americans to catch up. If there were to be no Nazi bomb, then an American monopoly might force an earlier end to the war. In some respects, then, it didn't matter if the Germans were building a bomb or not.

The likelihood of the nightmare being true was finally addressed in the fall of 1943. A new operation, called Alsos, was charged with finding out if the threat of a German bomb was real. *Alsos* is the Greek word for "grove," an association the general did not appreciate.[3]

At this same time, the Fascist government in Italy was collapsing, so the scientists of that nation were the first targets for Alsos. If other physicists the quality of Enrico Fermi were still in the country, perhaps they had firsthand knowledge of German progress toward a bomb.

The march of the U.S. Army up the Italian boot was slower than expected, and that delayed the opportunities for Alsos operatives to accomplish their purpose. Groves was always aware that the qualities that made these men and women so valuable were the same qualities that made them attractive to the Axis. To interrogate the Italian physicists, this special unit had to train its people in the fundamentals of atomic fission. Thus informed, they would have some understanding of the American progress toward a bomb, so they themselves were potential targets for German kidnapping.

Even operating at this slow pace, Groves was delighted with the work. In his memoirs, he makes a point that is instructive about the nature of the assignment: "In spite of their disappointment over the inability to enter Rome, this first Alsos mission was most successful.

Indeed, its accomplishment so far exceeded what we had considered possible that its conclusions were generally discounted, principally because its findings were essentially negative."[4]

The lack of evidence of progress toward a German bomb conceivably meant that the Germans had moved the research elsewhere. With the stakes so high, all that one could conclude was that no evidence of a bomb was found, not that it didn't exist anywhere. Even the optimistic Groves understood the problem: "We could not be absolutely sure that we were not being misled by the general lack of positive information."[5]

A year later, in the fall of 1944, Alsos targeted Werner Heisenberg, figuring that, if they removed him from the equation, any chance of a German bomb would be eliminated. At that point, Allied armies had been in France and the Low Countries for almost six months. They would cross the Rhine River into Germany at the end of the following March, so preventing an atomic knockout punch was a prudent piece of the Allied endgame strategy.

At this point, the tale assumes a Hollywood dimension. Heisenberg would not be wrapped up in an Allied advance. Rather, he would be kidnapped if at all possible. If not, plan B proposed his assassination. The key operative for Alsos in this venture was Morris Berg, known as Moe.[6] He was a multilingual intellectual, a graduate of Princeton, and a former Major League Baseball player. It was said that Moe could speak six languages and couldn't hit in any of them.

Berg worked as a civilian for the OSS, and he was an element of a scheme to sneak into Germany, find Heisenberg, and extract him for Allied interrogation. Groves's caution intervened.[7] Berg was another figure who had information that would have been more valuable to the Germans than anything Berg might have been able to get from Heisenberg. The intrusion into Germany was cancelled and replaced with a plan to take care of Heisenberg when he visited Switzerland to give a lecture.

The complexities with a kidnapping plan were augmented with another option for Berg. He was first instructed in the rudimentary aspects of fission, then supplied with a gun, and finally given instructions to stand midlecture, pull the gun, and kill Werner Heisenberg if he heard Heisenberg discussing fission in a way that made Berg suspect the Germans were closing in on a bomb.[8] Berg himself would be unlikely to survive; in fact, he was given a cyanide pill to use if his capture were imminent. So this was presumed to be a suicide mission for the purpose of securing the Allied victory in the most desperate war in human history.

In the late afternoon of December 18, 1944, Berg arrived for the lecture at the University of Zurich. Despite Heisenberg's fame and notoriety, only about twenty people were in attendance, and no security was present to interfere if bullets began to fly. Berg took cryptic notes on the lecture and his fellow attendees. His knowledge of German and physics were both very limited; if it were otherwise, he would have realized that Heisenberg was lecturing on S-matrix theory, a topic as obscure as it sounds and entirely unrelated to an atomic bomb.

Not having much direct material that he could have processed, Berg shifted to what is known in the law as "demeanor evidence." If two witnesses offer conflicting testimony, which one seems more credible? The obvious weakness in this approach is that a sociopath might be entirely persuasive, while a reliable innocent might be nervous and seem unsure, having sworn an oath in a courtroom. Heisenberg, we can believe, had no idea that he was lecturing for his life.

In his biography of Moe Berg, Nicholas Dawidoff writes, "Berg's assignment had been to look Heisenberg over. He was to fire only if he heard indisputable evidence that a German bomb was nearing completion. Berg wasn't exactly sure what he had heard, but it didn't seem terribly threatening, and nobody else seemed to find anything amiss either."[9]

Thomas Powers concludes about the encounter that "the truth probably is that Heisenberg would have had to click his heels and announce with evil laughter the imminent annihilation of the Allies with atomic fury before Berg would have drawn his pistol."[10]

Another reason for Berg's restraint would likely have been his keen awareness that, in killing Heisenberg, he would also be killing himself. Had he heard or intuited enough to sacrifice his own life? For Heisenberg's ideas on S-matrix theory? No, he had not.

Berg had another opportunity to render Heisenberg *hors d' combat*, an objective Berg had earlier decided was in order. The two men met later in the evening after the lecture. They left a dinner together after some fellow guests had berated Heisenberg for continuing to work in Germany. A casual conversation on a brief walk confirmed Berg's belief that Heisenberg was no threat to America.

What might be considered a plan C formed in Berg's mind. He suggested to other OSS officials that Heisenberg be approached about another lecture in Switzerland for which he would bring his family. All of them could then be "transferred" to America.

The idea went nowhere, meaning that kidnapping, killing, or transferring Heisenberg were all options that were not exercised.

In December of 1944 Groves and the Top Policy Group would have had no reason to believe that the Germans could produce an atomic bomb, yet the fear still kept its grip. At the time of Heisenberg's lecture in Zurich, the last great German offensive of the war was underway in the Ardennes. The Battle of the Bulge threatened to drag the war into a longer endgame than had seemed likely at Thanksgiving. More time meant more opportunity for some cataclysmic development from some laboratory somewhere in the Reich.

That same month, Groves informed Franklin Roosevelt that the Americans would need two atomic bombs to end the war and that both likely would be dropped on Japan. In Thomas Powers's account, FDR "told Groves he wanted the first bombs to be ready for use on Germany."[11] Not what the general had in mind: "This Groves did not at all want to do; he feared that if the bomb was a dud the Germans would acquire not only a working model of a bomb, but quite likely enough fissionable material to make one of their own as well."[12]

Groves didn't include his thoughts about the exchange with Roosevelt in his memoirs, but his caution is understandable. The attack in the Ardennes was a real shock. The slog through Italy had been more difficult than anticipated, and the Allies would not cross the Rhine into Germany for several more months. Might the final chapter of the war in Europe prove more difficult than seemed likely a few weeks before? If so, a hastily made and crude model of an atomic bomb could prove to be a tragic gift to the Nazis.

The general was showing a prudence that fit his responsibility. He had a better command of the complexities within the Manhattan Project than had the president, and he understood that nothing should interfere with strategy that was proving successful in pressing Germany from the west while the Red Army closed from the east.

As events developed, Germany surrendered before the Trinity test in New Mexico and months before bombs were ready for use. Racing to drop some kind of atomic device on Germany would have been reckless, but once the weapons were ready, the chance to end the war through a power that would shatter the tenacity of Japanese resistance would be irresistible.

A further point about Heisenberg. His famous meeting with Niels Bohr in Copenhagen in late October of 1941 remains intriguing perhaps more for dramatic reasons than for military strategy. No metaphor is needed about their being like actors in a play, since Michael Frayn actually wrote a play covering that mysterious week in Denmark. We can begin with what is certain.

Both Bohr and Heisenberg were as distinguished as any physicist in the world. The two had worked together in some of the most revolutionary days of quantum physics. Fifty-six years old at the time of the meeting in Copenhagen, Bohr was sixteen years older than Heisenberg. Since Heisenberg's work in quantum mechanics was as historic as any finding yet made, we might think of the two as colleagues. Expressions like *father figure* or *mentor* applied to Bohr tilt the relationship too far in his direction. An uncle or older brother perhaps, since Heisenberg traveled to Copenhagen apparently for some kind of personal exchange with Bohr.

Among the possibilities, Heisenberg might simply have wanted to reinforce a friendship that war had strained. Another explanation is that he sought some kind of absolution from Bohr for Heisenberg's acceptance of leadership of Germany's *Uranverein*, the Uranium Club, which would be the organization to pursue atomic fission. A bolder take is that Heisenberg wanted Bohr's complicity in a kind of strike by atomic physicists to prevent the building of a bomb by either Germany or the Allies. This last interpretation is compatible with the proposition that Heisenberg actually sabotaged the production of a German bomb, the theme of Thomas Powers's book.

The conversations between Bohr and Heisenberg over the course of a week ran through some complexities of friendship. At some point, Bohr became furious with his old friend, but later that week, he had subsequent meetings with him that appeared to be harmonious. The explanation for Bohr's rage may have had less to do with the atomic bomb and much more to do with Heisenberg's views on a very personal matter.

Without making a dangerous production of the point, Heisenberg was clear in certain circles that he was not a Nazi, nor did he support their most heinous policies. On the other hand, he mentioned a number of times, including his trip to Copenhagen as well as the dinner in Zurich with Moe Berg in attendance, that he hoped Germany would win the war. When he visited Bohr in October of 1941, German armies were closing on Moscow after subduing the European continent. England remained formidable, but if the United States continued its formal neutrality, a German victory might well come to pass.

During the Copenhagen visit, Heisenberg expressed an obscene hope. Three years later in Zurich, Berg heard the same sentiment expressed as a regret. Pressed by other dinner guests about his allegiance, Heisenberg acknowledged that the war was probably lost, but he insisted that Germany's defeat was regrettable because of the opportunity it opened to the Soviet Union. That argument was sobering to the Swiss in attendance, who would certainly have known the implications of Marx on marks, these reflections by Heisenberg on the outcome of the war bring up our second point about the man.

Heisenberg the diplomat may be an example of nature driving genius back to the mean. As brilliant as he was in physics, Heisenberg might have been every bit that obtuse about human relations and common decency. He might have thought that the Nazis were a temporary patch of nasty business. In time, Germany would assume her rightful place as hegemon of Europe, and the regime would be succeeded by a more tolerant collection. The injustices of the Treaty of Versailles would be reversed. Peace and prosperity would then reign. His failure to think *Peace and prosperity for whom?* is an indication that the genius in physics was elsewhere a very dim bulb.

Whether or not he approved of every step along the way, the potential golden age of Europe under German rule would include the deaths of every Jew, every Romani, every person with a disability, every homosexual, every person who could be considered a threat to the Nazis. In addition, people who did not show enthusiasm for the cult of Germany might be sentenced to a serfdom, slave labor that would crush their spirits and shorten their lives.

Few people could keep up a conversation with Werner Heisenberg on the characteristics of the atom, and few people could tolerate a conversation with him on the most important issue of the day.

For all the confusion and guessing about the prospects of a German bomb, a postwar assessment may be especially useful. An account by the Associated Press in February of 1946 relied on interviews with Otto Hahn and Werner Heisenberg. The press report claimed that Germany knew how to build an atomic bomb in 1942, but they were unable to do so because of the course of the war.

The press release quotes Heisenberg saying that the Germans had "an atomic energy machine" in 1941 that could generate power "from ordinary uranium," presumably U-238.[13] Any application was precluded by the drain on resources from the invasion of the Soviet Union. Heisenberg said, "Money and factory facilities could not be given for research and production when they were needed to replace tanks, airplanes and guns."[14]

In June of 1942, when Franklin Roosevelt and Winston Churchill were in Hyde Park concluding their gentlemen's agreement on atomic cooperation, Heisenberg sent a report to Albert Speer, advising him of the status of a German bomb. Upon reflection, Heisenberg claimed, "Then followed the great difference—America was able to start building the necessary factories on a huge scale. Germany could not even begin work on a scale large enough to produce just one bomb."[15]

Leo Szilard wasn't having any. Reacting to the AP report, Szilard wrote, "It may be categorically stated that the Germans did not have the atom bomb."[16] He explained that the American scientists who looked into the question concluded that the Germans had not discovered that plutonium is fissionable, nor was there any record of their knowing the volume of uranium needed for a bomb.

Samuel Goudsmit, a Harvard physicist, wrote an assessment for Alexander Sachs dated August 6, 1946, exactly one year after the bombing of Hiroshima. After noting the difficulties in finding the reasons for the failure of Germany to produce an atomic bomb, Goudsmit proposed one very interesting explanation. He wrote, "One serious mistake the Germans made was that even in their scientific work they indulged in some kind of hero worship."[17] Who was the hero? "The better physicists in Germany had kept their exclusive confidence in the judgment of one man, namely, Heisenberg."[18]

Goudsmit claimed that Heisenberg's views were never challenged, and Heisenberg generated the ideas that directed the program. Thus, "it is clear that a problem like the uranium project is too big for one man, even the great Heisenberg."[19] The last remark requires some context. Goudsmit had something of a professional rivalry with Heisenberg for a time, and he also thought that Heisenberg could have interceded to save Goudsmit's parents, who were murdered in a concentration camp.

Back to the letter to Sachs, Goudsmit added that Heisenberg was often mistaken in his thinking, but the Americans and British were probably making the same errors. He wrote, "I am certain that exactly the same scientific errors were made originally by our own physicists, but the divergence of opinions and an occasional strong friction between the men working over here helped the right ideas to come to the front."[20]

The contrast with the American and British effort is stark. We have often seen conflicts among scientists about matters like isotope separation, and we also know about the extensive battles over access and security, military versus commercial applications, and a range of organizational issues. In some respects, these conflicts are inefficient because they divert resources and delay final determinations. What Goudsmit contributes to our understanding is that the conflicts may serve a larger purpose of efficiency. In matters as complex as the Manhattan Project, bureaucratic battles and their subsequent obstruction and delay of an agreed-upon course are simply inevitable in assisting "the right ideas to come to the front."

Goudsmit gave a couple of examples of how the German effort was flawed. Heisenberg had decided that the simplest arrangement of an atomic pile was preferable. Some physicists in the German army built an alternative, and it proved better than Heisenberg's. Goudsmit wrote, "You can well understand the embarrassment and difficulties such an occurrence caused among the German physicists."[21]

Another problem for the Germans was their belief that the path to an atomic bomb went through the uranium engine. They may have thought that they needed to figure out the theory of a bomb before they could go into production. In the Manhattan Project, the decision to turn production over to the Army Corps of Engineers subordinated theory to manufacturing.

While scientists debated issues such as uranium or plutonium and the best means of separating the fuel, Gen. Leslie Groves, in effect, set up labs across the country to test the ideas. He went down several roads at the same time before deciding on the most promising course. He was able to do so because America was not being bombed as Germany was, nor did we have millions of men bogged down in the Soviet Union desperate for all the industrial goods the nation's economy could generate.

Goudsmit also found fault with the managers of the German effort. He distinguished between someone being a research scientist and someone else being able to manage research scientists. This issue has been long discussed in administration. Is an organization better off in the hands of someone who has specialized knowledge of a field or with someone who is skilled at personnel and budgeting issues? Goudsmit implied that either background might work, "but a man who guides science should have certain qualifications other than a doctor's degree and a membership card in the Nazi party."[22]

Looking at Germany's administrative equivalents of the American Office of Scientific Research and Development, Goudsmit found the Germans to be "second rate scientists, not so much because they were Nazis, but because they were bad administrators and lacked the confidence of the scientists for whose work they were responsible."[23] For future reference, he acknowledged that "the same thing can happen over here if a man or a committee in charge of scientific research is chosen merely on the basis of belonging to the proper political party or to the armed forces."[24]

Several episodes in the American experience come to mind. When Arthur Compton told the s-1 Committee of the OSRD about the chain reaction in Chicago scheduled for the very near future, James Conant and Leslie Groves were taken aback. Both men were troubled, but neither tried to block the experiment in the squash court. Compton's recollection of their shock may have been somewhat smug, but in their own memoirs, Conant and Groves simply acknowledged Compton's remark and gave him a pass with their own explanations to add to the record.

When a member of the Board of Trustees of the University of Chicago had asked Robert Hutchins if the atomic research on the campus was safe, Hutchins had to acquire more information and then report back. He offered his best estimate that all would be well, but he could not provide a guarantee. Again, Arthur Compton's account that he kept Hutchins out of the loop was inaccurate because Hutchins was aware that his university had become a war plant, but nothing in the American war effort was compromised by this personal wrinkle.

When Leslie Groves met Vannevar Bush, their initial exchange might have doomed their association. As it was, each gave the other the benefit of the doubt, and they developed a mutual confidence that was instrumental in the success of the program. As each saw that the other was serious and capable, they even found some humor in their initial misgivings. They were able to bring some grace to a very demanding set of circumstances.

Groves, Conant, Bush, and no doubt others were occasionally troubled by the behavior of their ultimate boss, yet no one tried to undermine Franklin Roosevelt even when they were baffled or frustrated by his directions. That speaks well of Roosevelt himself. It also indicates the enormous peril the nation would have faced had all of Europe fallen to the Nazis, all of Asia fallen under the control of the Japanese, and both Axis powers linked in the Middle East to control the oil fields that would feed their alliance against an isolated America.

The effectiveness of the Manhattan Project compared to the German *Uranverein* is also a testament to the character and talent of the top administrators. These were ambitious men who were major figures in their various fields before they were tapped for duty in the uranium project. Their egos were undoubtedly formidable, and they may not have been entirely comfortable in subordinate roles. But when Lyman Briggs had to answer to Vannevar Bush, he did so.

When it was time for Bush to turn over production of the bomb to the army, he complied. When Roosevelt and Stimson told Bush and Conant that good relations with the British were worth more than what might seem to be sound administrative practice, they found ways to reach an accord.

The evidence indicates that the civic cultures of the Americans and British encouraged vigorous conflicts . . . to a point. Even though Franklin Roosevelt had all but cut the other branches of government out of the Manhattan Project, the spirit of the Madisonian arrangement, that ambition would counter ambition, remained. Spirited battles sharpened ideas, forced advocates to accumulate more evidence, until a decision was finally reached.

We can assume that Germany also had able, bright people, but the hideous culture of the regime undermined those assets. People who might have aided the war effort escaped certain death. Others, like Otto Hahn, stayed but declined to cooperate in the research on a bomb. Heisenberg may or may not have sabotaged the German bomb, but if he was comfortable with the mindless obedience of his subordinates, he was undermining the atomic research, wittingly or not.

John Cornwell's book *Hitler's Scientists: Science, War, and the Devil's Pact* tries to look at atomic research through Hitler's eyes. Cornwell relies on Albert Speer's account in making some useful observations. In keeping with madness, Hitler seems to have had conflicting attitudes about modern weapons: "Hitler opposed the machine gun because, according to Speer, it made soldiers cowardly and made close combat impossible. He was against jet propulsion, because he thought its extreme speed was an obstacle to aerial combat, and distrusted German attempts to develop an atomic bomb, calling such efforts, according to Speer, 'a spawn of Jewish pseudo-science.'"[25]

Hitler's understanding of nuclear fission seems to have been very limited, but the same could have been said for the head of any nation state. The critical difference between the German and American experiences was that the American president reacted immediately in following up on the Einstein letter while the German chancellor's henchmen had driven Einstein from the country in 1933 shortly after Hitler's assuming power.

Cornwell notes that hundreds of German scientists were gathered at Peenemunde to work on long-range rockets. They were successful near the end of the war with both the v-1 and v-2. Cornwell speculates that if the warhead had been a dirty bomb, the result might have meant that "history would have been very different."[26] If the Germans were not able to build the equivalent of Little Boy and Fat Man, they could have mixed radioactive material in a conventional explosive and caused even more devastation than that suffered by the targeted populations.

At the outset of the war, the best estimates were that a bomb, if possible at all, would require a total effort by a very powerful economy and society. Those qualities describe the United States, but once bombs began to fall on Germany and the Soviets held the line at Stalingrad, they did not describe the Reich.

In addition to Germany being militarily vulnerable, Cornwell writes, "When Hitler went to war in 1939, Germany's education system, once the envy of the world, was in chaos, along with the country's national policies for the fostering and exploitation of science and technology."[27] Purging the universities of talented professors and stifling free inquiry and expression led to this predictable outcome.

Cornwell concludes, "In the absence of a rationalized, centralized executive, science and technology in the Third Reich were at the whim of competing warlords and commercial and bureaucratic fiefdoms. At the same time, Hitler deliberately generated rivalries between the main armed services and the ss, while failing to establish a policy for priorities in the complex mobilization and rearmament of a technologically advanced nation state."[28] This point is particularly helpful because it indicates a false assumption that, when a totalitarian regime issues orders, they are universally obeyed.

If we put Cornwell's observation together with Goudsmit, we find that both Germany and the United States had conflict within their military science sectors. In the American case, those conflicts were productive, and they were ultimately harmonized even if the direction from the top was vague. Franklin Roosevelt was not obeyed because dissenters were in terror of the consequences of defiance. His leadership was sought because the contending factors respected him sufficiently to put aside their differences, and certainly they acknowledged the legitimacy of his authority after he won his third presidential election. The same could be said for Winston Churchill, a figure respected even by skeptics, who was prime minister because king and country recognized him as the right person for a very daunting job.

In Germany the chancellor would have had the ultimate support only of those similarly deranged. Heisenberg stayed in Germany out of some questionable sense of attachment to the land of his birth. The top military officers had taken the Wehrmacht Oath, a pledge of honor focused on the person of Adolph Hitler. Other commercial and political factions realized too late that the clown whom they thought they could control would not relinquish his power until the nation was in ruins.

In one of the inevitably unpredictable courses of war, the threat of a German bomb did not lead to the destruction of Germany but to devastation for two Japanese cities. By the time of Japan's surrender on the deck of the USS *Missouri*, atomic bombs had established themselves as unprecedented in two respects. The lethal consequences of their use was matched to a degree by the strategic bombing raids that used conventional explosives, but no single weapon could deliver anything like the catastrophic effects of one *extraordinary bomb of a new type.*

Second, the threat of this devastation represented an unprecedented advantage for any nation that possessed atomic weapons. Among the first to understand this aspect of the new bomb was our ally Josef Stalin. With his country fighting for its existence against the German invasion, with Stalingrad and Leningrad under murderous sieges, with seemingly every resource hurled into national defense, Stalin still diverted assets into finding out what the Americans knew roughly at the same time the Americans knew it themselves.

The Soviet success in penetrating the imposing layers of security in the Manhattan Project not only gave Moscow atomic weapons years before they would otherwise have produced them. It also added a vein of treachery and distrust to a Cold War that would have had an abundance of both without the atomic dimension.

SEVEN

Secrets and Spies

If something can be both tragic and dreary, Soviet espionage and the American response may qualify. The spies included a number of pathetic, broken individuals trying to find purpose in a cause that slaughtered and enslaved millions while professing a utopian end for humanity. The American reaction to the discovery of spies among us was late, reactive, and often hysterical.

The Cold War combined aspects of international relations that we have already considered. The Soviet Union was our ally during World War II, but not in the way that the British were. We shared no common cultural heritage. Franklin Roosevelt and Josef Stalin had no friendship nor did they visit each other outside of three conferences that were also attended by Winston Churchill. As we have seen, figuring out what kind of information to share with the British occupied Roosevelt and his staff for several years. They faced no such complications with the Soviets, because helping them with an atomic bomb was out of the question. Sharing with London was difficult. Sharing with Moscow was impossible.

We have also seen that the threat of a German bomb drove the Manhattan Project from its earliest days. That danger never materialized, but American officials knew fairly early that the Soviets would possess an atomic bomb at some point, probably before 1950. A different totalitarian state with its own unhinged miscreant in command would challenge the United States as soon as the glow of victory in World War II dimmed. And that challenger would possess the terrible weapon that had finished the conflict just past.

The Cold War represented a collision at two levels. In the 1830s, Alexis de Tocqueville identified America and Russia as two nations on the rise: "Both of them have grown up unnoticed; and whilst the attention of mankind was directed elsewhere, they have suddenly placed themselves in the front rank among the nations, and the world learned their existence and their greatness at almost the same time."[1] Tocqueville proposed that the rest of world had reached a mature state, but the United States and Russia were "still in the act of growth."[2]

He claimed that the paths were different. The Americans faced a daunting wilderness and, in his regrettable expression, "savage life."[3] The Russians were challenged by "civilization with all its arms."[4] The implications were that "the conquests of the American are therefore gained with the ploughshare; those of the Russian by the sword."[5] As it was, about the time Tocqueville was writing his observations of American life, John Deere, a Vermont blacksmith who had moved to Illinois, was inventing a plow to cut the tough soil of the American Midwest. The Russian czar declined the sword that Tocqueville mentioned in favor of the hangman's rope to dispatch five who had rebelled against the monarchy.

Anticipating a difference that would be evident in the Cold War, Tocqueville argues, "The Anglo-American relies upon personal interest to accomplish his ends, and gives free scope to the unguided strength and common sense of the people; the Russian centers all the authority of society in a single arm."[6]

Seemingly looking directly into the 1950s, Tocqueville concluded, "The principal instrument of the former [the Americans] is freedom; of the latter, servitude. Their starting-point is different, and their courses are not the same; yet each of them seems marked out by the will of heaven to sway the destinies of half the globe."[7] With nuclear weapons coming to dominate each arsenal of the former allies, the entire globe had a vital interest in the rivalry between the two superpowers.

In addition to this national competition, the United States and the Soviet Union differed on a fundamental point of ideology even older than Tocqueville's observations. Both political cultures considered the significance of economic inequality. Once again, James Madison is central to the American understanding. He looked directly at the implications of some having more than others.

In *Federalist* No. 10, Madison considered the reasons why factions form; after a review of various causes, he wrote, "The most common and durable source of factions has been the various and unequal distribution of property."[8] He considered the option of eliminating this disparity of wealth, and he concluded that the leveling of material difference required the suppression of individual freedom.

He then insisted that the cure was worse than the disease. In his memorable metaphor, liberty is to faction as air is to fire. A forest fire conceivably could be extinguished by vacuuming the air from the forest. In addition to extinguishing the fire, all plant and animal life would perish as well. Less poetically, removing the unequal distribution of wealth would require a government that had the power and will to intrude into every aspect of a person's life, and such a government was exactly what the framers were trying to prevent.

Freedom, in this liberal tradition, means the individual's right to do what he or she wants. The community, and certainly the state, is in service to the individual, so the cause of faction will be tolerated while we control for the effects of factions in ways previously discussed, specifically the separation of powers along with checks and balances. Karl Marx saw the matter differently.

From a Communist perspective, the freedom to dissent publicly and unequivocally is something of an adolescent exercise. One can criticize the president of the United States on the sidewalk in front of the White House, and the state itself will station officers to protect that individual from anyone excessively provoked by the protest. Having vented displeasure, perhaps the dissenter goes home satisfied.

The Communist might point out that nothing of substance has changed. Poor people still live in squalor in this very rich country. Medical care is not available to everyone. Schools in some places are thoroughly inadequate. Markets allow the wealthiest to indulge whims of vanity while children may go hungry. Liberal freedom may reduce to the right to pop off, as a teenager might to parents or teachers. True freedom would mean access to a sufficient share of material goods. To achieve real freedom would require the very exercise that Madison rejected: the leveling of material inequality.

For fifty years, the United States and the Soviet Union faced off in a struggle to persuade other nations to a particular set of civic values. The Americans offered civil liberties that would allow free expression of even unpopular views. That political tradition was supplemented with economic markets and capitalism that promised prosperity for those willing to work and sacrifice.

The Soviets offered meaning and community. The individual would join the great class struggle to overthrow the privileged elite who had always used the state as an instrument of class oppression. For some time, a dictatorship of the proletariat would be needed, a concentration of power sufficient to challenge the favored rich. Once the economic leveling had occurred, the state would, in the phrase of Friedrich Engels, Marx's collaborator, "wither away." Ultimately, Communism is a theory of anarchy predicated on establishing the proper economic and social relationships.

The reality in both systems fell short of perfection. Throughout American history, we have not always been a tolerant lot, especially to the outsider, most especially if that outsider proposes to change us. And in some cases, members of the Communist Party in the Soviet Union reached the state of material prosperity before fellow countrymen, enjoying a comfortable home and late model car while comrades waited in the snow for toilet paper.

The rivalry between the Americans and the Soviets defined international relations for the duration of the Cold War. It also helped us to understand ourselves in a way that broke with our past. Because the Soviets had, in a sense, succeeded the Nazis as a threat to our values, we stayed engaged in the affairs of other nations. Instead of retreating to isolationism, we bolstered regimes in Greece and Turkey, drew lines across the globe, and fought wars in Korea and Vietnam.

Competing against the elaborate system of Marxist Leninism produced important, if indirect, benefits. It provided a boost to the civil rights movement since film of dogs and fire hoses turned on non-violent protesters in the South played right into the Soviet critique of American life. Cultural expressions of the competition brought artistic exchanges between the two countries, and track-and-field dual meets packed the largest stadiums in each country. When the rivalry went into space, it provided the incentive for the United States to put a man on the moon.

We can imagine a competition that was primarily about high jumpers and the Bolshoi, but the Cold War was a deadly serious matter, a relationship poisoned to a nearly lethal extent so that, even in its final years, Ronald Reagan could go no further than a standard of "Trust but verify." Two elements made the relationship as toxic as it was: mistrust and nuclear weapons. Both were joined in the Manhattan Project.

As we have seen, Klaus Fuchs arrived in America as part of the British delegation of physicists. He was given a position at Columbia University and later transferred to Los Alamos. Soon after reaching America, Fuchs met Harry Gold, a Soviet agent. Using Gold as a conduit, Fuchs began sending information to keep Moscow up to speed on the American-British atomic bomb program.

In classic fashion, Fuchs was later described as quiet and withdrawn. In the Manhattan Project he was another brilliant figure, but his personality left no impact on his colleagues. He maintained the deceit through the rest of the experiments in Los Alamos, through the Trinity test, and through Hiroshima and the end of the war. After Japan's surrender, he returned to England, where he resumed his espionage, keeping the Soviets aware of British and American progress on a hydrogen bomb.

Fuchs's treachery was finally uncovered in 1949, and he was taken into custody on February 2, 1950. He confessed almost immediately and gave up Harry Gold, his contact. The dominoes began falling. In May of 1950 Gold admitted his crimes to the FBI and gave them the name of David Greenglass, an enlisted army man who was also a Soviet agent. Greenglass was posted to Los Alamos during 1944 and 1945.

Greenglass had a sister named Ethel; when the FBI interrogated him, he had a story to tell.[9] He claimed that Ethel and her husband, Julius Rosenberg, had brought him to the Communist movement. The couple were arrested that summer, Julius in July and Ethel in August. They were indicted in October for conspiracy to violate the Espionage Act of 1917.

Greenglass's wife, Ruth, was also implicated in the spying. It was said that she typed material that Julius gave her, material that he had acquired as the head of a spy ring centered in New York City. David Greenglass pleaded guilty and testified against his sister and brother-in-law in exchange for having the charges against his wife dropped.

The Rosenbergs denied being involved in any espionage and, unlike the others arrested in the case, refused to plead guilty and implicate others.

On March 29, 1951, after one day of deliberation, a jury returned a verdict of guilty against the Rosenbergs and an associate Morton Sobell. They were sentenced a week later. Sobell received twenty years, and the Rosenbergs were sentenced to death by electric chair during the week of May 21 of that year.

For more than two years, judicial appeals and public protests drew attention to the case. The term that Harry Truman won in 1948 expired, and Dwight Eisenhower was inaugurated as the thirty-fourth president of the United States. Just three weeks after taking the oath of office, Eisenhower rejected an appeal for clemency for the Rosenbergs. He emphasized that their crime was worse than murder, because "it involves the deliberate betrayal of the entire nation and could very well result in the death of many, many thousands of innocent citizens."[10] He reviewed the history of the case, concluding "that the two individuals have been accorded their full measure of justice."[11]

Eisenhower declined clemency again on June 19, 1953, the date of their execution. He again insisted that the Rosenbergs had received "the fullest measure of justice and due process of law."[12] He acknowledged that the case had attracted international attention, but he could "only say that by immeasurably increasing the chances of atomic war the Rosenbergs may have condemned to death tens of millions of innocent people all over the world. The execution of two human beings is a grave matter, but even graver is the thought of the millions of dead whose death may be directly attributable to what these spies have done."[13]

Justice can be complicated. The Rosenbergs paid with their lives for their conviction of espionage. David Greenglass was sentenced to fifteen years in prison and served nine. Klaus Fuchs, meanwhile, was sentenced in England to fourteen years in jail, a relatively light sentence because the crimes for which he was convicted involved the Soviet Union when it was an ally. Nonetheless, Fuchs served nine years.

Another court case that caused turmoil in America was that of

Alger Hiss, a State Department official who had been charged by Whittaker Chambers with being a Communist. Chambers himself had been a Communist but had renounced the affiliation before claiming that he knew Hiss from their common commitment. The allegation was made before the House Un-American Activities Committee, where Chambers enjoyed protection from a libel suit.

Hiss challenged Chambers to make the claim in a setting where he could be challenged. Chambers did so on a newscast, and Hiss filed a libel suit. Hiss, in sworn testimony, insisted that he had never been a Communist; after Chambers produced evidence to the contrary, Hiss found himself charged with perjury. His first trial ended in a hung jury in 1949, but a retrial the following year resulted in his conviction. Hiss was sentenced to five years in prison and served three and a half.

Hiss, Fuchs, Greenglass, and the Rosenbergs were evidence of an inadequate system of safeguarding information vital to national security. At a minimum, their duplicity coincided with some troubling international developments.

After the Japanese surrender, the Americans faced a question: What should we do with the monopoly of atomic bombs? John Lewis Gaddis provided perspective in his history *The United States and the Origins of the Cold War, 1941–1947*: "American possession of this revolutionary new weapon drastically altered the postwar balance of power, making it at least technically feasible for the United States to impose its will upon the rest of the world."[14]

Some of our representatives were up to the challenge. As Gaddis quoted, "'God Almighty in His infinite wisdom [has] dropped the atomic bomb in our lap,' Senator Edwin C. Johnson of Colorado proclaimed in November, 1945; now for the first time the United States, 'with vision and guts and plenty of atomic bombs, . . . [could] compel mankind to adopt the policy of lasting peace . . . or be burned to a crisp.'"[15]

The Truman administration was not averse to using the bomb to apply some leverage to the Soviets. Stalin, however, seemed to understand a peculiar quality of this weapon: It lacked nuance. Either use it and set a new standard for the mass murder of innocents, or keep it in a holster while looking for economic and political means of persuasion.

One of the ways that physicists explained the quantum world was by pointing out that one could go to a market to buy a quart of milk or some fraction thereof, a pound of meat or some part of that pound, but it was not possible to buy part of an egg. You bought the entire egg or none at all. So it was with nuclear weapons. As the Cold War proceeded, those weapons would become ever more sophisticated and potentially smaller.[16] Nuclear torpedoes and land mines were conceivable. Even so, their nuclear quality meant that their use would cross a line, regardless of how much was blown up.

Realizing the limitations of the atomic monopoly, the administration looked for an alternative. They found it in the idea of international control of nuclear weapons. It could be an American gift to the United Nations, then, in the planning stage. Of course, if the Americans turned over our nuclear arsenal, any other nation building a bomb would have to do the same.

Henry Stimson favored the international option, but he understood the complication. How could the United Nations know that countries were turning over their entire arsenals? Even if Stimson anticipated President Reagan's *trust but verify*, how could anyone know that the verification was comprehensive? When the betrayal by Klaus Fuchs was subsequently revealed, any possibility of trust—verified or not—was negligible.

The product of Fuchs's spy craft became evident after August 29, 1949, the date the Soviet Union exploded its first atomic bomb. This was several years before American experts expected the Soviets to be able to develop the weapon, so the implication was that espionage had played a key role in accelerating the Soviet program.

The decision to keep every aspect of the Manhattan Project a secret is understandable, but when it was revealed that an Austrian working for the British had been keeping Stalin better informed about Los Alamos than members of Congress, the news was received by the American people with a fair bit of incomprehension and rage. Nor could the timing have been much worse.

Klaus Fuchs's arrest on February 2, 1950, came four months after the Soviets detonated their atomic bomb and Mao Zedong proclaimed the People's Republic of China. It was a week after Alger Hiss was sentenced to five years in prison and two days after Harry Truman announced that the United States would proceed to develop a hydrogen bomb.

The decision to build the Super, as the fusion bomb was called, was a matter of great controversy within the Truman administration.[17] The president had asked aides from the military and science agencies for their views, and he got two camps with people in each whom he respected immensely. Edward Teller, Ernest Lawrence, and Karl Compton, all veterans of the Manhattan Project, argued for building the weapon. They noted the failure to reach an international agreement on atomic weapons and thought for the United States to forego what the Soviets would try to build would be irresponsible.

Dean Acheson, Truman's secretary of state, came to the same view and rather sharply rebuffed George Kennan, who had urged that the United States should take a chance on leading the Soviets to the same position of not building the bomb. J. Robert Oppenheimer joined Kennan as, to a lesser degree, did David Lilienthal, the head of the Atomic Energy Commission (AEC).

People were applying lessons from the recent past. Advocates for the hydrogen bomb feared that Stalin would take a show of restraint as a sign of weakness, and the result could be even more tragic than Adolf Hitler's reaction to Neville Chamberlain's strategy of appeasement at Munich. As Acheson put it, "How can you persuade a paranoid adversary to 'disarm by example?'"[18]

Having seen the devastation in Hiroshima and Nagasaki, Albert Einstein and others recoiled from the concept of the superbomb. The fusion bomb would be many times more powerful than a fission bomb with a comparable amount of fuel, but why in the world would a bomb of such force be needed? In later years of the Cold War, the arsenals of the Americans and Soviets were sometimes compared in terms of overkill: How many times could one side utterly destroy the other? Even assuming sentience, very few species on the planet would find such a question significant.

Harry Truman's decision to build a hydrogen bomb was a product of the Cold War, which, in turn, represented a failure of diplomacy.

A few weeks after the Japanese surrendered, Truman learned from the Canadian prime minister of an extensive Soviet espionage ring working in Canada and the United States. The president thought that the American monopoly could hold for four or five years, which would be long enough to fashion the international controls that represented the best way to control these new instruments of destruction.

As the American public learned of Soviet spying and witnessed the Communist advance in China and the emergence of single-party Communist states in Eastern Europe in violation of the Yalta accords, they were not so optimistic as their president. The atmosphere of growing suspicion "created special problems for a nation which prided itself on reaching decisions democratically."[19]

John Gaddis continued, "Public knowledge of the issues had always been regarded, accurately or inaccurately, as a prerequisite for successful operation of the American political system."[20] Turning to the central theme of this book, Gaddis proposed that "nuclear energy was a totally new field which only a tiny minority of Americans could understand. The process of educating the public would take time and, because of the forbiddingly technical nature of the subject, could never be thorough."[21] The arcane nature of the field meant that "the formulation of United States policy on the control of atomic energy took place in an atmosphere of uncertainty, confusion and ignorance."[22]

To think that popular participation in atomic decision making could not be informed and thoughtful does not mean that participation itself was not possible. Since isolationism was no longer an option, the success or failure of diplomacy in a nuclear age could mean life or death for anyone in the United States, the Soviet Union, countries allied with either, or even potentially countries who thought of themselves as being apart from the rivalry.

The Roosevelt and Truman administrations operated on the premise that secrecy was fundamental to the success of an array of programs, especially in the area of international affairs. As the public inevitably saw the results of those policies, some reactions found the policies misguided, and people holding that view looked for explanations. Any number of reasons could be offered why the end of World War II had not brought immediate tranquility to the land. And some of those reasons could be offered that lay the blame at the feet of policy makers along with accusations of incompetence or worse.

The Republican Party had been in the political wilderness since FDR's victory in 1932. They saw the growing frustration in the country, and some of them were ready to pounce no matter the damage a strategy of vulgarity might cause. An opening came after the Hiss sentencing when Dean Acheson, Truman's secretary of state, was asked at a press conference if he stood by his former assistant.

Acheson, in fact, stood with Jesus. His father had been an Episcopal minister in Connecticut, so the secretary referred the reporters literally to chapter and verse. Just in case a member of the press was a little hazy on the Good Book, an aide was present with a Bible in hand.[23] When reporters looked up Matthew chapter 25, verse 34, they read about visiting the imprisoned, feeding the hungry, and other works of mercy. Gasoline had been poured on glowing embers.

Senator Joseph McCarthy, not yet fully aware of the potential for hysteria, asked on the Senate floor if Acheson would turn his back on any Communist in the State Department. A restrained remark compared to what he would offer in the near future. Richard Nixon declared Acheson's remarks "disgusting," and Senator Hugh Baker from Nebraska captured the essence of the seismic fault whose pressures were becoming unbearable.[24] Referring to Acheson—the impeccably dressed secretary of state; he of Groton, Yale, and Harvard Law; with moustache clipped and not a hair out of place—the Nebraska senator intoned, "I look at that fellow, I watch his smart-aleck manner and his British clothes and that New Dealism in everything he says and does, and I want to shout, 'Get out! Get out! You stand for everything that has been wrong in the United States for years.'"[25] There it was.

As Senator Hugh Baker saw it, the secretary had not made a mistake. He had not, in an emotional moment, put friendship ahead of the law. He had not made a serious error of judgment on the merits and a colossal blunder in the politics of Hiss. Rather, in the account of Senator Baker of Nebraska, Acheson had simply been himself. He had revealed that he thought he was better than everybody else, especially the good people of Nebraska who hadn't gone to an exclusive prep school or received an Ivy League education; who wore Levis rather than bespoke suits; who maybe slicked down their hair with Vaseline, not some sweet-smelling French stuff; who actually read and feared the Bible, instead of hauling it out to put a fig leaf over high treason.

One day in these strained times, Joe McCarthy of Wisconsin had lunch with Father Edmund Walsh, SJ, of Georgetown. For reasons passing understanding, the Jesuit thought that keeping McCarthy in the U.S. Senate was a good idea, but there was a problem. No one particularly liked McCarthy. He would not be riding to reelection on anyone's coattails or floating on a sea of money provided by wealthy patrons. He would need an idea, and Father Walsh had one: the government of the United States, which had recently led the victorious fight against aggressive totalitarian empires in Europe and Asia, was riddled with Communists.

McCarthy might have needed prompting, but having received it, he ran at full stride. His initial slap at Acheson's support for Alger Hiss was very thin soup. Refining the poetry of the smear, he later thundered, "When this pompous diplomat in striped pants, with the phony British accent, proclaimed to the American people that Christ on the Mount endorsed Communism, high treason, and betrayal of a sacred trust, the blasphemy was so great that it awakened the dormant indignation of the American people."[26] It awakened the dormant indignation of some people, but others were appalled at what looked like a rather hysterical attack.

For all the horror of World War II, the conflict did not lack for clarity. Almost as soon as peace was restored, confusion and frustration arrived. Where was the security and stability that should have rewarded the years of sacrifice? Why weren't the Yalta agreements being honored? Why were the Soviets being difficult?

These questions were painful, and they required answers. One theory was that American officials were naive and too trusting. The wily Soviets, tougher and more ruthless, took advantage of a gullible FDR at Yalta. Truman was in over his head, a political hack easily led by effete aides. When the loyalty of some of those aides was questioned, the frustration grew. When Alger Hiss was exposed, the theory crystallized on a theme of betrayal and treason.

A counter theory, what Richard G. Powers has called anti-anti-

Communism, saw every expression of concern about espionage or the Soviet appetite for expansion as a paranoid reaction or perhaps even a conspiracy of contrived convictions of innocents whose only crime was dissent.[27] All of that decades before dueling cable TV news shows.

This national argument had little room for complexity, when very little about civic life was simple. The notorious penetration of Los Alamos was not the result of a scheme hatched in Moscow. It turns out that Klaus Fuchs had taken the initiative in passing secrets to the Soviets. An even more peculiar case of what is known as a walk-in was that of Theodore Alvin Hall.[28]

Hall was recruited to work at Los Alamos while only nineteen. He was a Harvard undergraduate who was known in Cambridge for his brilliance in physics and his commitment to Marxism. His physics beat his politics, and he was hired by the Manhattan Engineering District and then sent to New Mexico. He passed secrets on nuclear implosion to the Soviets; when the war ended, he continued his spying, deciding for himself that the American atomic monopoly was dangerous.

An FBI memo from May of 1950 identified Hall as working with Saville Sax, a Harvard classmate in espionage at Los Alamos. The memo stated that Sax and Hall were working in Chicago, but apparently neither was even brought in for questioning. In time, Hall moved to England, where he lived out his life teaching physics and unapproached about his spying until decades had passed. Even then, he was able to return to the United States from time to time without any engagement from the authorities.

Before leaving for England, Hall and his wife were living in Westchester County, New York. One evening in 1953, they were driving to a dinner party and passed the penitentiary in Ossining, a town on the Hudson River where the Rosenbergs were being readied for execution. Two electrocutions, long prison sentences for other spies, jobs lost and reputations ruined for many innocent people, a country polarized—Theodore Alvin Hall walked through the entire storm without a scratch.

In the 1990s, reporters located Hall in Cambridge, England, where he had been teaching for over thirty years. They asked the questions we would expect, and Hall's answers don't do much to clarify his place in those earlier tumultuous times. He mentioned his own youth; his political views tilting left as a result of a childhood in the Great Depression; and a fear that war spending had been the only reason the economy had rebounded, so peace might mean a return to domestic misery. And then there was the monopoly.

Would the United States try to impose its will on others, as Senator Johnson had proposed? Even looking back, Hall wondered if the United States might have used atomic bombs in China after that revolution or in Korea. He expressed regret at any aid he might have given to Stalin, but if he had helped to stabilize international relations by breaking the monopoly? That was fine with him.

Theodore Alvin Hall was not old enough to vote when he decided that he should exercise an authority that the law confers on the president and Congress. In his mind, even in his final years, he had been an agent for peace. In other language, Hall, *with intent, delivered documents related to national defense to a foreign government for its advantage*; that language is a close paraphrase of section 2 of the Espionage Act of 1917. The statute allows for "imprisonment for not more than twenty years," unless *the violation occurs in time of war.* In that case, Hall could have joined the Rosenbergs, for section 2 of the Espionage Act of 1917 was the standard that they were convicted of violating and the basis for their executions.

What damage did the Soviet espionage cause? No doubt it helped in their production of an atomic bomb in 1949. Daniel Patrick Moynihan wrote that Hans Bethe had estimated in 1945 that Moscow would have the bomb by 1950. By this arithmetic, the spying gave it to them a year earlier. As Moynihan weighed the outcome, "That was the edge that espionage gave them: a year's worth, no more."[29]

Others might have a different calculation, but the Soviet bomb was not the only harm to come out of spying in the Manhattan Project and related perfidy. The Truman administration faced an array of very serious policy questions in the postwar period, and they would have to tackle those issues with a Congress eager to reassert its traditional role in American government. Central to every question in foreign policy was whether or not the Soviets could be trusted.

The first question was the atomic monopoly. As we have seen, the administration had an internal split on the issue. State Department officials tried to engage their Soviet counterparts on a number of issues and were puzzled to find little interest from the other side. Certainly, the Soviets were aware that they might receive some very useful information if they took a cooperative pose with the Americans. On the other hand, if they were getting inside information about bomb production, why would they consider adjusting their positions to accommodate the American administration?

By March of 1946 any good feelings from the Allied victory in World War II were gone. Winston Churchill, in forced retirement, travelled to Missouri and gave his famous address that an Iron Curtain had descended across Europe. Still unaware of the extent to which the Manhattan Project had been compromised, Truman began the consideration of pursuing the superbomb.

A nuclear arms race was almost the least appealing option for the administration. The economic transition to peacetime would be challenging, and a weapons race would put enormous fiscal pressure on the federal budget. All kinds of benefits would accrue if the president could believe that the Soviets could be trusted, but evidence continued to build that they could not.

The lack of progress in establishing international control of atomic bombs spurred those who were interested in the fusion, or hydrogen, superbomb. Edward Teller had been an early advocate, and he may have been given latitude to pursue that project by J. Robert Oppenheimer, who thought that a hydrogen bomb faced insurmountable technical obstacles and who also found Teller a difficult fellow to work with.

The option of a hydrogen bomb was kept so secret that not even Harry Truman knew of it until shortly after the Soviets' first atomic bomb test in the fall of 1949. Not long after the president learned about the possibility of the superbomb, the rest of the world did too. The grim business was not without some humor.

Senator Edwin Johnson, a member of the Joint Committee on Atomic Energy and the champion of burning to a crisp anyone who didn't share his desire for peace, appeared on a news program that focused on the question, "Is there too much secrecy in our atomic program?" The senator complained about scientists wanting to disclose that they were working on a bomb one thousand times more powerful than what was dropped on Hiroshima, thus disclosing the matter himself.[30]

Truman was enraged and sought to restrict any further talk about the new weapon, but the gaffe revealed some nearly impossible aspects of controlling scientific information. In this case, an advocate for secrecy had announced to the world the very information he had been insisting should remain secret. We might ascribe that breach to the human factor.

Soviet espionage was less colorful than a loose-lipped senator, but it too took information to an audience that was not supposed to receive it. A sound policy, but in the enforcement some violators went to jail, two were executed, and one of the most flagrant cases went all but unaddressed.

Spying was not the result of indifference by the officials of the Manhattan Project. General Groves was a stickler for the tightest security. He pressed the need to know as the standard for deciding whether information should be shared, even to a point of increasing tension with our British allies. We have also seen that any scientist who had been born elsewhere might face barriers to certain administrative positions simply because of that accident of birth. Security checks and compartmentalization didn't stop Klaus Fuchs from waltzing in through the front door.

President Truman could have been furious about Senator Johnson's security gaffe, but having served in the Senate himself, he should have appreciated that, even unwittingly, members of Congress would have their own calculus about disclosure.

[EIGHT]

Congress Rebounds

Senator Edwin Johnson's untimely notification about a pending hydrogen bomb program seemed to confirm the wisdom of Franklin Roosevelt's keeping members of Congress out of the atomic loop. Any president would be indignant about such a leak, and Harry Truman was beyond indignant. When his temper eased, he might have realized that his own hands weren't clean on matters of this kind.

Truman had made a name for himself in the Senate by investigating waste in military spending. While plenty of people focused on the urgency of defeating the Axis, he recognized the related issue of applying efficiency to the American war machine. Waste was not an abstract principle; it meant that resources, desperately needed in any number of combat zones, were diverted to unproductive ventures. The sloppiness didn't have to be criminal. If it denied combat units necessary supplies, it was at odds with the war effort, and it had to stop.

Truman had been elected to the Senate in 1934 and reelected six years later. In 1941, troubled by the waste that he found in defense contracts, he assumed the chairmanship of the newly created Senate Special Committee to Investigate the National Defense Program. Because of the enormous expense, the multiple locations, the number of employees, and the shroud of secrecy, the Manhattan Project was an inevitable target.

On June 17, 1943, Senator Truman called Secretary of War Henry Stimson to ask about an enormous expenditure that had been identified only as the "Manhattan Project." Stimson acknowledged that he knew about it, he and only two or three other people. He added that it was for "a very important secret development."[1] Truman immediately went into reverse, "Whenever you say that to me that's all I want to hear."[2]

That was the executive-legislative relationship that Franklin Roosevelt and Vannevar Bush favored. A question from Congress, a reply from a trusted administrative official, and end of story . . . but only for a few months. Lewis Schwellenbach, a former member of the Senate from the state of Washington, had left the Senate to become a federal district court judge in that state. He contacted his old colleague to ask about significant land condemnations, half a million acres, "for the DuPont Company along the Columbia River near a desolate railroad town called Hanford."[3] A month after the conversation with Secretary Stimson, Truman replied to Schwellenbach, "I know something about that tremendous real estate deal, and I have been informed that it is for the construction of a plant to make a terrific explosion for a secret weapon that will be a wonder. I hope it works."[4]

In David McCullough's superb biography, he captures the breadth of Truman's indiscretion: "This was a terrible breach of security on Truman's part, an astonishing lapse of simple good judgment—to have passed on such information in so offhand a fashion in an ordinary letter sent through the mail. It was exactly the sort of 'insider' talk, one member of the senatorial 'club' to another, that gave generals and admirals nightmares and little desire ever to tell politicians anything more than necessary."[5]

The elected officials, of course, have their own stories about the waste of their constituents' money on weapons systems that add little to the nation's security. If an administration sees the new weapon as vital, the appropriated funds might have to be spread among a variety of states and congressional districts, solving the political problem but adding to the waste and inefficiency.

McCullough noted that Truman's blunder was especially thoughtless because he had dictated the letter to his secretary. Mildred Dryden had given Truman loyal service for a number of years, so she kept the letter confidential. Schwellenbach did the same, but we can easily imagine how tempting it might have been to gain points with friends and relatives by passing along, in strictest confidence of course, some inside information about "a secret weapon."

Hanging over the Senate at this time was a recent episode that shook Truman's commitment to Stimson to back off Hanford. The Canol Project was a 1,200-mile petroleum pipeline from Canada to Alaska. The cost was $25 million, and it was justified by very little other than a memorandum about "military facilities." The army's adviser for the project was James H. Graham, who could not describe to the Truman committee the most elemental facts of the pipeline. Graham, like Vannevar Bush, was a "dollar-a-year-man"; in the words of Harold Ickes, the secretary of the interior, Graham was "worth every penny of it."[6]

The Canol hearings were frustrating for Truman. They consisted of the worst kind of bureaucratic temporizing. An army general admitted that the navy had been bypassed but claimed that they supported the project. Truman had been directly in touch with the navy and found no such endorsement.

With that episode as background, Truman heard complaints from other senators who were themselves learning about the spending in Hanford. Fred Canfil was an old associate of Truman, going back to the Kansas City days. Canfil's reputation was something like that of a tough, but a decent one as these things go. So Truman sent him to Washington to find out about Hanford.

Unsuccessful in his effort, Canfil told Truman by telegraph that Stimson had ordered Hanford officials to bar any senator or person acting for the Senate from entering the facilities or getting any information about the work there. Once again, Manhattan Project security: senators were blocked from learning the specifics about massive appropriations, but a vague notion that something big was in the works was now in the hands of a Western Union employee.

Congress was becoming a serious problem for the Manhattan Project but only because they were acting consistent with the nature of a legislative body that can be fractious in the best of times. Congress has no coordinating official to tell members of the House and Senate to get in line. So the Top Policy Group sent a delegation to the Hill to try to make peace with an increasingly unruly Congress.

Leslie Groves explained the problem: "We realized from the start that this could not go on forever, for our expenditures were too vast and the project was too big to remain concealed indefinitely. And, as always happens in the case of any large construction job, rumors and distortions of the facts abounded, and could understandably become a source of concern to any Congressman who heard them."[7]

In February of 1944 Secretary Stimson, Gen. George C. Marshall, and Vannevar Bush met with Speaker Sam Rayburn and the majority and minority leaders of the House, John McCormack and Joe Martin. They brought them into the tight circle that knew of the research on an atomic bomb.[8] They were told about the German threat, the design of the bomb, and its price tag. On top of nearly a billion dollars that Congress had spent to that point, the House leadership was told that another $1.6 billion would be needed. The petitioners added that they would be unwilling to provide any information to Congress to show how the money was being spent.

The Senate majority and minority leaders, Alben Barkley and Wallace White, received the same treatment; Elmer Thomas, chair of the Military Appropriations Subcommittee, and Styles Bridges, the ranking member, were also given the administration's instructions. Pointedly, Senator Harry Truman was kept out of the conversations and effectively frozen out of the Manhattan Project at Secretary Stimson's insistence. On April 12, 1945, after the death that afternoon of Franklin Roosevelt, it was Henry Stimson who told the new president that they needed to talk about something.

Peter Pry—an authority on national security issues, including the current threat of an attack by electromagnetic pulse (EMP)—wrote a report in 2010 titled *The Role of Congress in the Strategic Posture of the United States, 1942–1960*, for the National Institute for Public Policy. In it, he wrote, "One common historical myth is that Congress played no role in the Manhattan Project that developed the first atomic bombs."[9]

After reviewing the advising that members of the Top Policy Group gave to a handful of House and Senate members, Pry quoted Gen. Leslie Groves's memoirs on the essential matter of funding: "The Congressmen indicated their approval without reservation. They said that, while the amount of money needed was large, they were in full agreement that the expenditures were justified, and they would do everything possible to have the necessary funds included in the upcoming Appropriations Bill. It would not be necessary, they said, to make any further explanations to the Appropriations Committee."[10]

Pry is correct that it goes too far to claim that Congress played no role in the Manhattan Project, but their involvement was not at all a traditional one. Providing effective programs with the minimum resources necessary is one important standard, but elected officials also have to consider the reactions of their constituents. At another point in that same chapter of Groves's memoirs, the general described a request shortly after the Japanese surrender. Henry Stimson had resigned, and he was replaced by Robert Patterson, who advised Groves that he had received rumors of waste in the Manhattan Project. With the general's permission, Patterson sent Jack Madigan, a special assistant, to investigate.

Several weeks later, Madigan returned and told Patterson he had his report. Patterson said that he had to attend a cabinet meeting in five minutes, so he would meet Madigan later that day. In Groves's account, "Madigan replied, 'It won't take me five minutes—I can give you my report in thirty seconds.'"[11] That got Patterson's attention, so Madigan proceeded with the political calculus of Congress, "If the project succeeds, there won't be any investigation. If it doesn't, they won't investigate anything else."[12]

The logic is similar to that driving the decisions to drop the bombs, to try to maintain the atomic monopoly, to develop the hydrogen bomb, to ferret Communist spies out of American institutions, and other critical issues of the day. Any elected official has to have an elegant story to tell the voters. The story may reduce to "Everything's fine" or to "Everything's terrible," but it has to reduce to something that people can grasp after working all day at a tough job. All the better that Madigan's more thorough report concluded that the Manhattan Project had been run with remarkable efficiency for a program of that size.

In this account, the reason the administration got a pass was because of the authority of the congressional leadership: "The stature of these leaders was so great among members of Congress that they could direct Appropriations Committee and Subcommittee chairmen to 'look the other way' and not ask revealing questions of mysterious line items that were funding parts of the A-bomb program."[13] It's a fair characterization of what happened, but it may not stress how far from normal operations was the arrangement of limiting information to 7 members out of what then totaled 531 in both chambers.

By mid-April of 1945 acquiescence to the congressional leadership was wearing thin. Groves and Stimson were prepared to bring a few more representatives and senators into their confidence. On the verge of clearing the matter with the House and Senate leaders, Franklin Roosevelt died. At a later point, visits to Oak Ridge were conducted, and they satisfied the members of Congress that the taxpayers' money was being spent responsibly.

Peter Pry's report later quoted Vannevar Bush's assessment of why Congress was so cooperative in giving the administration all the funding it requested. In his memoirs, Bush asks the essential question: "How does it happen that a Congressman who was a small-town lawyer in private life can sit on a committee and judge wisely whether the military organization is running well, whether its proposals appear sound, and whether its appropriations should be cut or extended?"[14]

Bush answered his own question with a remarkable assumption: "Congress is composed of successful politicians. To be successful as a politician a man needs many talents. Especially he needs one attribute: the ability to judge men, the ability above all to know whom he can trust. Without that quality, he does not get to Congress."[15]

An interesting theory, but even more interesting is where Bush's conclusion leaves us. He wrote, "How did Congress decide during the war to throw billions into the race for the atomic bomb? Because there were leaders of Congress who had the confidence of their fellows and because those leaders trusted the elder statesman who was then Secretary of War, Henry L. Stimson."[16]

The acknowledgment all but characterizes Congress as a rubber stamp for the administration despite Pry's rejection of that term. If one were to blindly trust public officials, we would want those officials to be the quality of Stimson, Vannevar Bush, George Marshall, James Conant, Leslie Groves, and their colleagues. But members of Congress don't get elected to trust blindly. It's a fair question to ask how "a small-town lawyer" can possibly assess the testimony of an expert in the obscure. But in our system of government, we cannot think that the answer is to let the administration do what they want, literally bankroll their programs without asking a question except, "Are you sure we're giving you enough?"

As it was, Congressman John Taber of New York cornered Groves after one of the tours. Fearing an intrusive question or concern, Groves wrote, "I was utterly astounded when Mr. Taber said, 'There is only one thing that worries me, General. Are you sure that you are spending enough money at Oak Ridge?'"[17]

In addition to ascribing congressional cooperation with the administration to the personal character of Henry Stimson, Bush also indirectly gave a nod to James Madison. He proposed, "It is a sound political system that projects into power primarily men who know men."[18] He added a nod to the political culture in a syntactically challenged sentence: "When they are also men of high patriotism, as most of them inevitably and fortunately are, then, in spite of shenanigans, political maneuverings of questionable nature, occasional blatherskites, and sometimes profound ignorance, they can create and cause to function well all sorts of organizations that can deal effectively with the twisted strands of present-day science, technology, economics and military art, without understanding any one of these in its broad compass and without interfering improperly with the activities of those who do."[19]

He went on to describe such a condition as "democracy at its best."[20] He then acknowledged that the norm was something different: "We do not often see it at its best, we see a muddle, and cross-purposes, and small men on pinnacles, and all the tinsel and ballyhoo of a political merry-go-round. We see the reputations of sincere men smeared, and we believe there are hypocrisy and evil action, nepotism, and enrichment from the public purse that are never uncovered. We hear raucous cries and arguments that make no sense, and witness the hard labor of devoted men disregarded and the false front maintained in power by intrigue. We see a maelstrom in which men struggle and contend by methods of elementary barbarity. We see these things all exaggerated by the more lurid press and columnists, for a fight is news and harmony is not. Yet, if we see only these things, we do not see democracy as it exists."[21]

Bush wrote this evaluation in 1968, a turbulent year in American politics, but the assessment fits a number of periods in our history when hysteria seems to drive public affairs. Bush seemed to appreciate a democracy in which people know their places. He and his colleagues were brilliant men of high character in a traditional sense who dedicated themselves to the improvement of life through their professions in law, science, business, and government. His limiting his subject to "men" reflects the times, and that reflection suggests the subtlety and power of ingrained bias against historically beleaguered groups.

Bush's argument is a call to recognize that an elite lives among us. As he saw it, they are entitled to our deference. As he lost his temper at his first congressional hearing, his remarks may imply that, when men know men, the men in Congress will know that the men in the executive branch should be taken at their word. By 1968 Bush had lived through the McCarthy era. He had seen reputations ruined, as he mentioned; it is very unlikely that he had any use for campus demonstrations or other democratic movements to take power from its traditional sources.

The significance for our purposes is that members of the House and Senate need to explain themselves to the public. Appointed officials in the executive branch often do not, or they do so to follow a president's directive. The contact with the public means that members risk their seats if they project an attitude of noblesse oblige. As we will see, Congress's return to its traditional place in the constitutional system sometimes included vulgarity that disrespects the very people who are supposed to find such coarseness appealing.

When Congress returned to an active role in our government, numerous issues provided opportunities to restore a balance long distorted. Referring to Congress's being freed from the ties of wartime cooperation with the executive, John Gaddis wrote, "For reasons of national security, legislators during the war had allowed the Chief Executive almost a free hand in dealing with other countries."[22] Fine for the emergency, but "the wartime relationship between the White House and Capitol Hill was clearly an abnormal one, which legislators, at least, did not expect to continue after victory."[23] It did not.

The breakdown of the Yalta agreements and the onset of the Cold War meant that the victory in World War II would not mean complete stability and security; rather, a different conflict, a peculiar and frustrating one, replaced the open combat just concluded. The economic impact of returning veterans was another occasion for ideas to collide. Challenges to racial suppression would soon have to be addressed. And the control of atomic weapons was a policy in which members of Congress saw an opening to reassert their traditional authority.

The atomic monopoly became a public issue with many new factions weighing in. How spies penetrated the Manhattan Project concerned people regardless of factional affiliation, as did the matter of whether spies remained among us. The hydrogen bomb remained a secret for a few years, but the awareness, once that recognition developed, increased the tension in an already-difficult international climate.

A Communist revolution in China was successful in 1949, turning a wartime ally against Japan into an enemy perhaps more ferocious than the Soviet Union. The following year, North Korea invaded South Korea, beginning a war that would bring 33,652 American combat deaths. Elsewhere, an airlift was needed to sustain an isolated West Berlin after the Soviets closed roads supplying the city. In the Middle East, the State of Israel was declared in 1948, with war following immediately. Expecting Congress to continue to take its lead from the executive was unrealistic and a bad idea to begin with.

The reaction in the country to these international crises included a strain of vitriol that served no purpose other than releasing frustration. Accusations about motives, reputations smeared, insinuations, rumors, and gossip often drove out thoughtful deliberation. Many individuals and families had serious challenges adjusting to the postwar world, and some public figures traded on that anxiety with wild rhetoric void of substance, the "blatherskites" of Vannevar Bush's description.

These fears were not channeled into productive reform. They tended to concentrate on individuals or factions that were unnerving to other individuals and other factions. Liberals were smeared as pink; anyone leaning further left was accused of Communism. If one had any tangible connection to Communism, as some people did back in the 1930s, they could pay in middle age for what might have been youthful curiosity. They might have known people or attended a meeting, curious to learn what Marxism had to say about the Great Depression or the Spanish Civil War.

In a calmer period, others might be interested in learning more about those experiences, but the postwar era was not calm. Curious, though, that Leslie Groves and Vannevar Bush were among those whose thinking was stimulated by the reality of nuclear weapons, the recent war, and the emerging Cold War. Peter Pry described hearings before the Senate Select Committee on Atomic Energy in 1945 and noted that "General Groves testified that, because of the invention of atomic weapons, 'I think you have got, maybe, to change the world from feeling loyalty to nations.'"[24]

Bush added that "the United Nations Charter represented 'a high point' among the achievements of mankind, and that UN international control and an international inspection regime was the best future for atomic energy."[25] These sentiments could be characterized as favoring One World government, a threat to the sovereignty of the United States. This argument is familiar to us when regional trade agreements are under consideration. Will joining other countries, whose values may differ from ours, compromise American interests? Will jobs be exported? Will environmental standards be weakened?

These are reasonable questions, so we need to see that they are considered seriously and thoughtfully. Congress can be useful in that purpose, but that was difficult in the postwar period. Kept at bay during the war years, left in the dark about decisions on atomic fission, unclear about agreements with the Soviets—Congress was in something of a frenzy when it got back in the game.

The Manhattan Project required secrecy. Discovering the path to atomic fission and then the adjustments needed to make a bomb could not be available to the world when the world was at war. The essential secrecy, however, came at a price. The ultimate secret was enormously complex, but it boiled down to this: due to radical scientific discoveries, weapons of staggering power have been developed, they will soon be in the hands of other countries, so we will never again be as safe as we were before World War II.

That's a lot to digest. Receiving the news in more manageable amounts might have prevented our being overwhelmed and reacting with fear. We might have been able to craft policy without the hysterics that plagued those times. Congress conceivably could have been a place to digest a glut of unsettling information. Removed from the key events, it was as frantic to catch up as anyone; including all members of Congress in the progress of the Manhattan Project would have probably amounted to telling the world about the work. Secrecy was necessary to accomplish the purpose of the endeavor, but secrecy came at a price that was paid after the arrival of peace.

In October of 1945 the administration had a proposal introduced in Congress. An Act for the Development and Control of Atomic Energy would establish an administrative agency, the Atomic Energy Commission (AEC). Its purpose would be to manage the military purposes of atomic research while also promoting a nuclear power industry in the United States.

Congress balked at creating the AEC, fearing that it would be the bureaucratic instrument for giving up the atomic monopoly. While considering the administration's proposal for the agency, the Senate established its own means of keeping up with the rapidly developing science. A Select Committee on Atomic Energy was established, and it began with hearings that gave the members a chance to get up to speed with the latest developments.

In June of 1946 the enabling act for the AEC was finally passed. One significant modification from the original bill, however, changed the Special Committee on Atomic Energy to a Joint Committee on Atomic Energy (JCAE). The adjustment gave the House of Representatives an equal place with the Senate in congressional control of atomic energy.

Peter Pry's report on Congress's role in national security policy claims that "records of congressional hearings before the Joint Committee on Atomic Energy reveal that the JCAE probably saved the H-bomb from being scuttled."[26] In 1950 the committee provided Edward Teller with an opportunity to get the money he sought for additional research on the superbomb. The AEC tilted against development of the weapon, and they gave limited encouragement to Teller.

The specter of the Fuchs case rose. Senator Brien McMahon, chairman of the JCAE, suggested that spies had given the Soviets an advantage in building their recently detonated atomic bomb and that "Soviet spies might give them the lead on the H-bomb."[27] While factions within the administration battled about the new weapon, members of Congress generally took the hard line. It had been the same on the earlier issue of giving up the atomic monopoly, and now Congress tried to press the administration to go ahead with the hydrogen bomb.

Pry claimed that "Senator Millard Tydings spoke for the entire JCAE with the opinion that 'the Soviets will have a gun at our heart if they do it [develop the H-bomb] and we do not.'"[28] The prospect of a Soviet bomb was orders of magnitude more serious than the possibility of a German bomb had been. The latter was always in the imagination, admittedly an ominous place. The Soviets had managed to produce an atomic bomb, and there was no reason to think that the hydrogen bomb was beyond their capacity.

Teller and the JCAE were concerned that, as the Soviets went ahead, the American program would slow. Teller testified that many scientists had left Los Alamos when peace arrived. Some had moral objections to more weapons research, and an inadequate budget would be no inducement to bring some of them back. Congress provided the funds that Teller wanted, and they also leaned on the president to proceed with the program.

We miss a key point when we think of Congress as a bicameral legislature, a single unit of government with two parts. We better understand this branch if we think of the United States as having two autonomous legislatures, neither of which is exactly what the framers had in mind.

The House of Representatives is decidedly the most democratic part of the Madisonian system. Two year terms, the smallest constituencies, direct elections, and a qualifying age of twenty-five should tie the members closer to the voters than any other part of the system. Even then, the relationship between members and the electorate is very different from what was established at the end of the eighteenth century.

The first House of Representatives included fifty-nine members for a population of about 4 million, almost 700,000 of whom were slaves. The House increased with the population until the 1920s when the body was capped at its present 435 members. From 1790 to 1940, the population of the United States grew to roughly 132 million. If the House of Representatives had kept pace with that growth, it would have had 1,947 members to make policy during and after World War II. Improvements in the technology of transportation and communication are important factors in how members keep in touch with their constituents, but the possibility that today's House of Representatives is fundamentally the same as it was when Madison was a member is too remote to take seriously.

The Senate has gone through its own transformation. Article 5 of the Constitution stipulates that "no State, without its Consent, shall be deprived of its equal Suffrage in the Senate"—in other words, the system of awarding two seats to each state regardless of population cannot be altered, even through amendment, without the permission of the smaller state. The Seventeenth Amendment of 1913 is the most obvious change, with the senators now chosen directly by voters rather than through the state legislatures as the framers established. States with the smallest populations have the two senators that the Constitution requires but only one member of the House.

New York City currently has about 8.4 million residents. That number is approximately equal to the populations of the nine least populous states plus the District of Columbia. Those nine states have eighteen senators, giving them far more influence in the Senate than does one city of comparable size. The point is that representation is a complex subject, and this is a complex nation. When factions feel ignored, tensions rise, and they can be frantic and emotional when released. Those factions can be in rural areas troubled by what they see as urban values or in the nation's largest city, which wonders if antelopes in Wyoming have more representation in the U.S. Senate than does the borough of Staten Island, whose human residents number about the same as those in the Cowboy State.

Factions ignored will look for ways to apply pressure. The extensive use of the filibuster may be such an indication. From legislation to the confirmation of judges and other executive appointments, the Senate has become a body that may need a supermajority of sixty to conduct essential business. The filibuster was not a commonly used tool in the 1940s, but the pressures to which Gaddis referred had built to a point that would drive the members to find ways to rein in the executive branch.

Throughout the history of Congress, the dynamic of leadership versus the autonomy of the members has varied. Some speakers of the House have been legendary, while others, almost immediately forgotten. Some committee chairs have run their shops like feudal lords, while others have sought consensus.

As we saw, Congress in the age of Roosevelt could be a remarkably independent collection. In 1927 the Democrats were locked into a minority status that had held almost continuously since the Civil War. In 1937 Democrats had three-fourths majorities in both the House and Senate. The change was driven by the Great Depression, the Republicans' inept reaction to the crisis, and the beguiling charms of Franklin Delano Roosevelt; yet Congress remained an obstreperous lot.

After Roosevelt's reelection in 1936, Congress rejected his plan to create the Executive Office of the President and his court-packing scheme to dominate the Supreme Court. It passed neutrality acts that gave teeth to the country's isolationist spirit. If anything, FDR's successful pursuit of a third term heightened congressional wariness of this most ambitious president.

Article 1, section 9, clause 7, reads, "No Money shall be drawn from the Treasury, but in Consequence of Appropriations made by Law; and a regular Statement and Account of the Receipts and Expenditures of all public Money shall be published from time to time." "Appropriations made by Law" means that Congress has the power of the purse, that the taxpayers' money cannot be spent unless both Houses of Congress have approved a bill with identical language and then presented that bill to the president to be signed into law.

In fact, two laws are normally required. One of them authorizes a policy. In the case of the defense budget, that often means a weapons system. The Armed Services Committees of the House and Senate would hold hearings at which members of the military, civilian consultants, weapons manufacturers, and other interested parties would testify about the characteristics of the anticipated system. A ceiling on spending would then be attached to the bill.

In the normal process, the bill would work its way through the entire House and Senate, emerging from each body with differences that are ironed out in a conference committee comprised of senators and House members. The House and Senate would each vote up or down on the common bill. If passed, it would go to the president for signing into law or veto. If vetoed, back to the House and Senate to see if a two-thirds vote could be mustered to override the president's action.

At a later point, the process repeats for the actual appropriating of money. Congress can decide to spend up to the ceiling set in the authorization. Conditions, called riders, can be attached to the spending, and these riders sometimes collide with the policy standards that were set in the earlier authorizing process.[29]

The Manhattan Project was an extraordinary exception to a serious application of the constitutional standard and legislative practice. In a note from FDR to Vannevar Bush dated December 28, 1942, the president asked, "Please send me a memorandum as to how you think I should approach the Budget in asking for the appropriation."[30]

Bush finally got around to replying on February 2, 1943: "My suggestion is that you direct the Army to include the matter with its other requests for appropriation as a contingent percentage for reserves for one of the larger items. No detailed justification would be submitted, but a general justification could be made confidentially to the Chairman of each Appropriation Committee and to the Director of the Bureau of the Budget."[31]

Normally, a bill becomes a law after public hearings in which the merits of the proposal are debated openly with opportunities for affected parties to comment on the pending legislation. Nothing like that happened with the Manhattan Project. When it was no longer possible to bury the massive spending in a line item in the budget for the Army Corps of Engineers, three members of the Top Policy Group told three members of the House of Representatives and four senators about the atomic bomb. And the Top Policy Group demanded that they tell no one about the program nor ask any questions. Remarkably, the elected representatives of the American people complied.

Other members no doubt had many questions about the spending. Sure, war and all that, but $2.5 *billion*? At some point, the world would know the product of the spending, and what would they think? Most importantly, what will my constituents think? Even if the Army Corps of Engineers comes up with something amazing, what am I left to say? "I went along?"

After the end of the war, patience was over. Trust was frayed. Deference was finished. It was time for Republicans to assert a claim to national leadership. The Democrats were largely supportive of Franklin Roosevelt even when he sought a third and fourth term. Harry Truman? He was one of us in the Senate, and far from the most dazzling member.

The first opportunity for the Republicans to contend for regaining control of Congress was the midterm elections of 1946. The GOP won sweeping victories in both chambers. The Democrats had controlled the House of Representatives with 242 seats compared to 191 for the Republicans. After the 1946 vote, the Republicans had captured the House with 246 seats to 188 for the Democrats.

The Senate had a similar flip. Prior to the midterms, the Democrats had fifty-seven seats plus one Progressive Party ally against thirty-eight for the Republicans. After the election, the Republicans controlled the Senate with fifty-one seats to forty-five for the Democrats. With this popular support, the Republicans ripped into the Truman agenda.

They began by retaliating against a deceased tormentor. The Twenty-Second Amendment was passed, establishing a term limit for the president. The incumbent Harry Truman was exempted from the restriction, but few in either party thought that he could make it past the 1948 campaign.

In 1935, labor unions secured a statutory right to organize under the National Labor Relations Act, crafted by Senator Robert Wagner of New York. A decade later much of the public thought that unions had become too powerful, so the earlier legislation was modified through the Taft-Harley Act, which limited the impact of strikes and allowed states to pass so-called "right to work" laws that would permit nonunion employees to receive benefits won by unions that they would not be required to support. Tax cuts and the end of wartime economic regulations were proposed as additional ways to give the economy a boost.

Prior to the elections, Congress enacted an overhaul of bureaucracy. The Administrative Procedure Act of 1946 brought some order to the operation of the numerous agencies that had been created during the New Deal as well as the war. The clarification was overdue, but no one thought it was accomplished through any interest in making the agencies more powerful.

Truman found congressional support in foreign policy, sometimes more support than he might have wanted. In 1947 the National Security Act was passed. It reorganized the system of national defense and created some new agencies to deal with new threats. The Department of Defense (DOD) replaced the Department of War, one of the original cabinet departments that dated to 1789. More than a marketing update, the DOD also became the home of the Department of the Navy and the Army. The armed services lost some autonomy to civilian control; on the face of it, greater coordination of military force might be possible.

Congress also created the Joint Chiefs of Staff and determined that the body should have a chairman. This move was one of a number that reflected the growing complexity of war and the recognition that readiness included an effective administrative apparatus for national defense.

The National Security Council was set up in the Executive Office of the President to provide more-direct presidential control over this vital area. The position of national security adviser was created to help the president rein in troublesome cabinet secretaries and agencies.

When a review of the nation's readiness before Pearl Harbor revealed vital information that was in our possession but not brought together for comprehensive analysis, the Central Intelligence Agency (CIA) was established to provide the essential coordination.

The Truman Doctrine, a policy related to George Kennan's strategy of "containment," received Republican support when Congress approved aid to Greece and Turkey, who were battling Communist guerilla movements. Kennan's idea was that the Soviet Union would eventually collapse, without our having to go to war, if we held a line and blocked their attempts to expand their influence.

These moves appeared to fashion a stronger administrative system of national security, while it bolstered ideas of free enterprise and lower taxes. They eased concerns about those matters that might have troubled the voters and, in some way, put Harry Truman in a stronger position to seek election to a full term in 1948. The Republicans' greatest gift to him was nominating Thomas Dewey, described by Theodore Roosevelt's daughter Alice as looking like "the little man on the wedding cake." In case an inept opponent was not enough, Truman—overlooking the major, if not always brilliant, accomplishments of the nation's legislature—blistered the "do-nothing Eightieth Congress."

Truman faced an important complication of the most serious split in a major party since Theodore Roosevelt left the Republicans for the Progressives in 1912. In 1948, angered by a civil rights plank in the party platform, Strom Thurmond of South Carolina abandoned the Democrats to run on a Dixiecrat ticket. The move threatened to deprive the Democrats of the Solid South, one of the most reliable parts of the party's winning coalition.

Thurmond did break through, carrying the states of Louisiana, Mississippi, and Alabama, as well as his home state of South Carolina. He also picked up one electoral vote in Tennessee. His total was thirty-nine electoral votes from 2.4 percent of the popular vote.

Truman fell just short of a majority of popular votes with 49.6 percent, but he won a decisive victory in the electoral college with 303 votes to Dewey's 189. His win is often described as a great upset. More likely, it is a great indictment of the methods of prediction in that era.

The voters also responded with a repudiation of the Republicans' brief congressional reign. The Democrats gained seventy-five seats in the House of Representatives to reestablish their majority, and they also took back control of the Senate by adding nine seats to take their majority to fifty-four members.

The partisan swing did not indicate much of a tilt to the left. Henry Wallace, FDR's second vice president, ran for the presidency himself in 1948 and trailed even Strom Thurmond. The mood of the country seemed to be strong on national defense, fiercely anti-Communist, and nervous about the economy. A little incoherence solved a number of complications. We might think of the prevailing attitude as one in which once popular New Deal programs were now decried as creeping socialism, except for the ones that benefited the critic.

In his assessment of the failure of the Germans to produce an atomic bomb, General Groves wrote, "The status of the German effort at the close of the war in Europe was reminiscent of the early phases of our project in the United States, when committees were appointed only to be superseded by other committees. At times it seemed as though more thought had to be devoted to organization than to solving the problems under study."[32] Groves was critical of the bureaucratic battles in both countries, but it is impossible to imagine how such an original and momentous development as the atomic bomb could have failed to generate such conflicts.

The war had provided one point of focus: defeat the Axis. When another thought intruded, it would have been something of a vague aspiration for the future. The surrender of Japan meant that actual decisions had to be made almost immediately. How would we help devastated nations get back on their feet? What would we do with the atomic monopoly? What leverage might we have over the Soviets so that the Yalta accords were realized? Should Edward Teller's idea of a superbomb be pursued? How will the economy avoid a collapse back into the Great Depression?

The lessons of the Great War were not encouraging. Social, labor, and racial violence tore at the country. The economy buckled. Anticipating what America would face midcentury, some radicals had, in fact, set off bombs, and some of the reactions of the Wilson administration were hysterical and contrary to the values that Wilson had insisted we were defending in that conflict. After World War II, could laws be enforced and order secured while respecting the right to dissent?

The complexity of these questions would have overwhelmed any administration. The participation of Congress—welcome or not, wise or not—would mean that the array of interests in America would have a chance to be heard at some point in the process. No doubt that process would be more tumultuous than it had been during the war, because the nature of the new challenges would be an unprecedented test for the eighteenth-century model of government that we had just successfully defended.

The reengagement of Congress as an equal, albeit very different, policy-making body is perhaps the major factor in postwar national security. During World War II, the national legislature was little more than an ATM for the executive branch. The terrible urgency of that conflict explains Congress's acquiescence to presidential policy, but the constitutional structure and over a century and a half of practice guaranteed that, when peace returned, the friction among the branches would as well.

[NINE]

The Transition to Truman

In the summer of 1944 World War II had reached its endgame. Terrible battles remained. The death camps would continue their slaughter. Civilians would die in their homes and schools. In the following spring, children in German army uniforms would be killed in the defense of Berlin. These and other horrors would be suffered across the globe, but the outcome was no longer in doubt. The Allies would demand unconditional surrender and get it. The Axis could offer no terms that the victors would have to accept. The time was apt for the Allies to give consideration to the conditions of surrender as well as to policies that would guide the postwar world. At that critical point, the American commander in chief was a dying man looking at a reelection campaign.

The Democratic Party held its nominating convention in Chicago over June 19–21. Franklin Roosevelt would not attend. He had no significant opposition to his renomination, but if the delegates could have seen him, that might have changed quickly. By heading to Pearl Harbor for talks with Gen. Douglas MacArthur and other military figures, FDR was sending several signals. First, contrary to rumors about his health, he was vigorous enough to travel far from his base in New York and Washington DC. Second, his presence where the American war had begun demonstrated that a place of anguish was now securely in the hands of the United States. Third, in the refrain of the day, there was still a war on. This was not the time to be casting about for new leadership. America would be wise to let their president see things through to the finish.

Politics may have been another factor in the trip. Roosevelt may have been sizing up Douglas MacArthur. The general was a larger-than-life figure—much more flamboyant than Gen. George C. Marshall, Dwight Eisenhower, or any other top military figure, with the possible exception of George Patton. MacArthur had presidential ambitions but not for 1944. As an athlete looks at tape of a potential opponent, FDR may simply have wanted to see how he would do in the company of an up-and-coming contender.

They went together to see servicemen in military hospitals. One of FDR's top aides remembered, "At one of the hospitals, the President did something which affected us all very deeply. He asked a secret service man to wheel him slowly through all the wards that were occupied by veterans who had lost one or more arms and legs. He insisted on going past each individual bed. He wanted to display himself and his useless legs to those boys who would have to face the same bitterness."[1]

Doris Kearns Goodwin elaborated, "Roosevelt generally allowed himself to be seen in public in only two situations—either standing with his braces locked, or seated in an open car. But here, in the presence of so many young amputees, he was willing to reveal his vulnerability, to let them see that he was as crippled as they."[2] The ordeal of his paralysis had changed the upper-class courtesies in which he was raised into a genuine compassion for the cruelty of life that could strike anyone at any time.

The visits to the hospitals were not entirely grim business. The president had invited General MacArthur along; in MacArthur's own account, the president fouled off a pitch about the Republican nominee for president, Thomas Dewey, with an incredible reply that he had been too busy to keep up with politics. With that, MacArthur said, "I threw back my head and laughed. He looked at me and broke into a laugh himself."[3] The Roosevelt charm had again beguiled a prickly, ego-inflated character. Maybe their exchange was somewhere in the president's head when he met Josef Stalin at Yalta.

The return from Hawaii took Roosevelt through the Aleutian Islands, where the president shared a meal with the troops on a gray, dreary day. He cheerfully told them how much he enjoyed their food and their weather. They caught the tongue in cheek and appreciated him for it.

He later had one of those ideas that seem to have come from life at Hyde Park and his interest in engaging nature for some larger purpose. His time in Alaska convinced him that returning veterans, who might be eager for a fresh start, could begin anew in Alaska, taking advantage of the hunting, fishing, and farming.[4] He determined that conditions were not so different from Scandinavia, so the need of the veterans and the resources of the place seemed to be a sensible match.

Leaving the Aleutians set up one of those stories that becomes legendary. Based on who knows what, congressional Republicans decided that, when the president reached Seattle, he realized that his dog Fala had been left behind. At taxpayers' expense and servicemen's peril, the story went, Roosevelt sent some number of navy ships (depending on the telling) to retrieve the scotty. Revenge would be served cold when Roosevelt arrived back at the White House.

Still in the Pacific Northwest, FDR prepared to give a speech at the naval yard at Bremerton, Washington, in Puget Sound. It would be broadcast nationally and a chance perhaps for the country to learn if the rumors about his health had any substance. His speechwriter had flown back to Washington DC. But how many of these had he given, going back to his days as assistant secretary of the navy? The president dictated the speech himself. He then edited it. He then decided he could wing quite a bit of it. It would be like a fireside chat. Except, he was not beside a fire, and the speech was a brutal ordeal rather than a chat.

The first problem was that he stood to give the address. In Frank Friedel's account, "He had not used his braces for a year; they no longer fit well, and cut into his flesh. It was also agonizing for him to put his full weight on his feet. Although his muscles were atrophied, his nerves were sensitive."[5] The stress increased as a wind blew at the pages before him. The audience numbered ten thousand, not counting the millions listening across the land. The roar of the wind drowned out his amplified voice to the live audience, so Roosevelt had no signs of personal engagement to encourage him.

In physical pain, frustrated to be heard, probably anticipating the reaction to a poor performance, the president suddenly faced a far graver personal crisis. As Friedel described it, "During the early part of the speech, as his heart specialist, Dr. Bruenn, revealed years later, Roosevelt began to suffer for the first and only time in his life from an angina attack. An excruciating pain in his chest extended up into both of his shoulders, and only slowly, after fifteen minutes, subsided."[6]

Roosevelt did tell his doctor but insisted he was fine. He was not. In addition to his physical ailments, his emotional state was being taxed. While on the trip west, the president received word that Marguerite LeHand had died suddenly. "Missy" was his personal secretary and one of the people most devoted to him. Harry Hopkins, perhaps FDR's most important aide, was no longer living in the White House. His third wife had accommodated the arrangement as long as she could, but the Hopkins moved to Georgetown about Christmas of 1943. Having Harry living down the hall was an important convenience for the president, so the change was another burden at an especially difficult time.

The campaign in 1944 might have been a simple affair, a referendum on the first three terms. After twelve years in office with access to radio and countless newspapers, what could the electorate possibly need to know about their president? For one thing, a point that the Republicans hammered relentlessly, he was old and possibly no longer up to the job. Rumors abounded, and the mess in Bremerton lent some substance to the stories.

He also looked terrible. Doris Kearns Goodwin wrote, "His loss of weight made him seem much older than his sixty-two years. His color was bad. He had not given a major speech since his appearance at Bremerton, when he had suffered the angina attack in the middle of his delivery."[7] Roosevelt sought to bounce back with a major speech to the Teamsters on September 23. It would mark the start of the fall campaign, and he would have to show that he had a substantial future as well as a past.

Aides recommended that he no longer attempt to walk, since the braces had become as much a hindrance as a support. He continued to try to employ the braces, but in his one concession, he agreed to give the speech while seated. He began by joking about his age and then moved to an attack on the Republicans for trying to escape the shadow of Herbert Hoover. He excoriated the GOP mercilessly; then, having forgotten nothing, he tore into them for their treatment of Fala.

The performance was masterful. He delivered the remarks with a faux seriousness that made the Republicans look ridiculous: "Well, of course, I don't resent attacks, and my family doesn't resent attacks, but Fala does resent them. You know, Fala is Scotch, and being a Scottie, as soon as he learned that the Republican fiction writers in Congress and out had concocted a story that I had left him behind on the Aleutian Islands and had sent a destroyer back to find him—at a cost of two or three, or eight or twenty million dollars—his Scotch soul was furious. He has not been the same dog since. I am accustomed to hearing malicious falsehoods about myself . . . but I think I have a right to resent, to object to libelous statements about my dog."[8] Pandemonium from the Teamsters; roars of laughter; glasses smashed with glee; and more than a few of the truckers with tears in their eyes. The Franklin Roosevelt they saw was entirely ready for the campaign.

The speech was everything it needed to be in substance; in another arena, its delivery would have won an Oscar. But a fair question remains: Was Franklin Delano Roosevelt physically, mentally, and emotionally up to the task of being president of the United States for some or all of a fourth term?

In the British system, to draw the comparison again, the term of office for the prime minister is some part of five years. At that point, an election must be held, but the ruling party can call one at any time during that span. A coalition government can put contending factions together in a kind of unity regime. In America, of course, the Constitution requires our chief executive to be locked into a four-year stretch. Death, resignation, or impeachment and removal are the only escapes. Eight presidents have died in office, four of them assassinated, and Richard Nixon resigned the office. Andrew Johnson and Bill Clinton have been the only ones impeached, and the Senate convicted neither.

The Democratic Party had a decision to make in the summer of 1944, and the American electorate faced a related decision in the fall: stay with FDR or find an alternative. The Democrats ducked the issue at their convention, substituting an alternative that recognized the problem without having to engage it directly.

The party focused its energy on the vice presidency. No serious person could ignore completely the state of the president's health. He himself had talked about resigning once the war was won. In choosing a running mate, the delegates had to go beyond the normal calculations of geography and approving factions to recognize that they were quite likely determining the next president by their choice.

Henry Wallace was the incumbent. He had replaced John Nance Garner for the third term. Wallace was very much a Progressive, and the administration had been drifting to the right during the war. The president was no longer talking as he had in his first inaugural address. He had come to the view that the country and the Allies needed the enormous industrial output of the American economy, and the heads of corporations might need to be coddled a bit to get that level of production.

Wallace had worn on a number of the party elders. Too liberal for the southerners, too intellectual for the city bosses, Wallace was, as David McCullough wrote, "a mystic who spoke Russian and played with a boomerang and reputedly consulted with the spirit of a dead Sioux Indian chief."[9] On the other hand, as McCullough noted, "With the exception of Franklin Roosevelt, he was the most popular Democrat in the country. Those who loved him saw him as one of the rare men of ideas in politics and the prophet of a truly democratic America."[10] Choosing a vice presidential nominee had probably never been so important, and the party was split on the matter.

Alternatives were available. Harry Truman thought Sam Rayburn would be the best choice. A number of insiders thought Truman himself was the right call. FDR had told an aide that Jimmy Byrnes was the man best qualified to take over if necessary. Of course, Roosevelt had also indicated support for Wallace. Alben Barkley was another possibility.

The internal machinations worked their way; on the second ballot, Harry Truman was chosen to be one very short step from the Oval Office. Franklin Roosevelt admitted that he knew very little about Truman. Henry Stimson, the secretary of war, who was widely respected in both parties, had had a fairly serious difference with Truman over the Manhattan Project. Truman was a combat veteran of the Great War, and he was the ninth and last president to be without a college degree. In his defense, he might have pointed out that George Washington and Abraham Lincoln were fellow members on that list.

The Roosevelt-Truman ticket had one overarching challenge. It had to demonstrate that Franklin Roosevelt could carry on. The Republican Party platform offered little of difference except for some hysterical rhetoric: "Four more years of New Deal policy would centralize all power in the President, and would daily subject every act of every citizen to regulation by his henchmen; and this country could remain a Republic only in name. No problem exists which cannot be solved by American methods. We have no need of either the communistic or fascist technique."[11]

That critique was about as serious as the charge that a destroyer ferried the president's dog to Seattle. The Republicans harped on FDR's frailty, but they failed to offer any serious counterpoints of policy. To finally eliminate the concerns about his health, Roosevelt planned a full day in New York City on October 21, a Saturday. A cold rain fell throughout the day. The president required several changes of clothes and dismissals of his doctor's counsel, but he managed to maintain his enthusiasm throughout the day. He made an appearance at Ebbets Field; so if Brooklyn was in doubt, he no doubt secured it with that stop. He also told the crowd that he had rooted for the Dodgers; if so, like his other attachments, it wouldn't necessarily mean that the commitment was exclusive.

The Republicans had no serious argument to get traction with the voters. The electorate had not tired of Franklin Roosevelt, and he gave them reason to ignore their fears about his health. In the election, the Democratic ticket won 432 electoral votes to 99 for the Republicans. Roosevelt carried thirty-six states to Dewey's twelve, and the president—in his fourth time before the voters—won 53.4 percent of the popular vote.

Back in the summer, the Democratic Party leaders decided that, more than anything, they wanted to hold on to the White House. No serious alternative to Franklin Roosevelt was considered for the top of the ticket. Hedging the bet, they did look carefully at the vice presidency, finding Harry Truman to be acceptable to the dominant factions in the party, a boast that no other candidate could make with the same conviction.

The Democratic Party was not going to abandon Franklin Roosevelt in 1944, because he was their best chance to hold the White

House and the congressional majorities. The Republican Party was not going to defeat Franklin Roosevelt in 1944, because they never developed a serious campaign that made an argument about terms for peace, the postwar world, and the economic and social challenges the country would face when the guns fell silent. In 1944, while the Democrats practiced the politics of evasion, the Republicans went with the politics of ineptitude. Neither approach adequately served the republic.

Out of view of the nominating conventions, campaign speeches, and the election itself, the Manhattan Project advanced, tackling and solving the technical obstacles to making an atomic bomb. One can imagine a victorious Thomas Dewey being briefed on the project and declaring that it should come to a stop, but once the administrative and political factors are considered, reality returns. We might think that bureaucratic momentum had carried things too far to reverse, but that concept is an example of bad poetry more than a serious understanding of the forces in play.

The election of 1944 was held on November 7; from that date through January of 1945, decisions were made that kept the production of the atomic bomb on schedule. No single act was decisive, but the cumulative effect of the work at Oak Ridge, Hanford, and Los Alamos determined that a bomb would be built. Whether the weapon would be used or not was a separate decision, but the same forces would still be operating when that calculation was made. Meanwhile, the Manhattan Project had reached its final stage.

A bomb would be built. An airplane would deliver it to its target. A crew would fly that plane and do its very best to escape becoming a casualty of the explosion. Details remained: the physical dimensions of the bomb; the aircraft and its necessary modifications; the crew's need to account for the altitude at which the bomb should detonate for maximum effect, the extent of the blast, the maneuvers necessary to reduce the risk of becoming the ultimate in collateral damage. These details required around-the-clock work, and the specifics would mean life or death for hundreds of thousands of people.

Gen. Leslie Groves of the Army Corps of Engineers needed to extend his authority over the Army Air Corps. He did so by securing the cooperation of Gen. "Hap" Arnold, who was more than eager to help. At one point in their discussions, they realized that the American B-29 might not be able to accommodate the new weapon. Arnold asked Groves what he would do if the B-29 could not deliver the bomb. Groves replied that he would ask the British for the use of a Lancaster, one of their bombers.

Groves recorded Arnold's response: "This brought from him the characteristic reply that I had hoped and expected to hear: that he wanted an American plane to deliver our bomb, and that the Air Force would make every effort to ensure that we had a B-29 capable of doing the job."[12] The commitment was not easy to realize.

The B-29 was the most powerful bomber in the air corps. It was needed for the existing air war against Japan, and many of the planes were mechanically compromised from their extensive use. In further conversations between Groves and Arnold, Arnold asked how many B-29s would be needed. Groves gave the answer: one—the one that would carry the bomb. A few others would be nice to have along to record the effects, but *one* was the answer to the question.

Arnold had a different answer to his own question: "Immediately Arnold said that he would order fourteen new planes for us, and fourteen more to be placed in reserve to meet emergency needs. He repeated that no matter what else might go wrong, no one would ever be able to say that the Air Force did not do its utmost to support the Manhattan Project."[13]

An elite aircrew was then formed, led by Col. Paul W. Tibbets, who was described by Groves as "a superb pilot of heavy planes, with years of military flying experience, and was probably as familiar with the B-29 as anyone in the service."[14] Back in September, when FDR was entertaining the Teamsters, "the 393rd Heavy Bombardment Squadron was detached from the 504th Bombardment Group to form the nucleus of the new unit—the 509th Composite Group."[15]

The squadron was sent to Cuba for training. Bombing strategy had been based on flying within vast formations of aircraft. The mission for which they were training would include a single plane, so navigation and other tasks had to be as close to perfection as possible.

After the time in Cuba, where long flights over water were a constant exercise, the 393rd returned to the United States, where they practiced with dummy bombs that eventually were armed with conventional explosives. On separate tracks, the design of the bombs was nearing conclusion. Of particular interest to the crew, the Ballistics Group of the Los Alamos Ordnance Division focused on "the shock pressure that the B-29 could safely withstand, the flight maneuver that would carry the plane the greatest distance away from the burst in the least time, and the use of special shock-bracing for the crew."[16]

Groves recognized that, in normal circumstances, more tests and refinements would be ordered before a weapon would be used in combat. The circumstances in this case were far from normal. Imperfect bombs would be dropped as long as they could do the job. Groves was not willing to drop a potential dud on Germany, despite FDR's preference, but he would not drag out the war in pursuit of the ideal atomic bomb.

In its final months, the Manhattan Project increased its pace, and it pressed the integration of its various parts. The planes, the crews, and the bombs then had to be transported to the Pacific for preparation for the mission. Everyone involved had to be focused completely on their individual responsibility. And other aspects of the war continued.

At the end of January, days after his fourth inaugural address, Franklin Roosevelt began a journey to the Black Sea to fashion the postwar world. His own doctor had told him that he suffered from hypertension and high blood pressure and that his left ventricular chamber was compromised. When Lord Moran, Churchill's physician, saw the president, he concluded that he was looking at a dying man.

If Roosevelt had been in perfect health, the negotiations would still have been extremely difficult. Stalin had an army in Europe, moving west hard into Germany, and he could keep them there seemingly for as long as he wanted. The president had determined that a race to Berlin was not called for, and he knew that peace would trigger powerful calls to bring the troops home.

The talks were grueling. Years earlier, Roosevelt was a match for anyone in this kind of battling. Von Clausewitz had famously said that war is politics by other means. FDR might have reversed that, seeing politics as an all-consuming activity in which victory is the only purpose. He was not going to win this one.

He returned to the United States with a commitment from Stalin that the Soviets would join the war against Japan sometime after a German surrender. Roosevelt had agreed to $20 billion in German war reparations, with half going to the Soviet Union, but the Americans would largely control that transfer. In the same way, Stalin agreed to free elections in Eastern Europe, but with an army in place he would decide what satisfied that condition. Germany would have zones rather than formal partitions, and France would be part of the occupying force in Germany.

The agreements could be sold as fine under the circumstances. Churchill told his wife that he was "very pleased."[17] The president had a different take. He told an aide, "I didn't say the result was good. I said it was the best I could do."[18]

On March 1, 1945, he gave his last address to Congress, describing the Yalta Conference. More memorable was his calling attention to his leg braces, "ten pounds of steel around on the bottom of my legs."[19] But Frances Perkins, his labor secretary, said, "He did it with such a casual, debonair manner, without self-pity that the episode lost any grim quality and left everybody quite comfortable."[20]

People who knew him well would be shocked if they hadn't seen him in a couple of months. The symptoms could be a distraction from a reality that no one wanted to face: Franklin Delano Roosevelt was dying.

While having his portrait painted at Warm Springs on April 12, in the company of Lucy Mercer, his complicated life ended with a complicated death.

Harry Truman told reporters that he felt as if a bale of hay had fallen on his head. Eleanor Roosevelt learned of the final betrayal with Lucy and then discovered that her daughter had arranged the liaison. Churchill was devastated. Stalin seemed sincerely grieved. Vannevar Bush found his role diminished in the inevitable bureaucratic shuffling that followed the death. Robert Taft, a Republican senator from Ohio and son of a former president, expressed the real cause of

Franklin Roosevelt's passing: "He dies a hero of the war, for he literally worked himself to death in the service of the American people."

Taft's assessment was right on the mark. Roosevelt himself might have decided that a fourth term was too much. He might have worked to elect a Democrat to succeed him and then, if at all possible, focus on recovering his health. He had a great interest in the United Nations as the instrument of resolving disputes before they became causes of war. His regard for the UN revealed him again as a Wilsonian, but a realistic one.

As it was, Roosevelt made a different decision. He was not on a suicide mission. He probably had the denial of death that most humans cultivate. Though he had to know that he was taking an enormous risk with his health, this was a man who had endured paralysis for more than twenty years and who continued to believe that one day he would walk again.

Of all the repercussions, the major one perhaps least affected was the Manhattan Project. Leslie Groves's memoirs fail to address Roosevelt's death. He mentioned FDR and Truman together concerning the use of the atomic bomb, contending that no serious person, certainly neither president, had any expectation other than using the bomb if the war was still on when the weapon was ready.

Richard Rhodes conveyed Robert Oppenheimer's eloquence in addressing people at Los Alamos.[21] No doubt people there had the same reaction that people elsewhere did. Robert Taft was no friend of the president, but he understood the historical significance of the man. People in the Manhattan Project wept over Roosevelt's passing, as so many others did, but they kept at their work.

The puzzle here is the treatment of the new president. Harry Truman, as we have seen, had some vague knowledge about a special weapon. Trying to learn more had earned him a polite rebuff from Henry Stimson. When Truman later persisted, Stimson dealt with him with more clarity than courtesy.

On the terrible night of April 12, Stimson gave the new president the most basic information about the Manhattan Project. Jimmy Byrnes saw Truman the next day and added more information. Not until April 25 did Stimson give Harry Truman a full briefing. Leslie Groves joined Stimson after waiting in an outer office while the secretary and the president covered an array of foreign policy issues. A case of "need to know" being applied to the general.

Essential to our understanding of how experts were controlled in the Manhattan Project is that no one asked Harry Truman for permission to continue the work. Franklin Roosevelt and Harry Truman could have stopped the research and the production of an atomic bomb by a personal command.

Congress could have blocked the project by starving it of the necessary money. Members of the House and Senate might have refused to go along with the instruction to appropriate the money without knowing its purpose. Conceivably, since only a total of seven members of both chambers knew what $2.5 billion was buying, a majority of the uninformed could have said, "If we don't get a full briefing, we won't give you the money." Hard to say how that would have played.

If the briefing were denied or if its contents were unpersuasive, Congress could have shut down the Manhattan Project as a subsequent Congress ended the war in Vietnam, by cutting off the money. This option is another case of something being imaginable but unfeasible. The German bomb had launched the project; when that threat was exposed as unfounded, so much money had been spent that shutting things down would have been impossible to explain.

The long and short of it is that Harry Truman did not have to say *yes* for the atomic bomb to be produced. He would have had to say *no* to stop what was otherwise inevitable. Truman seems never to have thought of himself as an accidental president, a mistake who was in no position to challenge the people who had served Franklin Roosevelt. He put his own stamp on the office fairly quickly, facing monumental issues with apparent confidence. But there is no indication that, when he was in a position to shut down the Manhattan Project, he ever considered doing so.

Having briefed the president, Leslie Groves was ready to get back to work; when he did, he ran smack into the man who started it all. Leo Szilard had some ideas about atomic bombs; thinking about how to get those thoughts to someone who mattered, he again turned to Albert Einstein.

On March 25, 1945, Einstein wrote a letter of introduction on behalf of Szilard to Franklin Roosevelt.[22] The letter acknowledged that he had no specifics about Szilard's message, but he reminded Roosevelt of the earlier letter from 1939 and assured the president, "I have much confidence in his judgment and it was on the basis of his judgment as well as my own that I took the liberty to approach you in connection with this subject."[23]

Although Szilard's work in the Manhattan Project was classified, Einstein concluded, "I understand that he now is greatly concerned about the lack of adequate contact between scientists who are doing this work and those members of your Cabinet who are responsible for formulating policy."[24]

Szilard had less of a problem with Vannevar Bush, James Conant, and Henry Stimson than he might have known, but he had an impossible problem with General Groves. The general mentioned Szilard only twice in his memoirs. One reference described Szilard as one of the "brilliant Hungarian physicists," and the other mention was about a meeting with Szilard about a technical matter related to the atomic pile.[25]

If Groves did not want to discuss Szilard, Jim Baggott's history of the Manhattan Project clarifies the issue: "Groves had taken a dislike to Leo Szilard the very first time they had met in October 1942. Ever since then, Szilard had lodged like an increasingly painful thorn in Groves' backside. Growing ever more annoyed at Szilard's erratic behaviour, his outspoken criticism of the Manhattan Project's administration, unauthorized travels and intransigence over his chain-reaction patent claims, Groves had the FBI put him under close surveillance."[26]

For Leo Szilard, the Hahn-Strassman experiments late in 1938 were an alarm bell. As soon as anyone, Szilard saw the implications for an atomic bomb. Worse, much worse, the atomic bomb could display a swastika in the moment before detonating over London, New York, Moscow, his hometown of Budapest, or any other city of the Reich's determination. More than six years after those experiments, Szilard was disturbed by another prospect: that the United States would develop and use an atomic bomb.

An American bomb was better than a German bomb, but not by much. Szilard was not alone in his concerns. He discussed his fears with a number of his colleagues, "their moral responsibility growing along with their concern for the likely impact of the 'gadget' on future civilization."[27] Speculation about the implications for foreign affairs of nuclear weapons covered a range. Robert Hutchins at the University of Chicago had welcomed the development, because the horror and catastrophic effects might sober nations into rejecting war and resolving disputes through diplomacy.

Szilard, Niels Bohr, and others feared an arms race after a first use, as countries would realize their vulnerability. J. Robert Oppenheimer, tilting perhaps wistfully in Hutchins's direction, advised the dissenting scientists that an initial use would establish the devastation and reinforce the argument to find an alternative to war.

The issue was one we've seen before: What should the United States do with its monopoly over the new weapon? In the aftermath of the war, the administration had advocates for turning the bombs over to international control if other nations did the same. We saw that position resisted by others within the administration and certainly within Congress. Leo Szilard was looking to establish that policy prior to the first test in New Mexico and any subsequent use against Japan, and he hoped to persuade Franklin Roosevelt to stop the train that Szilard himself had put in motion in 1939.

Before hearing from the president, Szilard received a reply to another overture. He was to meet with Eleanor Roosevelt on May 8. Roosevelt's death on April 12 meant that Szilard had a different president to sway. Working a different contact, Szilard secured an appointment with Harry Truman on May 25.

When Szilard got to Washington DC, he found the president unavailable, but Jimmy Byrnes could see him . . . in Spartanburg, South Carolina. Byrnes's status at that point seemed to be that of a party elder, but he was on the verge of being appointed secretary of state.

The meeting was awful. The more Szilard talked about the effects of an atomic bomb, the more Byrnes thought it was a solid idea. Something like this: "That'll show the Soviets we mean business." "No, no, no—they'll think they have to get their own nukes." "No—they'll realize it's futile to try to keep up with us."

If Szilard had been aware of a memo that Byrnes had sent to FDR early in March, he might not have bothered with the meeting. Byrnes wrote the president when he learned of the price tag for the Manhattan Project. Looking at factors that might not have occurred to Szilard or been appreciated by him, Byrnes wrote, "I understand that the expenditures for the Manhattan Project are approaching 2 billion dollars with no definite assurance yet of production."[28]

The production, in fact, was all but assured, but a political factor was in play. Byrnes continued, "We have succeeded to date in obtaining the cooperation of Congressional Committees in secret hearings. Perhaps we can continue to do so while the war lasts. However, if the project proves a failure, it will then be subjected to relentless investigation and criticism."[29]

Szilard would then read about Byrnes's regard for his profession: "I know little of the project except that it is supported by eminent scientists. Even eminent scientists may continue a project rather than concede its failure."[30] He called for a review "by a small group of scientists not already identified with the project."[31] Showing his own blind spot, Byrnes seemed not to appreciate how bringing in the outsiders might compromise security. We could also ask who these reviewers might be. How many physicists would be able to understand the science of atomic fission?

If Szilard had any more doubts, Byrnes's memo would have cleared them up: "Such a review might hurt the feelings of those now engaged in the project. Still 2 billion dollars is enough money to risk such hurt."[32] If it's working, fine. We can continue. If not, it "would indicate the need for further justification by those who are responsible for the Project."[33]

He concluded, "In any event, it would be clear that we were mindful of the tremendous expenditure of men and materials."[34] In short, we're way out on a limb, and we better have a story in case the bomb doesn't work. These experts will keep their science project going indefinitely, but they won't be the ones who have to explain themselves to congressional committees or the American electorate.

Byrnes might still have been unsure if the bomb would be ready to use against Japan, but Szilard was raising an intriguing alternate justification. If the $2 billion had been spent before a bomb could be used in combat, maybe it could be used to intimidate the Soviets. We were probably going to be having problems with our ally once the war ended, so having an atomic bomb in our arsenal might be useful once the bargaining began.

Szilard was getting nowhere. Richard Rhodes identifies the problem between Szilard and Groves as "compartmentalization."[35] The general wanted people working on and thinking about only the part of the Manhattan Project that concerned them. "Need to know" meant that one needn't form an opinion about somebody else's work. Szilard, on the other hand, preferred an open exchange of ideas. The key insight might come from someone who is looking at an old puzzle with fresh eyes. These two perspectives are hard to reconcile, and when the advocates are driven by strong personalities, the reconciliation is extremely difficult.

Szilard, Bohr, and other scientists were starting to press considerations that had nothing to do with energy and mass. They were engaging foreign policy by advocating that the Soviets should be informed about the atomic bomb. In Szilard's case, he seemed ready to shut the project down. Cancel the test in New Mexico. Pursue the Japanese surrender through other means. Leave the atomic bomb as a horrifying idea, too terrible for any nation to pursue. The United States should set the example by refraining from taking the final steps to the new weapon.

The dissenting scientists were in a difficult position, because the Manhattan Project had moved past them. A few years earlier, their imaginations and conceptual skills were essential in figuring out if and how a bomb might be made. With every day after Leslie Groves's appointment in September of 1942, the project became more of a manufacturing challenge than a theoretical one. By the summer of 1945, physicists were still needed, but maybe carpenters and electricians were needed just as much. The daily grind of making the bomb was the principal task of Leslie Groves. The intrusions of Leo Szilard amounted to unpleasant noise, but Groves kept his focus.

The key figures in the Roosevelt-Truman administration had a different focus. They were considering conditions of surrender and the postwar world. Another Big Three conference was planned for Potsdam, Germany, from July 17 to August 2. At the outset, Stalin and Churchill needed to get a sense of the new president. If he seemed especially assured, it might have been because he learned the day before the opening of the conference that a plutonium implosion explosive had been successfully detonated at Alamogordo, New Mexico. Not exactly a bomb, but one step removed.

Enrico Fermi was curious, of course, about the strength of the upcoming blast, and he had a unique way to measure it. Nothing to do with spectrographs, computers, seismometers, or other tools of the trade. The "Italian Navigator," Fermi's identity after the squash court, dropped pieces of paper from his pocket just before the explosion. There was no wind at ground level, and he knew the distance from his hand to the ground. So their movement after the blast would tell him how powerful the device had been. Leslie Groves wrote that, after the test, Fermi "promptly announced the strength of the explosion. He was remarkably close to the calculations that were made later from the data accumulated by our complicated instruments."[36]

Truman was then the one person who could legitimately determine whether or not he should tell Stalin. On July 24 he informed the Soviet leader that the United States had tested a powerful new weapon. Stalin seemed not to be intimidated, curious, or shocked. While physicists, military brass, and administration officials had been exchanging their views on bringing the Soviets into the loop of the Manhattan Project, Klaus Fuchs and Theodore Hall were keeping Moscow informed. Stalin may have been placid about the news because it wasn't news to him.

The shock at Potsdam was not so much the test at Alamogordo as the election in Great Britain. Winston Churchill was out. Unlike incoming American presidents, who wait nearly three months between election and inauguration, Clement Atlee replaced Churchill the next day. We can imagine Stalin's thoughts about the changes since Yalta. The West would be pressing for democracy in countries liberated from the Nazis, but what would Stalin have thought about democracy, watching two strangers appear at the culmination of the Great Patriotic War?

Atlee arrived in time to join his counterparts in demanding that Japan surrender unconditionally. By this time, Henry Stimson was developing some doubts about following through with the bomb. Even more than Harry Truman, Stimson might have had the personal authority to break down the administrative barriers that kept the military, the politicians, the physicists, and the engineers in separate compartments. The moral argument was not a preposterous aside to him. He was troubled by the targeting of civilians, especially in the air war. He was ready to start asking questions himself before the United States changed the dimensions of warfare.

TEN

Hiroshima

Hiroshima has become a Rorschach test. Do you see a brutal, utilitarian calculation that saved more lives than it cost? Do you see an indulgence of revenge with a racist element as well? Were we trying to intimidate the Soviets? By having an actual example of the horror, were we showing the world that war was now obsolete? Was it simply an inevitable outcome of bureaucratic forces programmed for victory with no one able to arrest or divert the momentum? The scope of death and destruction from nuclear weapons is unprecedented in warfare, but is the individual suffering worse than the grisly accounts of combat from Homer and Virgil?

We can think of Hiroshima as war compressed to an instant. The casualties were similar to some conventional bombing raids. The destruction of property was less than some of the attacks on Tokyo. The injuries, especially the burns, were horrifying but not unique. Radiation sickness and death was unprecedented, but disease associated with combat is mentioned in the opening lines of the Iliad. As Vannevar Bush suggested, the fear associated with atomic bombs was that they were the beginning of the nuclear age.[1] Before Little Boy and Fat Man were dropped, Edward Teller and others were thinking about a hydrogen bomb that would use a small atomic explosion as only a fuse.

One more question persists: Was the bombing of Hiroshima justified? And there's a related question that pertains to Nagasaki: Wasn't one enough?

The moral questions are often considered in seminar rooms, pulpits, and television studios—places where sometimes opinion flows too easily. For our purposes, the more useful questions are: What did the decision to drop the bomb look like through the eyes of the key actors? Did their perspectives incorporate the information, values, and judgment that so momentous a decision warranted?

Jim Baggott provides the essential information: "The *Enola Gay* dropped the Little Boy U-235 bomb on Hiroshima at 9:15am (8:15am local time) on 6 August 1945. It exploded 43 seconds later, 1,900 feet above the city, with a yield of 12,500 tons of TNT equivalent. Ferebee [the bombardier] missed his aiming point by 550 feet. The temperature at the burst point reached 60 million degrees, about four times the temperature at the sun's core."[2]

Approximately seventy-five thousand people were killed instantly, and another sixty thousand died by the end of the year from injuries or radiation-related illness. The devastation was so complete that it was difficult for the rest of Japan to get a clear understanding of what had happened to Hiroshima, a city that seemed to have vanished.

Three days later, on August 9, "the Fat Man bomb was dropped on Nagasaki at 12:02pm, 11:02am local time. It exploded 1,650 feet above the city with a yield of about 22,000 tons of TNT equivalent. The steep hills surrounding the city helped to confine the explosion and reduce its impact, but 70,000 died in the blast."[3]

How did the people most responsible for the bombings see the essential questions before and after the bombs were dropped?

If Vannevar Bush had not shown up midsummer of 1940, the development and use of nuclear weapons might have occurred at a different time in some other country. Remember that he began from a place of skepticism about "the uranium headache" as well as concern that a pursuit of the bomb would divert necessary resources from more promising scientific contributions to the defeat of the Axis. Not until a year had passed and the MAUD reports arrived in the summer of 1941 did Bush think that an atomic bomb might be feasible.

He turned the original Advisory Committee on Uranium into a component of the National Defense Research Committee, which in turn became the Office of Scientific Research and Development. More than title changes, Bush guided the development of the administrative structure that would work out the theory of an atomic bomb. Having inherited a fairly unfocused operation, he organized scientists for coherent research.

By the fall of 1942, work had progressed to a point that production could begin under the direction of Gen. Leslie Groves. Bush concentrated on his original purpose, that of directing science for national defense. He retained an important position in the Manhattan Project, but rather than working toward the production of a bomb, he had an essential role in resolving differences with the British and keeping Franklin Roosevelt connected with the developments in the Manhattan Project.

The bombs were dropped on Hiroshima and Nagasaki three months before an invasion would have been launched and three months after Germany surrendered. If Bush had not shaped up the American effort, the atomic option might not have been available.

Since it was available, should it have been used?

In reflections after the war, Bush assessed the impact of the bombings. He showed no regret about using the bombs, but his reasoning was rather complex. It starts with a simple, declarative sentence: "The use of the atomic bomb ended the war."[4] The very next sentence heads in a different direction: "Without doubt, the war would have ended before long in any case, for Japan had been brought nearly to her knees."[5]

Bush explained that the Japanese fleet had been destroyed. Few functioning planes were left, and the nation's economy was no longer functioning. "In these circumstances, we needed merely to keep the pressure on, at minimum cost in casualties, and she would most certainly have collapsed into utter impotence, whether she formally surrendered or not, and she could then have been contained by our Navy without risk until she did yield."[6] So, why not go that route?

Bush explained that an invasion of the home islands was planned and scheduled, and the martial code of the Japanese had a major impact on the Americans' thinking. The refusal of Japanese troops to surrender and the brutal treatment of Allied troops who did surrender convinced Bush, other officials, and especially the military command that an invasion of Japan itself would likely be an extremely difficult venture.

This concern was tinged with a view of the Japanese that, if not racist, certainly saw the culture of that country as precluding negotiations: "With the experience of Okinawa, with the demonstrated fanaticism of the Japanese and the proved ability and intent of their masters to whip them into a frenzy, it was clear that such a campaign might have cost hundreds of thousands casualties among our troops."[7]

At the end of the war, the Japanese government was a fractured mess. Factions ranged from those who were willing to accept peace if only the status of the emperor remained to those who thought Japan should exercise a Masada option in which every person died, leaving Japan with its honor intact. Numerous groups held other views, but none could deliver the nation. Looking at an enemy that could neither accept nor reject the demand for unconditional surrender, the Allied military properly prepared for the worst. The invasion would have proceeded if the bombs had not been ready.

Bush not only anticipated a frantic defense by a militarized populace; he also put the atomic bombs into some perspective. Acknowledging that the bomb "was indeed a terrible weapon," he argued that "the fire raids upon Japan were much more terrible, they reduced a far-greater area of the frail Japanese cities to ashes, they caused far-greater casualties among civilians—panic, the crush of mobs, and horrible death; yet they occurred almost unnoticed and created few later arguments."[8] He concluded, "It was fear of the future that concentrated attention on the atomic bomb."[9]

One alternative to atomic bombs or an invasion would have been to blockade Japan until it surrendered. No ship and no plane in or out until the nation gave up. Japan would have been completely isolated; on the face of it, lives might have been spared. The problem with this approach is that we have no idea how long the siege would have taken. The war needed to come to an end, and the terms that had been demanded repeatedly by the Allies were unconditional surrender.

A besieged Japan would likely have sought some kind of negotiations. Keeping the American military disciplined and ready without actual combat would have been a task with a short shelf life. Some of the veterans had been in uniform for three or four years, serving for the duration of the conflict. A siege would have meant sitting idle thousands of miles from home, being stuck on a military base or battleship with no fight looming, dealing with frantic calls from families to public officials to bring things to an end—all of that would have become irresistible. Vannevar Bush also thought, somewhat along the lines of Robert Hutchins, that atomic bombs would awaken the world to the dangers of any future war.

Pascal Zachary made an insightful observation that Bush was one of a very small group who had both helped to produce the bomb and then, separately, decided to use it. Among the implications that Zachary noted, "No legislative body in the U.S. debated these momentous decisions. The public's participation was neither invited nor received. However compelling the case for secrecy, Bush's role in the atomic age invited a backlash from those who abhorred the effects of the bomb or believed that its existence mocked American democracy, perhaps even crippled it."[10]

The decisions about the Manhattan Project and the bombs dropped on Hiroshima and Nagasaki can be considered on their own. The process by which those decisions were made is another matter and one with enormous significance itself. While only a very small number of people had the talents and opportunity to participate in the highest administrative levels of the Manhattan Project, every person on earth was affected by their decisions. Is there any serious way that people so motivated can express their views on questions of this kind, and can those judgments merit sober consideration if the affected parties have not acquired an elementary understanding of the issues involved?

James Conant, Bush's top assistant, was a principal liaison among the various groups in the Manhattan Project. He wrote his memoirs in 1969, and he focused on the timing of the bomb's production. After reviewing some of the arguments against the bomb's use, Conant wrote, "My own misgivings have never been about the use of the bomb. I think the decision was correct. What has often worried me is the thought that if only this or that had been different, the first bomb might have been dropped in May."[11] He then discussed the overly optimistic early estimates that the bomb would be ready in the summer of 1944.

Looking back, Conant admitted, "The optimistic forecast was of short duration. I still recall my disappointment and frustration when I became convinced by Groves' figures that the summer of 1945 was the earliest possible date. I felt the difference between May

1945 and August 1945 was very large in terms of American casualties. And history proved that I was right."[12] He added that an earlier bomb would have ended the war with the United States in a better position to deal with the Soviet Union.

In something of a split with Vannevar Bush, Conant downplayed the potential peaceful benefits of nuclear power: "To my mind, the potentialities for destruction are so awesome as to outweigh by far all the imaginable gains that may accrue in the distant future when atomic power plants may exist all over the world."[13] He ended his reflections with the observation that "the verdict of history has not yet been given."[14]

Conant's point is both salient and sobering. The Cold War ended without the use of nuclear weapons. An almost fifty-year conflict of deep ideological and cultural differences, with colliding interests in developing nations; military face-offs on land and sea, under the sea, in the air, and in space—every place that humans have gone; savage proxy wars in Korea and Vietnam; crushing fiscal burdens; and occasional accidental provocations. And the resolution was remarkably peaceful.

Gen. Leslie Groves assumed control of the Manhattan Project in September of 1942. Theoretical work remained, but those determinations would be made in the context of producing an atomic bomb. Groves did not come out of the academic world or a science lab or a career in government and foreign policy. A warrior and an engineer, he was prepared to do two things: fight and build.

He is often characterized as hard-driving and even difficult, but he would have understood James Conant's concern that any delay in getting the weapon meant losing lives. Under that kind of pressure, Groves had to manage scientists from a range of fields other than physics, elected officials, other military officers, contractors for everything from construction to food, and suppliers of everything from U-235 to shoes. Has anyone ever faced such an array of responsibilities with stakes so high and a timetable written in blood?

In July of 1944 a strategy was developed to bring the Pacific war to a conclusion. Not knowing whether an atomic bomb would be part of the American arsenal, the plan was an invasion of the home islands beginning with Kyushu, the southernmost of the four main islands of Japan, on October 1, 1945, with the hope of reaching Tokyo by the end of that year.

Groves wrote that the invasion did not assume that the Soviets would be at war with Japan in the fall of 1945, but Franklin Roosevelt did secure that commitment from Stalin at the Yalta Conference in February of 1945. In that light, "after the Yalta Conference, however, a debate sprang up over whether it would not be better to encircle Japan and defeat her by attrition than to defeat her by direct attack."[15] It is not made clear who argued what, except that Gen. Douglas MacArthur and Adm. Chester Nimitz both urged the invasion.

The Joint Chiefs, in April of 1945, adopted a comprehensive strategy that included continued strategic bombing, a blockade, an invasion at the earliest, and an occupation "of such areas in the industrial complex of Japan as are necessary to bring about unconditional surrender and to establish absolute military control."[16] The force needed for the invasion was estimated to be more than 1.5 million, and casualties were expected to be heavy. The invasion would have been the means of bringing Japan to its knees.

In the middle of June, on the eve of the Potsdam Conference, President Truman signed off on the invasion. Groves reflected, "In such a climate, no one who held a position of responsibility in the Manhattan Project could doubt that we were trying to perfect a weapon that, however repugnant it might be to us as human beings, could nonetheless save untold numbers of American lives."[17]

Groves mentioned that some consideration was given to suspending plans for an invasion while waiting to see if atomic bombs would be ready. He was emphatic that "to any experienced soldier it was obvious that, once an advantage had been gained over an agency as dangerous as Japan, no respite should be given."[18] Proceeding with the preparations for invading Japan was prudent, but it also meant that the alternative to using atomic bombs was the enormously costly invasion in which very high casualties had been predicted.

Groves then turned to the decision to drop one or more bombs on targets within Japan. He acknowledged that, at the beginning of the Manhattan Project, the use of any atomic bomb was an open question. He referred to "the activation of the Manhattan Project," a phrase that equated to his being placed in charge of developing the bomb.[19] Once he had the reins in his hands, "the situation began to change."[20] He explained, "As time went on, and as we poured more and more money and effort into the project, the government became increasingly committed to the ultimate use of the bomb, and while it has often been said that we undertook development of this terrible weapon so that Hitler would not get it first, the fact remains that the original decision to make the project an all-out effort was based upon using it to end the war."[21]

The war was ending, but the specifics were not entirely determined. A blockade had some advocates but none with sufficient influence for that option to be seriously considered. An invasion was going to be the means of a final victory over Japan unless atomic bombs could preclude that course or unless the ruling authority in Japan realized the futility of continuing the war. Did Japan even have such an authority at that point?

Groves then recognized that using atomic bombs did not necessarily mean dropping them on cities. As Groves put it, "Should we conduct a demonstration of its power for all the world to see, and then deliver an ultimatum to Japan, or should we use it without warning."[22] It was not a difficult decision for Groves: "It was always difficult for me to understand how anyone could ignore the importance of the effect on the Japanese people and their government of the overwhelming surprise of the bomb. To achieve surprise was one of the reasons we had tried so hard to maintain our security."[23]

The impact of surprise, a vital consideration for General Groves, anticipated the "shock and awe" that was expected to be a major factor in our war against the regime of Saddam Hussein in Iraq. A variation was included in the April 1945 policy of the Joint Chiefs. Their reference to the need for continuing strategic bombing of Japan was, "to demoralize the country."[24] Put it another way, the policy amounted to killing civilians by the thousands.

Strategic bombing had been employed in Europe with brutal results. Vannevar Bush had proposed that the conventional bombing of Tokyo and other cities was more lethal than the ruin visited on Hiroshima and Nagasaki. No credible call for peace came from a population shattered by the conventional bombing. Would the impact of atomic weapons have an effect that conventional explosives had not?

The Truman administration was not completely united on the matter of using the atomic bombs. Secretary of War Henry Stimson was one of the most distinguished public officials in America. In 1945 he was seventy-seven years old, at the end of a long career serving his country. Stimson had the elite pedigree of Phillips Andover, then Yale, and then Harvard Law; in any blue blood competition, he could play the great-grandmother card since he could remember her stories of chatting with George Washington when she was a girl.[25]

Stimson had been the secretary of war for William Howard Taft and secretary of state under Herbert Hoover. In Hoover's administration, he shut down the cryptology office of the State Department with the naive but charming, "Gentlemen don't read each other's mail."

During the 1932 campaign, Hoover asked him to attack Franklin Roosevelt, and Stimson declined. He thought it beneath him personally and not a proper function for the nation's top diplomat.

As Jean Smith noted, "Hoover never forgave Stimson for not participating in the campaign. Roosevelt never forgot. When war clouds gathered in 1940 and bipartisanship became essential, FDR reached out to Stimson and asked him to become secretary of war for a second time."[26] The appointment was shrewd for lending weight to Roosevelt's attempts to lead the country in facing the challenge before it.

As Jim Baggott describes the secretary, "He possessed a strong sense of morality, of faith in humanity and international law. He was horrified by the way that war on such unprecedented scale had blunted this sense of morality among the Western democracies. The firebombings of Dresden, Hamburg, and then of selected Japanese cities, represented a kind of total war that he disliked intensely."[27]

Stimson may have comforted himself by relying on reports of precision bombing in Europe (i.e., hitting military targets and sparing civilians). Nothing that clear-cut describes the air war against Germany or theirs against Britain; making matters much worse, Japan generally lacked industrial areas. Much of their economy depended on families working in their homes. Destroying the Japanese economy meant killing tens of thousands of their citizens.

Stimson's reputation has grown as a man burdened with the implications of total war and the accompanying demand for unconditional surrender yet who tried to find a way to honor the best of America's traditions. Complications abounded in the effort. Groves related the story of a conversation he had with Stimson on the matter of the Japanese cities that were being targeted for an atomic attack.

Groves was seeing Stimson on a different issue, but Stimson brought up the question of the target. The general replied that targets were an aspect of military operations, that he should only discuss them with General Marshall. Not good enough for Stimson, their civilian boss. Groves relented and had the list brought to Stimson.

Four cities were on it: Kokura, whose arsenal was a sizeable munitions plant; Hiroshima, where troops left Japan for combat areas; Niigata, a port city with an ironworks and an oil refinery; and Kyoto, "an urban industrial area with a population of about one million inhabitants."[28] Stimson said "no." He argued that Kyoto was the ancient capital of the nation and an important city for both religious and cultural reasons. Stimson had once been the governor-general of the Philippines, and he had visited Kyoto in that capacity. Perhaps that gave him a personal connection that he may not have had with other targeted cities.

Stimson was also one of those who favored a demonstration of the bomb as a show of force to the Japanese that might bring them to surrender. Before the Potsdam Conference, where the Allies formalized the demand for unconditional surrender, Stimson sent Truman an assessment of Japan's impossible condition. He pointed out that Japan was all but helpless and the United States had an overwhelming material advantage as well as a much stronger moral position as the victim of the sneak attack at Pearl Harbor.

Richard Rhodes quotes Stimson insisting that the Japanese are not the fanatical robots sometimes depicted: "Japan is not a nation composed wholly of mad fanatics of an entirely different mentality from ours."[29] He argued that they had made a remarkable embrace of Western values over the previous hundred years. He added that it would be a good idea to indicate that we would let them keep the emperor.

Truman was not persuaded. Relying on Jimmy Byrnes, who, as the incoming secretary of state, was being counseled by Cordell Hull, FDR's appointment to that post, the president feared that the Japanese military would smell weakness. The Japanese assumption before Pearl Harbor was that the Americans would not pay the price of island hopping in the Pacific and would accept a negotiated peace that left Japan in a dominant position in Asia. Having dispatched that error of judgment, administration officials were generally unwilling to make any accommodation that might revive the notion in Japan.

Henry Stimson was not the only significant figure who was deeply troubled by the fate that awaited Japan. The Alamogordo test was conducted during the Potsdam Conference, and Stimson had dinner one evening with Dwight Eisenhower fresh from the Allied conquest of Nazi Germany.

All was well until Stimson received a cable about the successful result. It read, "Doctor has just returned most enthusiastic and confident that the little boy is as husky as his big brother. The light in his eyes discernible from here to Highhold [Stimson's home on Long Island] and I could have heard his screams from here to my farm."[30]

Years later, Eisenhower remembered the note with disdain: "The cable was in code, you know the way they do it. 'The lamb is born' or some damn thing like that."[31] Having been told by Stimson that the weapon would be dropped on Japan, Eisenhower kept his own counsel because, "after all, my war was over in Europe and it wasn't up to me. But I was getting more and more depressed just thinking about it."[32]

Stimson may have sensed the general's distress. He asked Ike for his views, and Eisenhower replied that he opposed the use on two counts. For one, Japan was effectively defeated. The bomb was not necessary for victory. The second point was that Eisenhower did not want the United States to be the first nation to use the weapon. For his trouble, Eisenhower got an interesting reaction: "Well . . . the old gentleman was furious. And I can see how he would. After all, it had been his responsibility to push for all the huge expenditure to develop the bomb, which of course he had a right to do, and *was* right to do. Still, it was an awful problem."[33]

Would Eisenhower have preferred an invasion? A blockade? As he suggested, it wasn't his piece of the war. We should also remember that in 1945 people like Eisenhower and MacArthur were first learning about a project that had been underway for years. Ike's reaction of revulsion is instructive. He had just finished his own experience of leading the Allies on the Western front. For over a year, he had battled the Germans on European soil; in addition to the inevitable horrors of war, he saw the concentration camps with the tortured survivors. Hiroshima promised all of that death and destruction in one place and one moment.

Some of these differences of opinion, even furious arguments, reflect people who were at different points of the same line of thinking. One reason why Stimson might have been angered by Eisenhower's confident rejection of the bombing was that Stimson had been urging that very position on President Truman, urging with no indication of success. Ike might have been reminding Stimson that the secretary was right, but what more could Stimson do?

At the same time, Groves wasn't hesitating to hector Stimson about Kyoto. Even while at Potsdam, the secretary heard from the general. Stimson replied that he was not convinced and that he had brought the question to Truman, who agreed with the secretary. Groves wrote, "There was no further talk about Kyoto after that."[34]

Groves continued, "Nothing is more illustrative of the relationship between Secretary Stimson and me than this episode. Never once did he express the slightest displeasure or annoyance over my repeated recommendations that Kyoto be returned to the list of targets. Nor did I ever feel that he wanted me to remain silent, once I had learned his views, on a matter of such great importance. I believe the affair was also typical of his attitude toward other senior officers."[35]

As much as any of the American officials, Stimson looked at the end of the war in terms of the postwar world. What would be our relationship with the Soviets? How would the rest of the world look at us? Our actions in the final months might well answer those questions.

Years after the war ended, Groves reflected, "Events have certainly borne out the wisdom of Mr. Stimson's decision. I think, however, he did not foresee that much of the criticism he so scrupulously sought to avoid would come from American citizens; certainly he never mentioned this possibility to me. After the sudden ending of the war I was very glad that I had been overruled and that, through Mr. Stimson's wisdom, the number of Japanese casualties had been greatly reduced."[36] That had not always been the general's view.

After Hiroshima, "General Marshall expressed his feeling that we should guard against too much gratification over our success, because it undoubtedly involved a large number of Japanese casualties. I replied that I was not thinking so much about those casualties as I was about the men who had made the Bataan death march."[37]

On August 9 a second atomic bomb was dropped on Japan. Leslie Groves later remembered conversations with Adm. William Purnell about an atomic strategy, "Admiral Purnell and I had often discussed the importance of having the second blow follow the first one quickly, so that the Japanese would not have time to recover their balance."[38]

The mission was different in several respects from the one that destroyed Hiroshima. For one thing, the bomb was different. The Hiroshima bomb used uranium for fuel and a gun device for the triggering mechanism. The second mission was carrying a plutonium bomb with an implosion device for detonation. A more critical difference in the two raids was that the one on Hiroshima was textbook and the second encountered serious problems.

A reserve fuel tank contained eight hundred gallons to make sure that the *Bock's Car* would be able to return to Tinian. A mechanical problem prevented access to that fuel, so an efficient flight was critical. Carrying eight hundred gallons of dead weight did not do much for efficiency.

Circling over a point for a rendezvous that never occurred burned more fuel, and then the *Bock's Car* headed for Kokura, the primary target. Promised clear skies, the crew encountered a cloud cover over the target. Their orders were to drop the bomb when the target was visible, but three passes did nothing but burn more fuel.

The crew then headed for Nagasaki, the secondary target. More clouds there, but the pilot and bombardier decided to drop the bomb by radar, if necessary, on the one and only run that their fuel would allow. A break in the clouds gave them a sight of the target, and they delivered Fat Man, the plutonium bomb, on the city.

The return was perilous. The crew landed on fumes at Okinawa with insufficient fuel to taxi to the end of the runway.

The next drop on Japan was scheduled to be pamphlets informing the populace of the new weapon, its destructive power, and the willingness of the United States to use it. Those missions were cancelled when the emperor broke a stalemate in his government to side with the peace faction.

In the narrowest sense, the Manhattan Project culminated on August 6 and 9 of 1945. As argued here, Hiroshima and Nagasaki can be considered as war encapsulated. The killing and torturous injuries of innocents have been a part of every war. The extent of the devastation was less than that of some conventional air raids. The appalling suffering described by John Hersey and others is similar to the poems of Siegfried Sassoon and Wilfred Owen in the Great War and those of Walt Whitman from the Civil War.

The one horror that was introduced at Hiroshima was radiation sickness, a fatal condition that the Manhattan Engineering District's official report failed to recognize nearly a year after the bombing.[39] Comparing Hiroshima and Nagasaki to the tragedies of other wars is not meant to minimize the torment of anyone; rather, it does suggest that the bombing of those cities should lead us to face the pain that humans have inflicted on one another down to the present day. Did any aspect of the decision to bomb Hiroshima and Nagasaki indicate that problems existed in the process that led to the missions of the *Enola Gay* and the *Bock's Car*?

Before the bombings, Niels Bohr, Leo Szilard, and other scientists with a thorough understanding of question advised against the use of the weapon. Dwight Eisenhower proposed to Henry Stimson a month before the raids that they were unnecessary. In his memoirs, published in 1963, Eisenhower persisted against "the use of a weapon whose employment was, I thought, no longer mandatory as a measure to save American lives."[40]

The objections were made in a timely manner by serious people and directed to other serious people with the authority to prevent the missions. What remains troubling is that all those serious people were never in the same room at the same time arguing to President Truman. We might also question the assumption that the United States would drop the bombs unless a case could be made not to do so. The impression that emerges is that the use of the bombs was inevitable unless some powerful individual made a case to Harry Truman that caused the president to freeze the Manhattan Project in place short of dropping the bombs.

The analysis here has been sympathetic to the urgency of ending the war at the earliest point, but any action that could bring about that result is inevitably one of such magnitude that it should be considered on its own. The momentum of winning the war should not control a decision so important. Possibly, Franklin Roosevelt's death came at an especially bad time to have that kind of reflection. No one who has written on the matter has suggested that FDR would have refrained from bombing Japan and Germany if the bombs had been ready in time, but having the Manhattan Project dumped on an unprepared Harry Truman was not an ideal circumstance.

Nine vice presidents in our history have succeeded to the presidency midterm, and only Gerald Ford took the vice presidency with the expectation that he would soon be president. If Harry Truman had started preparing for the presidency on election night in 1944, he would have had five months to ready himself for the burden that landed on April 12, but we have no reason to think that Franklin Roosevelt would have been a willing teacher.

We all know that we are going to die, but until the last, we may be just as certain that it is not going to happen today. The denial of death may postpone writing a will and cleaning out the attic. But it should not prevent presidents and aspirants to the office from assuming that their running mate will inherit the mantle, so the best possible preparation for that event becomes a very serious responsibility.

Harry Truman showed enough grit on other occasions that we should not think he was rolled into authorizing atomic bombings because his subordinates intimidated him. Nonetheless, we might want any president making so momentous a decision to have some kind of organizational reset button that requires one more fresh review of all the issues with a range of issues presented by people with the skill to make an argument in that kind of setting.

The calculus of death, the effect on the Soviets, the tenacity of the fighting in the Pacific, memories of Pearl Harbor and the Bataan Death March almost certainly meant that a fuller and more explicit consideration of using the bombs would have wound up in the same place it did on the morning of August 6, 1945. For the future, we may want to have some way to hit that reset button before initiating action.

In January of 1943 Franklin Roosevelt announced a momentous decision that may have complicated the conclusion of the war. On his own and impulsively, so he claimed, he declared that the war would end with the unconditional surrender of the Axis powers.

His remarks were delivered in Casablanca, Morocco, where he had traveled to meet with Winston Churchill near a vital theater in the war against Germany. To get there, FDR became the first president to fly while in office. A Pan Am seaplane took off near Miami, travelled to Brazil, crossed the Atlantic to Africa, and then rendezvoused to the north at the final destination. The journey required forty-eight hours.

Stalin was unable to join the conference because some of the worst fighting of the war was occurring in the city named for him. FDR and Churchill had to resolve some local disputes among unappealing characters; in the course of their diplomacy, Roosevelt mentioned Ulysses Grant and his demand that victory over the Confederacy would require their unconditional surrender.

The president said that the phrase popped into his head during postconference remarks. His exact words were, "The elimination of German, Japanese and Italian war power means the unconditional surrender by Germany, Italy, and Japan. That does not mean the destruction of the population of Germany, Italy, nor Japan, but it does mean the destruction of the philosophies in those countries which are based on conquest and the subjugation of other people."[41]

Not even Winston Churchill, sitting next to FDR, was aware that the president was going to announce publicly the terms that the two leaders had agreed to demand the Axis meet. The Stimson note to Truman, quoted earlier, recommended a warning to Japan and then proposed, "I personally think that if in [giving such a warning] we should add that we do not exclude a constitutional monarchy under her present dynasty, it would substantially add to the chances of acceptance."[42]

Jimmy Byrnes and others feared that this adjustment would be taken as a crack in a solid Allied position. If the emperor's place were to be acknowledged and respected, would that place include the authority to interfere with other plans that the Americans and their allies had in mind for the defeated Japan?

Howard Zinn offered a clear critique of the policy of unconditional surrender. A bombardier during the air war in Europe during World War II, Zinn concluded, "If only the Americans had not insisted on unconditional surrender—that is, if they were willing to accept one condition to the surrender, that the Emperor, a holy figure to the Japanese, remain in place—the Japanese would have agreed to stop the war."[43] Perhaps. Evidence can be selected to support that view, but the Japanese government had little coherence by the summer of 1945. Factions ranged from *peace now* to *resistance to the last*.

As FDR acknowledged, the American doctrine of unconditional surrender traces to the Civil War and Ulysses Grant, who had an aide who initiated the standard. The histories of that conflict generally celebrate Grant for the conciliatory approach that he demonstrated at Appomattox Courthouse. The doctrine implies that the foe should trust the victor, that conditions imposed after total surrender will be better for the defeated enemy than any outcome secured by continuing the conflict.

After giving his remarks in Casablanca, Roosevelt reflected on the end of the Great War. Freidel explains that "after his press conference at Casablanca, he told Harriman that he did not want to repeat Wilson's blunder in issuing the Fourteen Points, which Germany in advance of the armistice had regarded as a basis for the postwar settlement."[44] FDR worked on a postwar world that differed sharply from the one produced by the Treaty of Versailles. A central point would be to help the defeated countries rise again. The president was determined that bitterness, a seed for future conflict, would be drained from the cultures of all the belligerents.

Germany had been led by the cartoonish Kaiser Wilhelm in the earlier conflict and then by Adolph Hitler in the next act of what Churchill called a second Thirty Years War. Germany was weakened to a point that it could not resist the punitive terms of the Treaty of Versailles, but that nation rebounded quicker than the countries that had conquered it.

Roosevelt might have said, "Surrender unequivocally, and we will see that your economy is restored and the healthy aspects of your culture respected. We will do so because it is in our own interest to have you as a vital partner in peace and prosperity." An attractive message, but it asks a foreign nation to trust the American president more than their own leader. No doubt the guidance of the American president would have been a major improvement in many cases, but it would be a very hard sell in nearly all of them.

A number of people shaped the policies that drove the Manhattan Project, but two people bore the ultimate responsibility. Franklin Roosevelt and Harry Truman were the only people who could have shut down the development of the atomic bomb. Their refusal to do so has been criticized by numerous people, from Howard Zinn to Dwight Eisenhower. Interesting that Zinn quotes Eisenhower in his *People's History of the United States*, when he proclaims, "Every gun that is made, every warship launched, every rocket fired, signifies in a final sense a theft from those who are hungry and are not fed, those who are cold and not clothed."[45] And that is a sentiment with which Franklin Roosevelt would have agreed even while appointing the officials who spent $2.5 billion to build bombs that killed directly over two hundred thousand people.

If the moral issue is limited to one's opinion about the decisions of Roosevelt and Truman, the perspective is too narrow. Looking at the Manhattan Project through the eyes of the two presidents, we can see a flaw in much of the controversy about the bombings of Hiroshima and Nagasaki. Specifically, the answer to the question, "Were the bombings of Hiroshima and Nagasaki justified?" is, "That's the wrong question." If one is the person who makes the decision, the real question is, "What was the best way to end the war with Japan?"

Neither president had the luxury of rejecting all the miserable choices at hand. If not the bombings, what? We can compare various estimates about casualties from an invasion against the actual losses from the bombings, but what Harry Truman would have had to expect from an invasion was something even worse than Okinawa. That battle began on April 12, twelve days before Truman's presidency began, and it lasted until June 22. Three months to secure one island. The U.S. Navy controlled the seas, but nearly five thousand sailors were killed in kamikaze attacks launched from Kyushu. If even a fraction of Japanese civilians held the military's value of death over surrender, the invasion could have required months of conventional fighting before turning into a guerilla campaign against the American occupying force. What choices would then have to be made?

A second option would be the blockade and siege. Its appeal is that combat would appear to end, and surrender would simply be a matter of time. Almost every observer at the time acknowledged that Japan was defeated, but we should be precise about that word. Defeated in the sense of being unable to win the war, yes. Defeated in the sense that they could offer no resistance at all, no. Could the country have subsisted for an indefinite time? Living on fish, rice, water, some milk, and subsistence farming would be unappealing but perhaps more agreeable to people than surrendering to the enemy.

A variation of this option would have been to supplement the siege with a continuation of conventional bombing. If the cities were destroyed, survivors would empty into the countryside in a humanitarian catastrophe. Epidemics, crime, and other miseries might have been inevitable.

The demonstration of an atomic bomb is perhaps the most attractive alternative. Leslie Groves rejected it because he wanted the bomb to have the most powerful psychological impact possible. Groves, however, saw the Trinity test at Alamogordo, and he would have been entirely aware of its effect on Robert Oppenheimer, Vannevar Bush, and others who had been as prepared for the result as possible. Despite their knowing the estimates about the force of the blast, the brilliant light, the heat, the boiling mushroom cloud—all had a nearly overwhelming impact on the men who had built the device.

Groves also wrote of his concerns if a test failed. The intent would have been to show the Japanese their fate; the impact might have been to encourage them to continue the fight. But what would have been lost? The other options would have remained.

At this point, we are well into the realm of speculation about a demonstration test, what-ifs piled upon what-ifs. One complication to a demonstration is abundantly evident. The logistics might have been impossible. Where would the blast occur? Who would witness it? The peace faction in the Japanese government would not have been the problem. They were ready to surrender as things were. Would the militarists cooperate? Some of them mounted a coup against the emperor when he opted for surrender after Nagasaki and then killed themselves after the coup failed. What would they see that would have turned them from death?

Would it be possible to reach the emperor himself? Wrapped in the preposterous cloak of divinity, Hirohito lacked an essential quality of sound leadership: he had no one to tell him he was wrong, that he needed to head in a different direction. Might it have been possible for the Americans to communicate with him directly? The pamphlets prepared to saturate Japan with news about the atomic bombs included a request: "We ask that you now petition the Emperor to end the war."

Petition the emperor? How would that happen? If the circumstances weren't so tragic, the request would be charming. Something like getting a referendum on a ballot in California through an initiative that collects signatures at shopping centers, in movie lines, and outside churches. Still . . .

Why not try everything imaginable to get to the emperor for a chance at the one and only bloodless way to end the war.

The price of this option would have been time—time to establish who the witnesses would be; time to figure out the mechanics for a safe and certain detonation; time to determine the place where the test would occur; time for the witnesses to communicate their experience to the emperor if he hadn't been there himself.

Would it take days or weeks at the earliest to set up the test? Could a cease-fire have been arranged while the preparations were made? Would local Japanese commanders, who tended to choose death over surrender, honor a cease-fire when a disgraceful surrender was being contemplated? If a cease-fire could be achieved, how would commanders keep their troops ready for renewed combat if that proved necessary?

Arranging a test of an atomic bomb would necessarily require some kind of negotiation, and that could easily lead to delay with consequences unforeseen.

Here again, we do well to try to get the presidential perspective. From December 7, 1941, to September 2, 1945, Franklin Roosevelt and Harry Truman received daily updates on the progress of the war, and casualty reports were part of those updates. Any American even remotely aware of those figures would have endured some measure of distress and grief. For millions, the news was personal. A son, brother, husband, father, or friend had been killed or wounded or was missing. For a commander in chief, these reports must have been hammer blows.

In some way, wasn't a president personally responsible? Franklin Roosevelt sought the extraordinary third term with World War II underway. Harry Truman accepted the vice presidential nomination with at least some expectation that it would make him the next president and perhaps before the war ended. Why did they take those jobs if they didn't think they could lead the country through the war better than anyone else? And if they were so sure about their capacity for that leadership, didn't every single playing of "Taps" at a graveside mock that confidence?

Franklin Roosevelt was born to wealth and privilege. He was an alumnus of Groton and Harvard. He was a member of the New York bar and a governor of that state, having sufficiently overcome the paralysis that attacked him when he was thirty-nine years old. He won the presidency in 1932 and over two terms changed the relationship between the American government and the people it serves.

In 1940, at the age of fifty-eight, he might have retired to a life of comfort. He might have focused all his resources on finding a cure for his impairment. He might have assisted his successor in some way. He might have done anything he wanted to do other than bear the burden of a wartime presidency. In that role, as surely as if he had been slain in combat—Robert Taft's point—Franklin Roosevelt worked himself to death.

In his forty months of combat, Roosevelt pressed the Manhattan Project, an effort he initiated after learning about the Einstein letter from Alexander Sachs. He put talented people in key positions and then gave them room to work. He made adjustments in the administrative structure even though the specifics of the project were quite beyond him. In an aspect closer to his own talents, he navigated the difficult atomic relationship with the British while deferring the even more troubling relationship with the Soviets to a later point.

Franklin Roosevelt was a complicated man, and his reasons for wanting the third term and for pursuing an atomic bomb were likely complex as well. No one who knew him thought that he would have refrained from using the weapon against the Japanese, and his conversation with Leslie Groves in December of 1944 indicates a willingness to use it against Germany. If we want to think about his reaction to appeals from Leo Szilard or Henry Stimson, we have to reenter the realm of speculation to do so. The certainty is that he wanted to beat the Germans to the bomb; when that outcome was secure, he wanted to proceed with the production so that the United States would have the widest range of options at the end of the war.

Harry Truman was not born to wealth or privilege. Two years younger than Franklin Roosevelt, Truman's boyhood was spent on a farm. Food was abundant, and his family was loving. He attended no college but served in France near the end of World War I, where he had firsthand experience in combat.

His political career began with support from the political machine of Tom Pendergast. He went from a county position in the 1920s to the U.S. Senate in the election of 1936. His brief vice presidency did little to prepare him for the White House. While figuring out a best friend for Franklin Roosevelt is difficult, Truman's personality seemed to be more open, maybe less wary.

His experience with the Manhattan Project was distinctly different from FDR's. Truman inherited all the issues on Roosevelt's desk, and he needed to get up to speed as fast as possible. He learned of his new responsibilities on the afternoon of April 12, and Adolf Hitler killed himself eighteen days later. Germany's surrender followed a week after that on May 7, 1945. The war seemed to be winding down before Truman could fully grasp it.

In this crash course in the American presidency, Truman learned that the Germans had accepted the Casablanca terms of unconditional surrender. The Italian government had made the same capitulation in 1943, but Stimson urged language that would give the Japanese some reassurance that the emperor could stay. Byrnes countered that any equivocation would be taken as appeasement and might be a political disaster when the American people learned of the accommodation.

Having seen an enemy he had faced on the battlefield in the Great

War rise again to inflict a historic catastrophe on the world, Truman may have thought that the warrior culture of Japan needed to be destroyed beyond repair. He may also have appreciated that delay in getting that unequivocal surrender meant death for Americans, either by an attack in violation of the cease-fire or by inefficiency in future battles if the demonstration failed in its objective.

As David McCullough points out in his masterful biography, the war in the Pacific might have been coming to a conclusion, but it was not winding down. He wrote, "Some critics and historians in years to come would argue that Japan was already finished by this time, just as Eisenhower had said and as several intelligence reports indicated. Japan's defeat, however, was not the issue. It was Japan's surrender that was so desperately wanted, since every day Japan did not surrender meant the killing continued."[46]

McCullough added that, in the brief time of Truman's presidency, American casualties in the Pacific amounted to half of the total from the previous three years. He concluded, "The nearer victory came, the heavier the price in blood. And whatever the projected toll in American lives in an invasion, it was too high if it could be avoided."[47]

Harry Truman was the only person with the final authority to approve the use of atomic bombs on Japan. And we should understand that he did not exactly say "yes" to their use; rather, he refrained from saying "no." McCullough thinks, "Very possibly there was no one, clearcut moment when he made up his mind, or announced that he had. Most likely, he never seriously considered not using the bomb. Indeed, to have said no at this point and called everything off would have been so drastic a break with the whole history of the project, not to say the terrific momentum of events that summer, as to have been almost inconceivable."[48]

Of all the options that Truman had, the demonstration was the one that might have held some promise, but it came with enormous complications as we have seen. We can think that the risk should have been taken anyway, that the horrific suffering of hundreds of thousands of innocent Japanese people merited an attempt at that alternative. The possibility of Japanese militarism reviving could have been dealt with at a later time; if diplomatic and commercial pressures had been more sensibly applied, a resumption of war might not have occurred.

If we wonder about that road not taken, we should remember that we do so in relative comfort and security. The only person who had to make that decision did so amid the daily drumbeat of casualty reports. By August of 1945 the deaths on his watch would be in a war that the bombing pamphlets described as "useless." Should he have taken a chance rather than visited certain death on thousands of Japanese? Perhaps, but Harry Truman found no consideration sufficient to put the lives of any more Americans in jeopardy.

ELEVEN

Science and Democracy

Poets and artists have created stories that celebrate the history of a people, warn of perils, and plead with gods for protection. Mythology developed to explain critical aspects of human life and to propose the virtues that would meet the challenges that every society faces.

In that regard, about 2,700 years ago, Hesiod presented the figure of Prometheus in his *Theogony*. Having brought fire to humans, Prometheus has been a convenient metaphor for those who developed atomic fire in the twentieth century, especially J. Robert Oppenheimer. His biographers have drawn the comparison that both were punished by those in authority—the god for his audacity in bringing life-changing energy to our world, the man for suggesting that atomic energy needed to be confined to nonmilitary purposes. For their trouble, Oppenheimer lost his security clearance, but Prometheus so angered Zeus that his punishment was to have his liver devoured each day by an eagle.

The Promethean myth is useful beyond its attachment to Oppenheimer or any one of a number of individuals central to the Manhattan Project. Fire in any form is a mixed blessing, so understanding its benefits and risks is crucial. Just as important, we need to determine who has the ultimate authority to act on the risk-benefit assessment. Finally, how might vulnerable parties try to shape the policies that will affect them? A closer look at the myth is instructive.

Hesiod described Prometheus as wily and cunning, twice defying Zeus to secure the fire that had been denied to mortals. The Lord of Gods and Men had considerable patience with Prometheus, who had stayed out of the fray when Zeus's Olympians overthrew the Titans, an earlier generation of gods into which Prometheus had been born. Zeus had been clear that mortals were not to have fire, but "the noble son of Iapetus outwitted him and stole the far-seen gleam of unwearying fire in a hollow fennel stalk."[1] Zeus, we learn, was "stung in spirit."[2]

In the tradition of punishing the whole class for the transgressions of a single student, Zeus "made an evil thing for men as the price of fire."[3] Specifically, Zeus made Pandora, and "from her is the race of women and female kind: of her is the deadly race and tribe of women who live amongst mortal men to their great trouble."[4]

Skipping past Hesiod's misogyny, we read the conclusion, "So it is not possible to deceive or go beyond the will of Zeus; for not even the son of Iapetus, kindly Prometheus, escaped his heavy anger."[5] In time, in a very long time, Prometheus was freed from his personal punishment. Heracles (Hercules to the Romans) killed the liver-eating eagle and freed Prometheus from his chains because Zeus had become more interested in exalting Heracles than in continuing the torment of Prometheus.

In his classic work on mythology, Thomas Bulfinch explained that Prometheus secured fire for mortals because he and his brother Epimetheus had been charged with creating humans and other animals but hit a complication. Epimetheus dispensed qualities to a range of creatures but failed to budget well. As Bulfinch explained, "Epimetheus accordingly proceeded to bestow upon the different animals the various gifts of courage, strength, swiftness, sagacity; wings to one, claws to another, a shelly covering to a third, etc."[6] He had nothing left for humans. Therefore, according to Bulfinch, "In his perplexity he resorted to his brother Prometheus, who, with the aid of Minerva, went up to heaven, and lighted his torch at the chariot of the sun, and brought down fire to man."[7]

Bulfinch's account of the mythology lost some perspective on the gift of fire. He saw only its benefits, writing, "With this gift man was more than a match for all other animals. It enabled him to make weapons wherewith to subdue them; tools with which to cultivate the earth; to warm his dwelling, so as to be comparatively independent of climate; and finally to introduce the arts and to coin money, the means of trade and commerce."[8]

In other words, as Bulfinch saw it, fire was a key to modern civilization. It allowed us to survive as hunter-gatherers during ice ages, and perhaps ten thousand years ago, it allowed us to transfer to agriculture and to begin building large complex societies. No fire—no cities, no capacity to develop and store wealth, no permanent art, no records of daily life, no science of medicine, no development of sources of energy, no systems of transportation beyond walking and sailing short distances, no possibility to explore the planet.

Bulfinch neglected other aspects of fire. Weapons that could subdue other animals have also subdued other humans, none more so than nuclear weapons. Some tools have cultivated the earth, but others have ravaged natural resources to a point that some places on earth are uninhabitable by our species. Dwellings are warm, but sometimes fires have spread beyond control, destroying vast areas of such cities as London, New York, and Chicago. Fire has introduced art, but some of that art has been entertainment that has degraded its participants for the amusement of others. Fire has served money, trade, and commerce but not always in ways that have ennobled us.

Hesiod's account of Prometheus demonstrates that, from the early times of Western civilization, people have thought about the proper relationship among the gifts of technology, the dazzling figures who bring those gifts, and the possible impacts on the rest of us. Did Zeus know best what humans were capable of handling? Was Prometheus a hero who suffered to provide us with a critical means of progress? Was he a reckless egotist who put us in peril with an offering for which we were unprepared?

Through millennia of polities, through any number of arrangements of civic power, we find those questions as compelling and germane as ever. Perhaps Zeus thought that we weren't ready for the gift because its implications were yet beyond us. But in the context of World War II, the fire of the atom represented the assurance of victory, and that prospect proved irresistible.

The Manhattan Project included a number of issues that would give a deity pause. But Franklin Roosevelt didn't think we had the luxury to stop and reflect, so he tapped a classical option in our constitutional system, one that has been used to meet the gravest crises in our history. Garry Wills has described George Washington as an American Cincinnatus; the title, in a different sense, fits Franklin Roosevelt as well.[9] Lucius Quinctius Cincinnatus lived from 519 BCE to 430 BCE, and he was the citizen-farmer who, according to the story, left his plow in the field to save Rome from the Aequi, a neighboring tribe that was clobbering the Roman army. Cincinnatus was given the office of dictator, did his job successfully, and returned to his farm at the earliest possible time. In the Second World War, with congressional acquiescence, FDR exercised more power than perhaps any other president, including Abraham Lincoln, who had to contend with Congress's Joint Committee on the Conduct of the War.

In Roosevelt's case, he indicated in his first inaugural address that he planned to tackle the Great Depression as he would a foreign invasion. When enemies rose in Europe and Asia, Roosevelt was constrained by the separation of powers from mobilizing the country, until the attack on Pearl Harbor. But even before the day of infamy, FDR had taken the research into atomic fission out of the Madisonian model and placed it into something like the Cincinnatus alternative. For the duration of the war and for the purposes of the Manhattan Project, Congress was a seven-member, unicameral legislature that rubber-stamped $2.5 billion of appropriations, no questions asked.

In the most favorable reading of the case, the atomic bomb would have ended the German war if the Nazi regime had not collapsed two months before the Trinity test. The bombs may have ended the war against Japan with fewer lives lost than any other strategy available. They may also have kept the Cold War from turning into World War III. At the same time, despite that success, the Manhattan Project was not without terrifying risks and actual disasters.

Affected parties is a legal concept referring to the people most likely to take the impact of a proposed government action. In most instances, these people have a right to know about the action and to have the opportunity to express their views about it, but Chicago on December 2, 1942, was not offered such an opportunity. If a worker building Chicago Pile No. 1 had made a Daghlian-Slotin blunder, might a radioactive hole have been blown in the middle of the city? It didn't happen, but the lesson from Los Alamos is that people take shortcuts and drop things, sometimes with catastrophic results.

Two and a half years later, on July 16, 1945, Enrico Fermi was at Alamogordo, New Mexico, for the Trinity test. The night before,

Fermi opened a book—not a physics or math book but a betting sheet. He took wagers "on whether or not the bomb would ignite the atmosphere, and, if so, whether it would merely destroy New Mexico or destroy the world."[10] Leslie Groves persuaded himself that the intent was to break the tension, and he mentioned that Fermi himself seemed completely at ease. Having called for lunch after the control rods in Chicago had temporarily stopped that experiment with a thunderclap, Fermi was probably very hard to unnerve.

Graveyard humor was the last stop for several of the geniuses. Robert Oppenheimer instructed Edward Teller to keep thinking about any possible way the Trinity bomb could have a force beyond the one anticipated. The evening before the test, Teller, who had been starting the work that would lead to the hydrogen bomb, ran into a colleague, Robert Serber. Oppenheimer had warned those who would witness the early morning test to watch out for rattlesnakes. Teller asked Serber what he planned to do about the risk of the snakes. Serber said that he would bring a bottle of whiskey. Teller then asked about the risk of an explosion beyond the calculations. Serber replied that he would bring a second bottle of whiskey.

Back to the people in New Mexico and the world. They had no chance to place a bet, to stockpile liquor, to scatter to Utah or Colorado, to ask for essential information about the experiment or why New Mexico was so fortunate; certainly they had no chance to comment on the test. At some level, everyone at Los Alamos was a volunteer, but aside from them, none of the 537,000 people living in New Mexico that day had any knowledge that they were participating in an experiment that had Robert Oppenheimer asking questions upon questions.

New Mexicans were not relocated for Trinity, but an evacuation did take place in 1943 in Hanford, Washington, the location that Henry Stimson told Harry Truman to ignore. Over fifteen hundred residents were moved so that facilities could be built for plutonium research. According to an account from the Environmental Protection Agency (EPA), "A camp for workers set up on the site eventually swelled to a population of 50,000. The camp included many trailers, mess halls, and other standard facilities as well as dance halls, ball fields, and other entertainment venues."[11]

As with other aspects of the Manhattan Project, the community operated outside our system of constitutional government: "Progress at the Hanford Site occurred quickly and secretly and, as a security measure, local and state officials were not even informed about the purposes of the Site."[12]

Again according to the EPA report, Hanford "was considered an ideal place because of the remote location, the access to railroad systems, the proximity to the Columbia River needed for cooling the reactors, and the abundance of hydroelectric power generated from dams along the river."[13] Passive voice is a particular problem in public affairs because, as in this case, we need to know "considered an ideal place" *by whom*? The immediate answer is Gen. Leslie Groves, and the ultimate answer is Franklin Roosevelt. But that raises another question: How did they balance the advantages of the site to the Manhattan Project against the risks to the people in the area, then and in the future?

The urgency of the war seems to have precluded any serious calculations along those lines. Hanford expanded and contracted according to the state of the Cold War, and then "beginning in 1989, the primary mission at the Hanford Site switched from production to waste cleanup. In May of that year, the USDOE [U.S. Department of Energy], EPA and Ecology signed the Tri-Party Agreement and, since then, no plutonium has been produced for defense purposes at the Site."[14]

The EPA's home page for the site further reviews the damage to the area: "The operations at Hanford created one of the largest and most complex cleanup projects in the U.S. Weapons production resulted in more than 43 million cubic yards of radioactive waste, and over 130 million cubic yards of contaminated soil and debris. Approximately 475 billion gallons of contaminated water was discharged to the soil. Some of the contaminants have made it to groundwater under the site. Over 80 square miles of groundwater is contaminated to levels above groundwater protection standards."[15]

Hanford produced Fat Man, the bomb dropped on Nagasaki, and other weapons that were instruments of deterrence in the Cold War. Hanford is now a Superfund site, an environmental disaster whose cleanup will require resources far beyond those of the Manhattan Project.

The state of Oregon is an affected party even though the Hanford site is thirty miles north of the border with Washington. Poison doesn't respect federalism, so state borders don't stop the damage from the production of toxins. The Oregon Department of Energy estimates that the total cost to clean up Hanford is $150 billion dollars.[16] Adjusting for inflation, that represents about five times the money spent to produce the first atomic bombs.

Hanford also includes a cost that historically has been easy to overlook in our country. Turning again to the EPA report, "Long before construction of the Hanford Site, the area had been inhabited by various Native American tribes, including the Yakama, Nez Perce, Umatilla, Cause and Walla Walla. However, in 1855 many of these tribes signed treaties with the United States government and a reservation system was devised. The tribes reserved the right to continue many practices on the ceded lands, such as to fish from any stream within or adjacent to the territory, to hunt, to graze their horses and cattle on open and unclaimed land, and to practice religious traditions at locations they consider sacred."[17] The environmental conditions of Hanford are a long way from sacred.

Combining the Manhattan Project with the current Superfund effort is instructive. Both are monumental commitments of public resources, but they are conducted in very different political settings. From December of 1941 to the late summer of 1945, the American government had one overarching purpose: win the war. From the late 1960s to the present, the wheels of bureaucracy turn much more democratically than they once did. Hearings, review, meetings, deliberation, more hearings—all drive up costs. That extra procedure is good if you want affected interests to receive proper consideration, bad if you want to get something important accomplished expeditiously.

Secrecy was essential to the Manhattan Project, but the way it was pursued left a record of very mixed results. Franklin Roosevelt's decision to give the production of an atomic bomb to the Army Corps of Engineers determined the way that vital information about the bomb would be managed. Leslie Groves relied on organizing the work by compartment and then dispensing information on a need-to-know basis. This model was very different from the usual practice of scientific research in which discoveries are widely disseminated for replication and review, but Enrico Fermi had acknowledged early in the study of fission that physicists were voluntarily limiting the knowledge of their work so that they would not inadvertently assist the Nazis in getting an atomic bomb.

The military model assumes discipline for the purpose of advancing the interests of the nation, but due to the spies who had penetrated Los Alamos, Josef Stalin knew more about the development of Fat Man and Little Boy than did all but a few members of Congress. When Leslie Groves wrote about Klaus Fuchs, he revealed a very interesting aspect of our alliance with the British: "Our acceptance of Fuchs into the project was a mistake. But I am at a loss when I try to determine just how we could have avoided that mistake without insulting our principal ally, Great Britain, by insisting on controlling their security measures."[18]

Groves reviewed the conversations with the British before their physicists arrived after the Quebec Agreement. He rejected the suggestion that he should have conducted his own review even after the British had vouched for the scientists: "This would have been most presumptuous and, in fact, impossible without complete infringement of British rights and without the co-operation of the British government which we would not have obtained."[19]

The general then insisted that it was the British who dropped the ball, and he proposed an explanation: "I have always felt that the basic reason for this [failure] was the attitude then prevalent in all British officialdom that for an Englishman treason was impossible, and that when a foreigner was granted citizenship he automatically became fully endowed with the qualities of a native-born Englishman."[20] Whatever merits Groves's sociology deserves, another way to tell the story is that the general declined to ruffle British feathers rather than verify that their physicists were reliable.

General Groves used the word *treason* to describe Fuchs's activities. The Constitution itself defines treason in article 3, section 3, clause 1, which reads in its entirety, "Treason against the United States, shall consist only in levying War against them, or in adhering to their Enemies, giving them Aid and Comfort. No Person shall be convicted of Treason unless on the Testimony of two Witnesses to the same overt Act, or on Confession in open Court."

Treason is the only crime defined in the Constitution, and one way to read the definition is that it is a very high bar, a standard that precludes a sloppy application of the term to people who have opinions different from ours. The word *only* establishes that nothing fits the legal definition of treason against the United States other than *waging war against them, or in adhering to their enemies, giving them aid and comfort.*

Conviction of this crime requires the testimony of *two witnesses to the same overt act* or a *confession in open court.* One person's accusation is insufficient. When one person sees an overt act and another sees something else, that is insufficient evidence of treason. An opinion about someone's state of mind is insufficient. An act is required, an act performed in the open. A confession must be made in open court with a judge able to evaluate the state of mind of the accused. Hearsay about a confession in a dungeon is insufficient.

The framers would have understood that treason historically had often meant that someone had annoyed authority. The constitutional standard has significantly limited the cases in which treason has been charged. Among the few convicted of treason in World War II were Mildred Gillars and Iva Toguri D'Aquino, known to American servicemen as Axis Sally and Tokyo Rose. The spies of Los Alamos escaped the charge.

Some who knew him admired the treachery of Theodore Hall. In that respect and others, he anticipated the revelations of Edward Snowden. The two cases are distinct, but they do have an important aspect in common. Like Snowden, Hall saw himself as a patriot. Neither man limited himself to dissent against the policies of the nation's officials, whether elected or appointed to public service. Rather, they presumed to substitute their judgment for those of people on whom the American electorate conferred the authority.

In Hall's case, treason would be a perfect fit if he had given atomic secrets to the Nazis. Passing them to the Soviets during World War II meant that he was giving them to an ally, an admittedly difficult one. If he had passed them to the British, he would still have been in violation of the administration's policy. As we have seen, the relationship with our closest ally was seriously complicated. More to the point, deciding what foreign powers would be privileged with the secrets of Los Alamos was not Theodore Hall's decision to make.

We can reach legal and moral conclusions about those who act contrary to official policy because they presume to know better than presidents what national security requires. Looking at the spying from a civic perspective, we see other issues. Start with the question, "Why did Hall not trust the lawful authority to follow a proper course?" The discussion about sharing information about the atomic bomb, thereby ending the American monopoly, was argued at the highest levels of government. A range of views was presented, including some from the legislative branch. Under the circumstances, it is hard to imagine a more thorough consideration of the issue.

On his own initiative, Theodore Hall reversed the decision to maintain the monopoly as long as possible. He was a young man who thought that an atomic monopoly was a bad idea. He believed that providing the Soviet Union with the means to develop their own nuclear weapons would contribute to a more stable postwar world. He was guessing at that outcome. He reached his personal policy by relying on few conversations with anyone else.

When he was near the end of his life, Hall still seemed to be less than entirely confident about the consequences of his actions.[21] He hoped that he had contributed to the tense stability of the Cold War. He feared what might have happened if the Americans alone had had nuclear weapons when the various international provocations occurred. His hopes and fears over a long span are not the same as sound judgment and certain conviction.

Theodore Hall also falls short of the model of Mohandas Gandhi and Martin Luther King. His was not civil disobedience for the purpose of exposing an inequity inherent in a civil order that boasted of its justice. He never accepted imprisonment as a way to scandalize the public into demanding action to correct practices that belied the values that are celebrated so widely. He took no action to prevent Hiroshima other than to give the Soviet Union and the murderous Stalin a weapon with which to threaten the world with potential annihilation from a more mercurial regime than that of the Americans.

The adjustment in government that we need for future challenges needs to include augmenting the authority of the state to minimize the number of people who put themselves ahead of the Constitution and the electorate. We will always have some people with malevolent motives and others with romantic delusions of themselves as protectors of everything that is good and true. Those in either camp can stand for public office or make an argument to persuade the rest of us of the justice of their cause.

The stakes in the crises yet to come are too high to have self-anointed saviors make policy all by themselves. These confident souls are always with us, but we need to anticipate and prevent their disruptions as far as possible and to limit the likelihood of their interference in the first place. A state that can take decisive action while making every effort to minimize adverse impacts is central to that objective.

Assassination is especially troubling when used as an instrument of foreign policy. Millions of people were killed in World War II in all kinds of terrible ways. No doubt a comparatively small number of them were shot with a handgun while they themselves were unarmed. Such could have been the death of Werner Heisenberg at the hands of Moe Berg, who operated under conditional orders from the Office of Strategic Services on behalf of the people of the United States. Heisenberg, however, saved his own life by talking about S-matrix analysis.

Fortune spared Adolf Hitler on July 20, 1944, when he survived an explosion meant as part of a coup to save Germany from complete destruction in the war. Hitler's case presents the utilitarian question starkly: If killing one person would save the lives of millions, what reason would justify sparing that person's life?

At the time of World War II, civilians in belligerent countries had little protection in international agreements. Hitler was certainly no civilian, but Heisenberg? The record is that anyone with a connection to a military resource, including living in the general area, could be slaughtered with impunity. Similarly, Heisenberg's connection with the German atomic bomb project would have made him fair game, although Switzerland, where the killing would have occurred, might have disagreed.

Executive Order 12,333, promulgated by Ronald Reagan on December 4, 1981, eight months after surviving an assassination attempt, states in its relevant part, "Prohibition on Assassination. No person employed by or acting on behalf of the United States Government shall engage in, or conspire to engage in, assassination." *Black's Law Dictionary* provides the key definition that assassination is "murder committed, usually, though not necessarily, for hire, without direct provocation or cause of resentment given to the murderer by the person upon whom the crime is committed."[22]

This executive order was an attempt to put some coherence into the very difficult matter of setting standards for killing people. In the absence of a declaration of war, the difficult question becomes even less clear. Congress passed the last declarations of war by the United States on June 2, 1942. The targets were Bulgaria, Hungary, and Romania, minor allies of the Axis. Since then, we have fought wars that were undeclared, sent troops into combat without any mention of war, and had them posted in the world where they have been killed in attacks by individuals or nongovernmental actors.

Moral and legal lines can be drawn between justifiable and unjustifiable killing, but they rarely stay straight. Michael V. Hayden, a former director of the Central Intelligence Agency in the George W. Bush administration, proposed that the policy of the Barack Obama administration regarding the killing of suspected terrorists should be made public: "This program rests on the personal legitimacy of the president, and that's not sustainable. I have lived the life of someone taking action on the basis of secret OLC [Office of Legal Counsel] memos, and it ain't a good life. Democracies do not make war on the basis of legal memos locked in a DOJ [Department of Justice] safe."[23]

Democracies do make war in that way, and we have. But it comes at the expense of some of the values for which we initially fought. American involvement in assassinations was a focus of the Senate Select Committee to Study Government Operations with Respect to Intelligence Activities in 1975. Known as the Church Committee for its founder Senator Frank Church of Idaho, the committee attempted to clean the stables of intelligence gathering and other activities to that point in the Cold War. The Senate investigation collided with the Ford administration's desire to confine these matters to the executive branch with occasional updates to a few members of Congress, a variation of the practice for the Manhattan Project.

President Ford issued Executive Order 11,905 in February of 1976 to clarify the responsibilities of various agencies for intelligence gathering. The order included a statement on assassinations that read, "Prohibition of Assassination. No employee of the United States Government shall engage in, or conspire to engage in, political assassination." This was the first of three executive orders prohibiting assassination. Presidents Ford, Carter, and Reagan were the authors, and the orders read as almost identical.

These executive orders clarify that assassination is illegal, but their application is less certain. According to Attorney General Eric Holder, the killing of Osama bin Laden by American forces in 2011 was legitimate because bin Laden was an enemy combatant subject to being killed or captured as if in uniform in a war zone.[24]

The use of drones to kill people plotting against the United States has also been considered something other than assassination. One controversial case was the killing of Anwar al-Awlaki on September 30, 2011, in Yemen. He had been born in the United States and was an American citizen. An article in the *New York Times* maintained that President Obama personally reviews every name on the "kill list" and that the decision to kill al-Awlaki was, according to the president, "an easy one."[25]

The administration also claimed that it had "informed the relevant congressional oversight committees that it had approved the use of lethal force against al-Aulaqi [sic] in February 2010—well over a year before the operation in question—and the legal justification was subsequently explained in detail to those committees, well before action was taken against [al-Aulaqi]."[26]

The article made no mention of the killing of al-Awlaki's sixteen-year-old son two weeks after the father was killed. The boy's killing seems to have been collateral to a deliberate strike, or else it was a very serious blunder. A federal district court for the District of Columbia dismissed a subsequent lawsuit by the boy's grandfather.[27]

　　　　　　　　SCIENCE AND DEMOCRACY

Part of the court's reasoning was that the matter was left to the discretion of the executive branch and that it was beyond the authority of the courts to consider.

Killing an individual by drone or by other explosives will inevitably lead to killing innocent bystanders. Courts have deferred to the executive branch to set the standards to guide such operations, but the public needs to know, as far as possible, what its representatives are doing. In addition, we need to know that some kind of legislative and judicial review of the executive action has been made.

Millions of people were in potential danger through experiments into atomic fission. Hanford, Washington, remains an environmental catastrophe from decades of plutonium production. An unprecedented standard of secrecy was introduced to the operation of American government, yet spies roamed freely at Los Alamos. Two cities were blown up, and a Nobel Prize–winning physicist was targeted for assassination. All of this was done in the name of the American people but without the knowledge of any but a very small number of them. For all of that, the principal goal was accomplished: the threat of totalitarian systems killing those who would not submit was defeated.

We also won the war, which wasn't inevitable simply because that's what happened. German hegemony in Europe would have given the Nazis the time and security to fashion the bomb that triggered the Einstein letter. The Manhattan Project didn't prevent the German bomb. American and British bombers, the counterattack from Allied armies in the east and west, courageous resistance movements in the occupied countries, code breakers, and the suddenly democratic workforce in American factories were key instruments in precluding the development of an atomic bomb by the Reich.

The Manhattan Project showed that, if necessary, our Madisonian government can transform itself into the most powerful public authority in the world. It cannot make that adjustment without complications, but if national security or another vital issue is at stake, the evidence is that the challenge can be met. This point matters greatly because an assortment of public goods and services may well be desperately needed in our lifetimes and those of our children.

Bioterrorism, a mutated virus, an asteroid on a collision course, a cyberattack, a natural disaster that overwhelms public health resources—these nightmares require little imagination because we have already suffered some version of them. Anthrax has been sent to members of Congress; AIDS seemed to appear suddenly in 1981; space rocks have hit the planet in the past few years, though relatively small and colliding in comparatively convenient places; SONY has had its corporate secrets revealed to the world; Hurricane Katrina destroyed much of New Orleans after being weakened from a category 5 hurricane at sea to a category 3 at landfall. Very slight changes could have made any of these tragedies far worse, so we have to assume that someday we will face even greater threats than those previously met.

From time to time, we will need a stronger government, one that inspires confidence rather than fear and contempt; so we must find a way to balance the powerful, focused state of the Manhattan Project with the Madisonian constraints that protect individual rights. We have recalibrated that balance between power and constraint a number of times in our history.

The Manhattan Project was one such adjustment. It began as an idea in the mind of Leo Szilard. It became a stumbling administrative program and then shaped up, acquiring resources and focus. It transformed from a physics experiment to an engineering project that produced the most powerful weapons in history. The weapons were then used to bring the war in the Pacific to an end.

The question at the center of this book has been: How do we control experts in a democracy when we can't understand their arguments? The answer is that we become sufficiently informed to elect men and women who can distill the public interest even in fields with the most obscure concepts, people who may be limited in physics and neuroscience but who have the intelligence, emotional makeup, and character to discern the public interest.

C. P. Snow concluded his reflections on *the two cultures* by proposing that "we can educate a large proportion of our better minds so that they are not ignorant of imaginative experience, both in the arts and in science."[28] The democratic question, of course, is: What did Snow mean by "better minds"?

Franklin Roosevelt might not have made the cut, since he was allegedly described by Oliver Wendell Holmes Jr. as having "a second rate intellect but a first rate temperament.[29] And Harry Truman would have lacked the academic pedigree that Snow might have required for admission to a *better minds* fraternity. Neither president would have understood the intricacies of Little Boy and Fat Man, but they did have the wherewithal to direct science to serve the purposes of the war. Their decisions may not always have been correct, but they reflected a thoughtful understanding of the public interest. The presidential aides and some members of Congress had their factional battles, but they ultimately trusted and accepted the decisions of the commanders in chief.

The challenge of experts to a democracy is not ultimately met by a spectator sport in which we cheer or boo an elite that watches over us. Nor will we find a resolution to the complications of science in any particular structure or process of government, though some are certainly more helpful than others. In this area, as in others, the balance of contending values has to be struck by people trusted with authority over experts. Since an electorate selects those people, we have an ever-greater responsibility to acquire enough scientific literacy to understand the fundamental qualities of issues that are looming.

For those of us who missed that knowledge in school, we are fortunate that books, online courses, and other resources are available for us. We will then be able to choose serious people for those offices that are removed from our direct engagement, allowing us to become more involved in tough issues in our own communities. We owe it to our heritage and to our futures to do so. In America we are ultimately the powers that be.

[NOTES]

Introduction

1. See Hargittai, *Martians of Science*.
2. Snow, *Two Cultures*, 98.
3. Snow, *Two Cultures*, 99.

1. A Squash Court in Chicago

1. Compton, *Atomic Quest*, 137.
2. Compton, *Atomic Quest*, 137.
3. Compton, *Atomic Quest*, 137.
4. Compton, *Atomic Quest*, 137–38.
5. Compton, *Atomic Quest*, 138.
6. Compton, *Atomic Quest*, 138.
7. Mayer, *Robert Maynard Hutchins*, 250.
8. Mayer, *Robert Maynard Hutchins*, 250.
9. Rhodes, *Making of the Atomic Bomb*, 436.
10. Smyth, *Atomic Energy for Military Purposes*.
11. Compton, *Atomic Quest*, 138.
12. Conant, *My Several Lives*, 289.
13. Conant, *My Several Lives*, 289.
14. Compton, *Atomic Quest*, 138.
15. Groves, *Now It Can Be Told*, 53.
16. Groves, *Now It Can Be Told*, 53.
17. Groves, *Now It Can Be Told*, 53.
18. Groves, *Now It Can Be Told*, 53.
19. Groves, *Now It Can Be Told*, 53.
20. Mahaffey, *Atomic Accidents*, 57–60.
21. Dion, "Acute Radiation Sickness."
22. Mahaffey, *Atomic Accidents*, 62–66.
23. The problem persists. On September 18, 1980, in Damascus, Arkansas, a worker on a Titan II missile, armed with hydrogen bombs, dropped a wrench socket down the missile's silo. The socket punctured the missile's exterior, causing a fuel leak. The next day, the fuel exploded, killing one airman, injuring oth-

ers, and sending a hydrogen bomb flying out of the silo to the ground nearby. The locks on the bomb held, and a greater catastrophe was averted. The cleanup cost over $250 million.

24. Enrico Fermi, "Fermi's Own Story."

25. Enrico Fermi, "Fermi's Own Story," 22.

26. Enrico Fermi, "Fermi's Own Story," 23.

27. Enrico Fermi, "Fermi's Own Story," 23.

28. Enrico Fermi, "Fermi's Own Story," 23.

29. Rhodes, *Making of the Atomic Bomb*, 433.

30. Rhodes, *Making of the Atomic Bomb*, 430.

31. Rhodes, *Making of the Atomic Bomb*, 434.

32. Enrico Fermi, "Fermi's Own Story," 24.

33. Enrico Fermi, "Fermi's Own Story," 24.

34. Rhodes, *Making of the Atomic Bomb*, 439.

35. Enrico Fermi, "Fermi's Own Story," 25.

36. Compton, *Atomic Quest*, 132.

37. Compton, *Atomic Quest*, 132.

38. Compton, *Atomic Quest*, 132.

39. Compton, *Atomic Quest*, 132.

40. Enrico Fermi, "Fermi's Own Story," 25.

41. Compton, *Atomic Quest*, 143.

42. Compton, *Atomic Quest*, 143.

43. Compton, *Atomic Quest*, 144.

44. Compton, *Atomic Quest*, 144.

45. Laura Fermi, *Atoms in the Family*, 177.

46. Laura Fermi, *Atoms in the Family*, 179.

47. Laura Fermi, *Atoms in the Family*, 179.

48. Laura Fermi, *Atoms in the Family*, 179.

49. Laura Fermi, *Atoms in the Family*, 179.

50. Smyth, *Atomic Energy for Military Purposes*, 98.

51. Smyth, *Atomic Energy for Military Purposes*, 99.

52. Laura Fermi, *Atoms in the Family*, 176.

2. FDR and the Einstein Letter

1. All quotes from Einstein's August 2, 1939, letter to F. D. Roosevelt (from the President's Secretary's Files, Franklin D. Roosevelt Presidential Library and Museum, Hyde Park, New York) can be found online at http://www.fdrlibrary .marist.edu/archives/pdfs/docsworldwar.pdf.

2. Hewlett and Anderson, *History of the United States Atomic Energy Commission*, 17.

3. Hewlett and Anderson, *History of the United States Atomic Energy Commission*, 17.

4. Riordon, *Plunkitt of Tammany Hall*.

5. Croly, *Promise of American Life*, 158.

6. Kennedy, *Over Here*, 97.

7. Burns, *Roosevelt: The Lion and the Fox*, 51.

8. Bureau of the Census, *Historical Statistics of the United States, 1789–1945*, 299.

9. Bureau of the Census, *Historical Statistics of the United States, 1789–1945*, 299.

10. Bureau of the Census, *Historical Statistics of the United States, 1789–1945*, 299.

11. Bureau of the Census, *Historical Statistics of the United States, 1789–1945*, 299.

12. Bureau of the Census, *Historical Statistics of the United States, 1789–1945*, 299.

13. Kennedy, *Over Here*, 94.

14. Burns, *Roosevelt: The Lion and the Fox*, 52.

15. Burns, *Roosevelt: The Lion and the Fox*, 52.

16. An article published in 2003 presents recent analysis by doctors who concluded that FDR suffered the paralysis because of Guillain-Barre, not polio. See Goldman et al., "What Was the Cause of Franklin Delano Roosevelt's Paralytic Illness?," quoted in Oshinsky, *Polio*, 28.

17. Black, *Franklin Delano Roosevelt*, 245.

18. Alexander Hamilton, *Federalist* No. 70, in Rossiter, *Federalist Papers*, 423.

19. Hamilton, *Federalist* No. 70, 423.

20. Quotations from the inaugural address are from Franklin D. Roosevelt, "Inaugural Address," March 4, 1933, The American Presidency Project, ed. Gerhard Peters and John T. Woolley, http://www.presidency.ucsb.edu/ws/?pid=14473.

21. James Madison, *Federalist* No. 10, in Rossiter, *Federalist Papers*, 79.

22. See A. L. A. Schechter Poultry Corporation v. United States, 295 U.S. 495 (1935).

23. Alexander Hamilton, *Federalist* No. 78, in Rossiter, *Federalist Papers*, 465–66.

24. See Humphrey's Executor v. United States, 295 U.S. 602 (1935).

25. See West Coast Hotel Company v. Elsie Parrish, 300 U.S. 379 (1937).

26. See Commager, *American Mind*.

27. From Wilfred Owen's poem "Dulce et Decorum Est," The War Poetry Website, ed. David Roberts, http://www.warpoetry.co.uk/owen1.html.

28. Barry, *Great Influenza*.

3. A Bungled Start

1. Smyth, *Atomic Energy for Military Purposes*, 47.

2. Cochrane, *Measures for Progress*, 362.

3. Rhodes, *Making of the Atomic Bomb*, 361.

4. Cochrane, *Measures for Progress*, 362.

5. Hewlett and Anderson, *History of the United States Atomic Energy Commission*, 19–20.

6. Rhodes, *Making of the Atomic Bomb*, 316.

7. Rhodes, *Making of the Atomic Bomb*, 316.

8. Leo Szilard to Alexander Sachs, November 5, 1939.

9. Rhodes, *Making of the Atomic Bomb*, 309.

10. Hewlett and Anderson, *History of the United States Atomic Energy Commission*, 23.

11. Hewlett and Anderson, *History of the United States Atomic Energy Commission*, 23.

12. Hewlett and Anderson, *History of the United States Atomic Energy Commission*, 23.

13. Hewlett and Anderson, *History of the United States Atomic Energy Commission*, 23.

14. Hewlett and Anderson, *History of the United States Atomic Energy Commission*, 23.

15. Hewlett and Anderson, *History of the United States Atomic Energy Commission*, 19.

16. Hewlett and Anderson, *History of the United States Atomic Energy Commission*, 19.

17. Wills, *Cincinnatus*, 196.

18. Cohen, *Science and the Founding Fathers*.

19. Bailyn, *Ideological Origins of the American Revolution*, 27.

20. Cochrane, *Measures for Progress*, 16.

21. See Hepburn v. Griswold, 75 U.S. 603 (1870).

22. Cochrane, *Measures for Progress*, 161.

23. Cochrane, *Measures for Progress*, 161.

24. Cochrane, *Measures for Progress*, 161.

4. The President's Man

1. Meacham, *Franklin and Winston*, 74.

2. Zachary, *Endless Frontier*.

3. See Lombardo, *Three Generations No Imbeciles*.

4. See Buck v. Bell, 274 U.S. 200 (1927).

5. Zachary, *Endless Frontier*, 99.

6. Zachary, *Endless Frontier*, 99.

7. Zachary, *Endless Frontier*, 111.

8. Zachary, *Endless Frontier*, 112.

9. Hewlett and Anderson, *History of the United States Atomic Energy Commission*, 25.

10. See Halberstam, *The Best and the Brightest*.

11. Zachary, *Endless Frontier*, 191.

12. Conant, *My Several Lives*, 278.

13. Smyth, *Atomic Energy for Military Purposes*, 50.

14. Smyth, *Atomic Energy for Military Purposes*, 51.

15. Smyth, *Atomic Energy for Military Purposes*, 51.

16. Zachary, *Endless Frontier*, 192.

17. Zachary, *Endless Frontier*, 193.

18. Hewlett and Anderson, *History of the United States Atomic Energy Commission*, 41.

19. Hewlett and Anderson, *History of the United States Atomic Energy Commission*, 45.

20. Hewlett and Anderson, *History of the United States Atomic Energy Commission*, 45–46.

21. Hewlett and Anderson, *History of the United States Atomic Energy Commission*, 46.

22. Zachary, *Endless Frontier*, 197.

23. James Madison, *Federalist No. 51*, in Rossiter, *Federalist Papers*, 322.

24. Madison, *Federalist* No. 51, 322.

25. Madison, *Federalist* No. 10, 77.

26. Madison, *Federalist* No. 10, 79.

27. Madison, *Federalist* No. 10, 79.

28. See Ex parte Merryman, 17 F. Cas. 144 (C. C. D. Md. 1861).

29. See Fred Korematsu v. United States, 323 U.S. 214 (1944).

30. U.S. Department of Energy, *Manhattan Project*, 5.

31. U.S. Department of Energy, *Manhattan Project*, 6.

32. U.S. Department of Energy, *Manhattan Project*, 6.

33. U.S. Department of Energy, *Manhattan Project*, 6.

34. U.S. Department of Energy, *Manhattan Project*, 20.

35. U.S. Department of Energy, *Manhattan Project*, 21.

36. U.S. Department of Energy, *Manhattan Project*, 32.

37. Groves, *Now It Can Be Told*, 89.

38. Groves, *Now It Can Be Told*, 90.

39. Groves, *Now It Can Be Told*, 90.

40. Groves, *Now It Can Be Told*, 20.

41. Groves, *Now It Can Be Told*, 20.

42. Groves, *Now It Can Be Told*, 20.

43. Groves, *Now It Can Be Told*, 21.

44. Conant, *My Several Lives*, 246.

45. Conant, *My Several Lives*, 246.

46. Conant, *My Several Lives*, 247.

5. MAUD—Working with the British

1. Madison, *Federalist* No. 10, 78.

2. See Meacham, *Franklin and Winston*.

3. Hewlett and Anderson, *History of the United States Atomic Energy Commission*, 256.

4. Hewlett and Anderson, *History of the United States Atomic Energy Commission*, 257.

5. Hewlett and Anderson, *History of the United States Atomic Energy Commission*, 257.

6. Hewlett and Anderson, *History of the United States Atomic Energy Commission*, 261.

7. Hewlett and Anderson, *History of the United States Atomic Energy Commission*, 261.

8. Hewlett and Anderson, *History of the United States Atomic Energy Commission*, 261.

9. Hewlett and Anderson, *History of the United States Atomic Energy Commission*, 263.

10. Hewlett and Anderson, *History of the United States Atomic Energy Commission*, 264.

11. Hewlett and Anderson, *History of the United States Atomic Energy Commission*, 264.

12. Hewlett and Anderson, *History of the United States Atomic Energy Commission*, 265.

13. Churchill to Hopkins, cablegram, February 16, 1943.

14. Hopkins to Churchill, cablegram, February 24, 1943.

15. Hopkins to Churchill, cablegram, February 24, 1943.

16. Bush to Churchill, memo, February 26, 1943.

17. Bush to Churchill, memo, February 26, 1943.

18. Churchill to Hopkins, cablegram, February 27, 1943.

19. Churchill to Hopkins, cablegram, February 27, 1943.

20. Churchill to Hopkins, cablegram, February 27, 1943.

21. Churchill to Hopkins, cablegram, February 27, 1943.

22. Churchill to Hopkins, second cablegram, February 27, 1943.

23. Churchill to Hopkins, second cablegram, February 27, 1943.

24. Churchill to Hopkins, second cablegram, February 27, 1943.

25. Churchill to Hopkins, second cablegram, February 27, 1943.

26. Churchill to Hopkins, second cablegram, February 27, 1943.

27. Churchill to Hopkins, second cablegram, February 27, 1943.

28. Churchill to Hopkins, second cablegram, February 27, 1943.

29. Churchill to Hopkins, cablegram, March 20, 1943.

30. Hopkins to Churchill, cablegram, March 20, 1943.

31. Conant to Bush, memo, March 25, 1943.

32. Conant to Bush, memo, March 25, 1943.

33. Conant to Bush, memo, March 25, 1943.

34. Conant to Bush, memo, March 25, 1943.

35. Conant to Bush, memo, March 25, 1943.

36. Conant to Bush, memo, March 25, 1943.

37. Bush to Hopkins, memo, March 31, 1943.

38. Bush to Hopkins, memo, March 31, 1943.

39. Bush to file, memo, May 25, 1943.

40. Bush to file, memo, May 25, 1943.

41. Hewlett and Anderson, *History of the United States Atomic Energy Commission*, 275.

42. Churchill to FDR, memo, July 9, 1943.

43. Hewlett and Anderson, *History of the United States Atomic Energy Commission*, 274.

44. Hewlett and Anderson, *History of the United States Atomic Energy Commission*, 274.

45. Hewlett and Anderson, *History of the United States Atomic Energy Commission*, 276–77.

46. Groves, *Now It Can Be Told*, 133.

47. Hewlett and Anderson, *History of the United States Atomic Energy Commission*, 279.

48. Zachary, *Endless Frontier*, 214.

49. Zachary, *Endless Frontier*, 215.

50. Meacham, *Franklin and Winston*, 245.

51. Meacham, *Franklin and Winston*, 171.

52. Meacham, *Franklin and Winston*, 171.

53. Hewett and Anderson, *History of the United States Atomic Energy Commission*, 279.

54. Hewett and Anderson, *History of the United States Atomic Energy Commission*, 282.

55. Hewett and Anderson, *History of the United States Atomic Energy Commission*, 310.

56. James Madison, *Federalist No. 55*, in Rossiter, *Federalist Papers*, 342.

57. A. L. A. Schechter Poultry Corporation v. United States, 295 U.S. 495, 551 (1935).

58. *Schechter*, 295 U.S. at 551.

59. *Schechter*, 295 U.S. at 552.

60. *Schechter*, 295 U.S. at 553.

61. *Schechter*, 295 U.S. at 553.

62. *Schechter*, 295 U.S. at 553.

63. Wilson, "Study of Administration."

64. Wilson, "Study of Administration," 24.

65. Wilson, "Study of Administration," 24.

6. The German Bomb

1. Cornwell, *Hitler's Scientists*, 394.

2. Lindley, *Uncertainty*, 214.

3. Groves, *Now It Can Be Told*, 191.

4. Groves, *Now It Can Be Told*, 194.

5. Groves, *Now It Can Be Told*, 194.

6. See Dawidoff, *Catcher Was a Spy*.

7. Groves, *Now It Can Be Told*, 217.

8. Dawidoff, *Catcher Was a Spy*, 205.

9. Dawidoff, *Catcher Was a Spy*, 204.

10. Thomas Powers, *Heisenberg's War*, 399.

11. Thomas Powers, *Heisenberg's War*, 404.

12. Thomas Powers, *Heisenberg's War*, 404.

13. Associated Press interview with Otto Hahn and Werner Heisenberg, quoted in Szilard, "Conference with Dr. Szilard," note, February 4, 1946, Manhattan Project files, Franklin D. Roosevelt Presidential Library and Museum, Hyde Park, New York.

14. Associated Press interview with Otto Hahn and Werner Heisenberg, quoted in Szilard, "Conference with Dr. Szilard," February 4, 1946.

15. Associated Press interview with Otto Hahn and Werner Heisenberg, quoted in Szilard, "Conference with Dr. Szilard," February 4, 1946.

16. Associated Press interview with Otto Hahn and Werner Heisenberg, quoted in Szilard, "Conference with Dr. Szilard," February 4, 1946.

17. Goudsmit to Sachs, August 6, 1946.

18. Goudsmit to Sachs, August 6, 1946.

19. Goudsmit to Sachs, August 6, 1946.

20. Goudsmit to Sachs, August 6, 1946.

21. Goudsmit to Sachs, August 6, 1946.

22. Goudsmit to Sachs, August 6, 1946.

23. Goudsmit to Sachs, August 6, 1946.

24. Goudsmit to Sachs, August 6, 1946.

25. Cornwell, *Hitler's Scientists*, 25.

26. Cornwell, *Hitler's Scientists*, 26.

27. Cornwell, *Hitler's Scientists*, 27.

28. Cornwell, *Hitler's Scientists*, 28.

7. Secrets and Spies

1. Tocqueville, *Democracy in America*, 452.

2. Tocqueville, *Democracy in America*, 452.

3. Tocqueville, *Democracy in America*, 452.

4. Tocqueville, *Democracy in America*, 452.

5. Tocqueville, *Democracy in America*, 452.

6. Tocqueville, *Democracy in America*, 452.

7. Tocqueville, *Democracy in America*, 452.

8. Madison, *Federalist* No. 10, 79.

9. See Roberts, *Brother*.

10. Eisenhower, *Mandate for Change*, 224.

11. Eisenhower, *Mandate for Change*, 224.

12. Dwight D. Eisenhower, "Statement by the President Declining to Intervene on Behalf of Julius and Ethel Rosenberg," June 19, 1953, The American Presidency Project, ed. Gerhard Peters and John T. Woolley, http://www.presidency.ucsb.edu/ws/?pid=9617.

13. Eisenhower, "Statement by the President Declining to Intervene on Behalf of Julius and Ethel Rosenberg."

14. Gaddis, *United States and the Origins of the Cold War*, 245.

15. Gaddis, *United States and the Origins of the Cold War*, 245.

16. Broad and Sanger, "As U.S. Modernizes Nuclear Weapons, 'Smaller' Leaves Some Uneasy."

17. McCullough, *Truman*, 757.

18. McCullough, *Truman*, 758.

19. Gaddis, *United States and the Origins of the Cold War*, 247.

20. Gaddis, *United States and the Origins of the Cold War*, 247.

21. Gaddis, *United States and the Origins of the Cold War*, 247.

22. Gaddis, *United States and the Origins of the Cold War*, 247.

23. McCullough, *Truman*, 760.

24. McCullough, *Truman*, 760.

25. McCullough, *Truman*, 760–61.

26. McCullough, *Truman*, 760.

27. See Richard Gid Powers, *Not without Honor*.

28. See Albright and Kunstel, *Bombshell*.

29. Moynihan, *Secrecy*, 143–44.

30. McCullough, *Truman*, 757.

8. Congress Rebounds

1. McCullough, *Truman*, 289.

2. McCullough, *Truman*, 289.

3. McCullough, *Truman*, 289.

4. McCullough, *Truman*, 230.

5. McCullough, *Truman*, 230.

6. McCullough, *Truman*, 280.

7. Groves, *Now It Can Be Told*, 362.

8. McCullough, *Truman*, 291.

9. Pry, *Role of Congress in the Strategic Posture of the United States*, 3.

10. Pry, *Role of Congress in the Strategic Posture of the United States*, 6.

11. Groves, *Now It Can Be Told*, 360.

12. Groves, *Now It Can Be Told*, 360.

13. Groves, *Now It Can Be Told*, 362.

14. Bush, *Free Men and Modern Arms*, 259.

15. Bush, *Free Men and Modern Arms*, 259.

16. Bush, *Free Men and Modern Arms*, 259.

17. Groves, *Now It Can Be Told*, 365.

18. Bush, *Free Men and Modern Arms*, 259.

19. Bush, *Free Men and Modern Arms*, 259.

20. Bush, *Free Men and Modern Arms*, 259.

21. Bush, *Free Men and Modern Arms*, 259.

22. Gaddis, *United States and the Origins of the Cold War*, 254.

23. Gaddis, *United States and the Origins of the Cold War*, 254.

24. Pry, *Role of Congress in the Strategic Posture of the United States*, 17.

25. Pry, *Role of Congress in the Strategic Posture of the United States*, 17.

26. Pry, *Role of Congress in the Strategic Posture of the United States*, 38.

27. Pry, *Role of Congress in the Strategic Posture of the United States*, 38.

28. Pry, *Role of Congress in the Strategic Posture of the United States*, 39.

29. See Mayhew, *Government without Passing Laws*.

30. FDR to Bush, memo, December 28, 1942.

31. Bush to FDR, memo, February 2, 1943.

32. Groves, *Now It Can Be Told*, 245.

9. The Transition to Truman

1. Freidel, *Franklin D. Roosevelt*, 542.

2. Kearns Goodwin, *No Ordinary Time*, 532.

3. Freidel, *Franklin D. Roosevelt*, 542.

4. Freidel, *Franklin D. Roosevelt*, 543.

5. Freidel, *Franklin D. Roosevelt*, 544.

6. Freidel, *Franklin D. Roosevelt*, 544–45.

7. Kearns Goodwin, *No Ordinary Time*, 547.

8. Freidel, *Franklin D. Roosevelt*, 558.

9. McCullough, *Truman*, 294.

10. McCullough, *Truman*, 294.

11. Republican National Committee, "Republican Party Platform of 1944," June 26, 1944, The American Presidency Project, ed. Gerhard Peters and John T. Woolley, http://www.presidency.ucsb.edu/ws/?pid=25835.

12. Groves, *Now It Can Be Told*, 254.

13. Groves, *Now It Can Be Told*, 258.

14. Groves, *Now It Can Be Told*, 258.

15. Groves, *Now It Can Be Told*, 259.

16. Groves, *Now It Can Be Told*, 261.

17. Smith, *FDR*, 632.

18. Smith, *FDR*, 632.

19. Smith, *FDR*, 632.

20. Smith, *FDR*, 632.

21. Rhodes, *Making of the Atomic Bomb*, 613.

22. Einstein to FDR, March 25, 1945.

23. Einstein to FDR, March 25, 1945.

24. Einstein to FDR, March 25, 1945.

25. Groves, *Now It Can Be Told*, 39, 41.

26. Baggott, *First War of Physics*, 299.

27. Baggott, *First War of Physics*, 300.

28. Byrnes to FDR, memo, March 2, 1945.

29. Byrnes to FDR, memo, March 2, 1945.
30. Byrnes to FDR, memo, March 2, 1945.
31. Byrnes to FDR, memo, March 2, 1945.
32. Byrnes to FDR, memo, March 2, 1945.
33. Byrnes to FDR, memo, March 2, 1945.
34. Byrnes to FDR, memo, March 2, 1945.
35. Rhodes, *Making of the Atomic Bomb*, 502.
36. Groves, *Now It Can Be Told*, 296.

10. Hiroshima

1. Bush, *Free Men and Modern Arms*, 91.
2. Baggott, *First War of Physics*, 333.
3. Baggott, *First War of Physics*, 335–36.
4. Bush, *Free Men and Modern Arms*, 91.
5. Bush, *Free Men and Modern Arms*, 91.
6. Bush, *Free Men and Modern Arms*, 91.
7. Bush, *Free Men and Modern Arms*, 91.
8. Bush, *Free Men and Modern Arms*, 91.
9. Bush, *Free Men and Modern Arms*, 91.
10. Zachary, *Endless Frontier*, 285.
11. Conant, *My Several Lives*, 304.
12. Conant, *My Several Lives*, 303.
13. Conant, *My Several Lives*, 304.
14. Conant, *My Several Lives*, 304.
15. Groves, *Now It Can Be Told*, 263.
16. Groves, *Now It Can Be Told*, 263–64.
17. Groves, *Now It Can Be Told*, 264.
18. Groves, *Now It Can Be Told*, 264.
19. Groves, *Now It Can Be Told*, 265.
20. Groves, *Now It Can Be Told*, 265.
21. Groves, *Now It Can Be Told*, 265.
22. Groves, *Now It Can Be Told*, 266.
23. Groves, *Now It Can Be Told*, 266.
24. Groves, *Now It Can Be Told*, 263.
25. Rhodes, *Making of the Atomic Bomb*, 617.
26. Smith, *FDR*, 286.
27. Baggott, *First War of Physics*, 302.
28. Groves, *Now It Can Be Told*, 273.
29. Rhodes, *Making of the Atomic Bomb*, 684.
30. Rhodes, *Making of the Atomic Bomb*, 688.
31. Rhodes, *Making of the Atomic Bomb*, 688.
32. Rhodes, *Making of the Atomic Bomb*, 688.
33. Rhodes, *Making of the Atomic Bomb*, 688.

34. Groves, *Now It Can Be Told*, 275.

35. Groves, *Now It Can Be Told*, 275.

36. Groves, *Now It Can Be Told*, 275.

37. Groves, *Now It Can Be Told*, 324.

38. Groves, *Now It Can Be Told*, 342.

39. Manhattan Engineer District, *Atomic Bombings of Hiroshima and Nagasaki*.

40. Eisenhower, *Mandate for Change*, 312.

41. Smith, *FDR*, 567.

42. Rhodes, *Making of the Atomic Bomb*, 684.

43. Zinn, *People's History of the United States*, 423.

44. Freidel, *Franklin D. Roosevelt*, 464.

45. Zinn, *People's History of the United States*, 661.

46. McCullough, *Truman*, 437.

47. McCullough, *Truman*, 437.

48. McCullough, *Truman*, 437.

11. Science and Democracy

1. Hesiod, *Hesiod's Theogony*, 15.

2. Hesiod, *Hesiod's Theogony*, 15.

3. Hesiod, *Hesiod's Theogony*, 15.

4. Hesiod, *Hesiod's Theogony*, 15.

5. Hesiod, *Hesiod's Theogony*, 16.

6. Bulfinch, *Bulfinch's Mythology*, 13.

7. Bulfinch, *Bulfinch's Mythology*, 13.

8. Bulfinch, *Bulfinch's Mythology*, 13.

9. Wills, *Cincinnatus*.

10. Groves, *Now It Can Be Told*, 296–97.

11. U.S. Environmental Protection Agency (EPA), "Hanford Superfund Site History."

12. EPA, "Hanford Superfund Site History."

13. EPA, "Hanford Superfund Site History."

14. EPA, "Hanford Superfund Site History."

15. EPA, "Hanford—Washington."

16. Oregon Department of Energy, "Frequently Asked Questions (FAQ's) about Hanford," 4.

17. EPA, "Hanford Superfund Site History."

18. Groves, *Now It Can Be Told*, 143.

19. Groves, *Now It Can Be Told*, 144.

20. Groves, *Now It Can Be Told*, 144.

21. Albright and Kunstel, *Bombshell*, 288–89.

22. *Black's Law Dictionary*, s.v. "assassination."

23. Becker and Shane, "Secret 'Kill List' Proves a Test of Obama's Principles and Will."

24. Becker and Shane, "Secret 'Kill List' Proves a Test of Obama's Principles and Will."

25. Becker and Shane, "Secret 'Kill List' Proves a Test of Obama's Principles and Will."

26. Becker and Shane, "Secret 'Kill List' Proves a Test of Obama's Principles and Will."

27. See al-Aulaqi v. Panetta, No. 2012-1192 (DC Apr. 4, 2014).

28. Snow, *Two Cultures*, 100.

29. Smith, *FDR*, 311. Smith describes the Holmes quote as "apocryphal."

[BIBLIOGRAPHY]

Archival Sources

Cablegrams, memos, and letters come from the two boxes on the Manhattan Project at the Franklin D. Roosevelt Presidential Library and Museum, Hyde Park, New York.

Published Sources

Albright, Joseph, and Marcia Kunstel. *Bombshell: The Secret Story of America's Unknown Atomic Spy Conspiracy.* New York: Times Books, 1997.

Alperovitz, Gar. *The Decision to Use the Atomic Bomb and the Architecture of an American Myth.* New York: Alfred A. Knopf, 1995.

Baggott, Jim. *The First War of Physics: The Secret History of the Atom Bomb, 1939–1949.* New York: Pegasus, 2010.

Bailyn, Bernard. *The Ideological Origins of the American Revolution.* Cambridge MA: Belknap, 1967.

Barry, John M. *The Great Influenza: The Story of the Deadliest Pandemic in History.* New York: Penguin, 2005.

Baxter, James Phinney, III. *Scientists against Time.* Boston: Little, Brown, 1946.

Becker, Jo, and Scott Shane. "Secret 'Kill List' Proves a Test of Obama's Principles and Will." *New York Times,* May 29, 2012. http://www.nytimes.com/2012/05/29/world/obamas-leadership-in-war-on-al-qaeda.html.

Bernstein, Jeremy. *Hitler's Uranium Club: The Secret Recordings at Farm Hall.* New York: Springer Science+Business Media, 2001.

Bird, Kai, and Martin J. Sherwin. *American Prometheus: The Triumph and Tragedy of J. Robert Oppenheimer.* New York: Vintage, 2006.

Black, Conrad. *Franklin Delano Roosevelt: Champion of Freedom.* New York: Public Affairs, 2003.

Black's Law Dictionary. 6th ed. Eagan MN: West Publishing, 1990.

Bowen, Catherine Drinker. *Miracle at Philadelphia: The Story of the Constitutional Convention, May to September 1787.* Boston: Little, Brown, 1966.

Brinkley, Alan. *The End of Reform: New Deal Liberalism in Recession and War.* New York: Vintage, 1995.

Broad, William J., and David E. Sanger. "As U.S. Modernizes Nuclear Weapons, 'Smaller' Leaves Some Uneasy." *New York Times*, January 11, 2016.

Bulfinch, Thomas. *Bulfinch's Mythology*. New York: Gramercy Books, 2003.

Bureau of the Census. *Historical Statistics of the United States, 1789–1945*. Washington DC: U.S. Department of Commerce, 1949.

Burns, James MacGregor. *Roosevelt: The Lion and the Fox, 1882–1940*. New York: Harcourt Brace Jovanovich, 1956.

————. *Roosevelt: The Soldier of Freedom, 1940–1945*. New York: Harcourt Brace Jovanovich, 1970.

Bush, Vannevar. *Free Men and Modern Arms: A Discussion of the Role of Science in Preserving Democracy*. Cambridge MA: MIT Press, 1968.

Cantelon, Philip L., Richard G. Hewlett, and Robert C. Williams, eds. *The American Atom: A Documentary History of Nuclear Policies from the Discovery of Fission to the Present*. 2nd ed. Philadelphia: University of Pennsylvania Press, 1991.

Cochrane, Rexmond C. *Measures for Progress: A History of the National Bureau of Standards*. Washington DC: U.S. Department of Commerce, 1966.

Cohen, I. Bernard. *Science and the Founding Fathers: Science in the Political Thought of Thomas Jefferson, Benjamin Franklin, John Adams and James Madison*. New York: W. W. Norton, 1995.

Commager, Henry Steele. *The American Mind: An Interpretation of American Thought and Character since the 1880's*. New Haven CT: Yale University Press, 1950.

Compton, Arthur Holly. *Atomic Quest: A Personal Narrative*. New York: Oxford University Press, 1956.

Conant, James B. *My Several Lives: Memoirs of a Social Inventor*. New York: Harper and Row, 1970.

Cornwell, John. *Hitler's Scientists: Science, War, and the Devil's Pact*. New York: Penguin, 2003.

Croly, Herbert David. *The Promise of American Life*. Minneapolis: Filiquarian Press, 2007. Originally published Boston: Northeastern University Press, 1909.

Dahl, Robert. *On Democracy*. New Haven CT: Yale University Press, 1998.

Dawidoff, Nicholas. *The Catcher Was a Spy: The Mysterious Life of Moe Berg*. New York: Vintage, 1994.

Dion, Arnold S. "Acute Radiation Sickness." *Harry K. Daghlian, Jr.: America's First Peacetime Atom Bomb Fatality*, accessed February 29, 2016. http://arnold_dion.tripod.com/Daghlian/sickness.html.

Eisenhower, Dwight D. *Mandate for Change: The White House Years, 1953–1956*. New York: Doubleday, 1963.

Fermi, Enrico. "Fermi's Own Story." In *The First Reactor*, 21–26. 40th Anniversary ed. Washington DC: U.S. Department of Energy, 1982. http://www.osti.gov/accomplishments/documents/fullText/ACC0044.pdf. Originally published in the *Chicago Sun-Times*, November 23, 1952.

Fermi, Laura. *Atoms in the Family: My Life with Enrico Fermi*. Chicago: University of Chicago Press, 1954.

Freidel, Frank. *Franklin D. Roosevelt: A Rendezvous with Destiny*. Boston: Little, Brown, 1990.

Gaddis, John Lewis. *The United States and the Origins of the Cold War, 1941–1947*. New York: Columbia University Press, 2000.

Goldman, Armond S., Elisabeth J. Schmalstieg, Daniel H. Freeman Jr., Daniel A. Goldman, and Frank C. Schmalstieg Jr. "What Was the Cause of Franklin Delano Roosevelt's Paralytic Illness?" *Journal of Medical Biography* 11, no. 4 (2003): 232–40.

Groves, Leslie. *Now It Can Be Told: The Story of the Manhattan Project*. New York: Da Capo, 1962.

Halberstam, David. *The Best and the Brightest*. New York: Random House, 1972.

Hargittai, István. *Martians of Science: Five Physicists Who Changed the Twentieth Century*. Oxford: Oxford University Press, 2006.

Hersey, John. *Hiroshima*. New York: Vintage, 1989.

Hesiod. *Hesiod's Theogony*. New York: Classic Books International, 2010.

Hewlett, Richard G., and Oscar E. Anderson Jr. *A History of the United States Atomic Energy Commission*. Vol. 1 of *The New World, 1939/1946*. University Park: Pennsylvania State University Press, 1962.

Hofstadter, Richard. *The Paranoid Style in American Politics*. New York: Vintage, 2008.

Isaacson, Walter. *Einstein: His Life and Universe*. New York: Simon and Schuster, 2007.

Jefferson, Thomas. *Notes on the State of Virginia*. Chapel Hill: University of North Carolina Press, 1982.

Jones, Vincent C. *Manhattan: The Army and the Atomic Bomb*. Washington DC: Center of Military History, United States Army, 1985.

Kearns Goodwin, Doris. *No Ordinary Time: Franklin and Eleanor Roosevelt; The Home Front in World War II*. New York: Simon and Schuster, 1994.

Kelly, Cynthia C., ed. *The Manhattan Project: The Birth of the Atomic Bomb in the Words of Its Creators, Eyewitnesses, and Historians*. New York: Black Dog and Leventhal, 2007.

Kennedy, David M. *Freedom from Fear: The American People in Depression and War, 1929–1945*. New York: Oxford University Press, 1999.

———. *Over Here: The First World War and American Society*. New York: Oxford University Press, 1980.

Kumar, Manjit. *Quantum: Einstein, Bohr, and the Great Debate about the Nature of Reality*. New York: W. W. Norton, 2008.

Lindley, David. *Uncertainty: Einstein, Heisenberg, Bohr and the Struggle for the Soul of Science*. New York: Anchor, 2008.

Lombardo, Paul A. *Three Generations No Imbeciles: Eugenics, the Supreme Court, and Buck v. Bell*. Baltimore, MA: Johns Hopkins University Press, 2008.

Mahaffey, James. *Atomic Accidents: A History of Nuclear Meltdowns and Disasters from the Ozark Mountains to Fukushima*. New York: Pegasus, 2014.

Manhattan Engineer District. *The Atomic Bombings of Hiroshima and Nagasaki*. Los Alamos NM, 1946.

Mayer, Milton. *Robert Maynard Hutching: A Memoir*. Berkeley: University of California Press, 1993.

McCullough, David. *Truman*. New York: Simon and Schuster, 1992.

Meacham, Jon. *Franklin and Winston: An Intimate Portrait of an Epic Friendship*. New York: Random House, 2003.

Moynihan, Daniel Patrick. *Secrecy: The American Experience*. New Haven CT: Yale University Press, 1998.

Norris, Robert S. *Racing for the Bomb: General Leslie R. Groves, the Manhattan Project's Indispensable Man*. South Royalton VT: Steerforth, 2002.

Oregon Department of Energy. "Frequently Asked Questions (FAQ's) about Hanford." Oregon Department of Energy, March 2014. http://www.oregon.gov /energy/NUCSAF/docs/FAQs_for_Nuclear_Safety-Hanford.pdf.

Oshinsky, David M. *Polio: An American Story*. New York: Oxford University Press, 2005.

Powers, Richard Gid. *Not without Honor: The History of American Anticommunism*. New York: Free Press, 1995.

Powers, Thomas. *Heisenberg's War: The Secret History of the Atomic Bomb*. New York: Da Capo, 1993.

Pry, Peter. *The Role of Congress in the Strategic Posture of the United States, 1942–1960: Manhattan Project to the New Look*. Report no. ASCO 2010 011. Ft. Belvoir VA: Defense Threat Reduction Agency, 2010. http://www.dtic.mil/get-tr-doc /pdf?AD=ADA556982.

Rhodes, Richard. *The Making of the Atomic Bomb*. New York: Simon and Schuster, 1986.

Riordan, William L. *Plunkitt of Tammany Hall*. New York: Signet Classics, 1995.

Roberts, Sam. *The Brother: The Untold Story of Atomic Spy David Greenglass and How He Sent His Sister, Ethel Rosenberg, to the Electric Chair*. New York: Random House, 2001.

Rossiter, Clinton, ed. *The Federalist Papers*. New York: Mentor, 1961.

Schlosser, Eric. *Command and Control: Nuclear Weapons, the Damascus Accident and the Illusion of Safety*. New York: Penguin, 2013.

Smith, Jean Edward. *FDR*. New York: Random House. 2007.

Smyth, Henry D. *Atomic Energy for Military Purposes: A General Account of the Scientific Research and Technical Development That Went into the Making of Atomic Bombs*. Princeton NJ: Princeton University Press, 1945.

Snow, C. P. *The Two Cultures*. Cambridge: Canto Classics, 1998.

Tocqueville, Alexis de. *Democracy in America*. Vol. 1. New York: Vintage Books, 1945.

U.S. Department of Energy. *The Manhattan Project: Making the Atomic Bomb*. Washington DC: U.S. Department of Energy, 1999.

U.S. Environmental Protection Agency (EPA). "Hanford Superfund Site History." U.S. Environmental Protection Agency, Region 10: The Pacific Northwest, last updated January 12, 2016. http://yosemite.epa.gov/R10/CLEANUP
.NSF/0903AE66D99736E188256F04006C2D3A/045F8399CAA1B6BD882573
FC0069B078?OpenDocument.

———. "Hanford—Washington." U.S. Environmental Protection Agency, Region 10: The Pacific Northwest, last updated January 12, 2016. https://yosemite.epa
.gov/r10/cleanup.nsf/sites/Hanford.

Wills, Garry. *Cincinnatus: George Washington and the Enlightenment.* New York: Doubleday, 1984.

Wilson, Woodrow. "The Study of Administration." *Political Science Quarterly* 2, no. 2 (June 1887): 197–222. Reprinted in *Classics of Public Administration*, 2nd ed., edited by Jay M. Shafritz and Albert C. Hyde, 10–25. Boston: Wadsworth, 1987. Page references are to the 1987 reprint edition.

Zachary, G. Pascal. *Endless Frontier: Vannevar Bush, Engineer of the American Century.* New York: Free Press, 1997.

Zinn, Howard. *A People's History of the United States, 1492–Present.* New York: Harper Perennial, 2003.

[INDEX]